THE
CHANGING
ENGLISH
COUNTRYSIDE
1400–1700
Leonard Cantor

The History of the British Landscape

Editor: Michael Reed

THE
CHANGING
ENGLISH
COUNTRYSIDE
1400-1700
Leonard Cantor

Routledge & Kegan Paul

London and New York

First published in 1987 by
Routledge & Kegan Paul Ltd
11 New Fetter Lane, London EC4P 4EE

Published in the USA by
Routledge & Kegan Paul Inc.
in association with Methuen Inc.
29 West 35th Street, New York, NY 10001

Set in 10/11 pt Erhardt
by Columns of Reading
and printed in Great Britain
by Thetford Press,
Thetford, Norfolk

Library of Congress Cataloging in Publication Data

Cantor, Leonard Martin.
The changing English countryside, 1400–1700.

(The History of the British landscape)
Includes Index
1. Land use, Rural—England—History.
2. Agriculture—Economic aspects—England—History.
3. England—Economic conditions.   4. England—Rural
conditions.   I. Title.   II. Series.
HD604.C36   1987   333.76'13'0942   86–6676

British Library CIP Data also available
ISBN 0–7102–0501–5

Contents

Illustrations

Plates

Figures

Preface

Throughout its history, the English countryside has been affected by change, and the long period of three hundred years covered by this book was no exception. However, due largely to the much slower rate of technological development, change occurred at a much more leisured pace than the one we have to live with today. At the beginning, the Middle Ages had not yet run its course, the English economy was still overwhelmingly an agricultural one, and over 90 per cent of the population lived in the countryside, earning their living by methods of farming which had changed little over the centuries. England in 1400 was, moreover, a thinly populated country with a population of only 2¼ million, about the population of the West Riding of Yorkshire today.

Three hundred years later, the country was on the brink of the Agricultural and Industrial Revolutions which were to wreak changes on the English countryside that were vastly greater than any that had preceded them. The seeds of these traumatic changes were sown in the earlier period covered in this book. By 1700, the population had more than doubled, industry had expanded and now employed approximately twice as high a proportion of the working population, major agricultural improvements were taking place, the transport network had expanded and its carrying capacity was greatly enhanced. Thus, the three hundred years between 1400 and 1700 span two very different Englands: on the one hand, the England of the later Middle Ages, very underdeveloped by comparison with its Continental neighbours and almost entirely dependent on a primitive agricultural economy; and, on the other, the wealthier, more sophisticated England of 1700, poised to usher in the major agricultural and industrial developments of the eighteenth century.

Two other major points about the book need to be made. The first is that it is concerned only with the English countryside and not with the urban landscape. Towns have been left out of consideration because a very considerable literature on the subject already exists, whereas much less has been written about the countryside during the period under review. Secondly, the book aims to give as vivid a picture as possible of the appearance of the English rural landscape between 1400 and 1700 and, where appropriate, to identify and describe those features of that landscape which are still to be seen in the present-day countryside.

Acknowledgements

I wish to thank Dr Michael Reed, Reader in Archives and Landscape Studies, Department of Library and Information Studies, Loughborough University, for his help in bringing this book to fruition. I am also grateful to Marjorie Salsbury for the enormous amount of typing and retyping that was necessary before the typescript achieved its final form; to Tracey Geary, and to Anne Tarver, cartographer in the Loughborough University Department of Geography, for drawing the maps.

Acknowledgement is given to the Committee for Aerial Photography, University of Cambridge, for permission to reproduce Plates 1, 40 and 46; to Patrick Bailey for Plates 2, 3 and 42; to the Warden and Fellows of All Souls College, Oxford, for Plates 4 and 6; to Tony Squires for Plate 5; to the Museum of English Rural Life, University of Reading, for Plate 7; to Tom Worcester for Plate 16; and to David Popham for Plates 25 and 26. Plates 10, 11, 12, 13, 14, 15, 17, 18, 19, 20, 21, 22, 23, 24, 28, 29 and 41 are by the author.

Above all, I am grateful to my wife for so tolerantly and encouragingly enduring the protracted labours associated with the writing of this book.

Leonard Cantor
Loughborough

CHAPTER 1

The English countryside in 1400

England in 1400 was overwhelmingly a rural country and, by today's standards, very thinly peopled, its total population being probably about 2¼ millions. Over 90 per cent of the people obtained their livelihood from farming and lived in villages, hamlets and isolated farmsteads in the country, though, as we shall see, both the size of the population and the extent of the cultivated land were smaller than they had been fifty years earlier. Industry employed very few people full-time, possibly little more than 1 per cent of the population, although it provided part-time work for many more, as a supplement to peasant agriculture. Scattered up and down the countryside were a large number of market towns, but they were very small and probably fewer than twenty provincial centres had as many as 3000 people. Even London, by far the largest town, had a population of only about 40,000 and, like every other town in the kingdom, had the countryside immediately at its doorstep. Nevertheless, the towns played a key part in the rural economy, providing markets for agricultural produce, supplying traded and manufactured goods to the rural population, and acting as social, cultural and religious centres.

However, for the vast majority of the population, who lived in the countryside, their overwhelming preoccupation was to obtain from the land they farmed the basic needs of food and shelter for themselves and their families. Virtually everything they ate, drank, wore and used for fuel they obtained from the crops which they grew, the animals which they reared and from the raw materials of the countryside outside their homes, which they built for themselves. Peasant life in the late Middle Ages was a hard one. Medieval food was often distasteful, with heavily salted meat, for those who could afford it, throughout the winter, and rancid butter in the hot weather of summer. Farming life was extremely demanding and more often than not very hard: the peasant rose with the sun and went to bed when it got dark. He had few mechanical aids to assist him and for many, especially those farming on poor soils, crops were thin and food barely adequate. Bad harvests caused real hardship and a succession of two or three could result in disaster and starvation.

1

The typical English peasant in 1400 was understandably of smaller stature than the Englishman of today and was a Catholic in a country which was part of Catholic Europe and in which religion played a dominant role. In terms of landholding, however, there was no such thing as a typical peasant in late medieval England. Although they all worked on the land, some peasants were free men and some were of servile status, though more and more of the latter obtained their freedom as time went on. By 1400 some had acquired substantial farms and might even employ labourers to work on them, while others occupied only enough land to sustain themselves and their families. They all had in common, however, the fact that they held their land by right of the lord of the manor, from whom they either rented the land, held it in copyhold, that is by custom of the manor, or in the case of a few, by freehold.

For all of them, life was made no easier by the fact that turbulence and lawlessness, both nationally and locally, were rife. Corruption was endemic in all strata of society and for the privileged few at the top of the social pyramid it was, by today's standards, a very small society indeed in which everyone knew everyone else. Yet the peasant's geographical horizons were very limited and he would typically spend all his life in one region of the country. This was largely the result of lack of transport and a primitive road system which, with the vagaries of climate to which the country was, and is, liable, could result in prosperity in one part of the country and the threat of starvation in another.

The English countryside was, above all, a mosaic of heterogeneous regions and of great diversity within those regions. In broad terms, the physical characteristics of the country created two principal divisions, as they still do today, between the lower-lying south and east and the hillier north and west, either side of the geographer's line drawn between the River Exe in the south-west and the River Tees, in the north-east (Figure 1). To the north and west of this line was the 'upland zone', with its cooler and wetter climate, its relatively thin soils, and its large expanses of moorland, mountain and fell separated by only relatively few areas of flatland suitable for cultivation. Here, grass was by far the most important crop and pasture farming was dominant. For the most part, settlement consisted of scattered hamlets and isolated farmsteads. Quite different was the 'lowland zone', lying to the south and east of the Exe-Tees line. Here mixed farming in which grain was cultivated and livestock kept was dominant. Settlement was mainly in the form of nucleated villages, and large, open fields were widespread.

However, within these two broad areas considerable variations were to be found, the product of the complexity of relief, aspect, soil and micro-climate, which are more characteristic of England than perhaps any other country in the world. Added to this complexity were the local differences brought about by human and historical factors. This resulted in an enormous variety of field

Figure 1 Upland and lowland England

0	80 km
0	50 miles

R. Tyne

CUMBRIA

R. Tees

NORTH YORKSHIRE MOORS

YORKSHIRE WOLDS

R. Humber

THE PEAK

LINCOLNSHIRE WOLDS

R. Trent

THE FENS

EAST ANGLIA

MIDLAND PLAIN

R. Ouse

WALES

COTSWOLD HILLS

R. Severn

R. Thames

MENDIP HILLS

SALISBURY PLAIN

THE WEALD

NORTH DOWNS

SOUTH DOWNS

EXMOOR

BODMIN MOOR

R. Exe

DARTMOOR

CORNWALL

PENNINES

Land over 800 feet (approx.244m)

—— The Exe-Tees Line

systems and agricultural organisations which led Postan to contend that

> it is even more dangerous to generalise about the organization of medieval agriculture than about its physical and demographic background. The rules and institutions which regulated medieval agriculture and ordered rural society differed in almost every particular from place to place as from generation to generation.[1]

Moreover, the identification and interpretation of the main features of the English countryside in all its regional variation at a

3

particular date in time like 1400 are made no easier by the relative paucity of documentary and map evidence. Nor is it to be supposed, of course, that the year 1400 has any particular significance except in the statistical sense of marking the commencement of a new century. The English countryside then, as now, was evolving and changing, though, in a society of relatively primitive technology, the rate of change was slow. Nevertheless, the previous fifty years or so had witnessed very considerable developments in the agricultural economy of the country which by 1400 were affecting the landscape considerably. These developments will be analysed more fully later in the chapter. In the meantime, it is possible to make some reasonably valid generalisations about the nature of the agricultural landscape at the beginning of the fifteenth century. By and large, the country was divided into two main forms of agricultural economy, determined mainly by relief and soil conditions. These were the 'fielden' or 'champion' areas in which arable farming largely prevailed, and the 'forest' or wood-pasture and upland areas, where pastoral and dairy farming predominated.

The 'fielden' form of agriculture, in which the plough predominated, extended over large parts of lowland England, especially in the fertile Midland plain, between the Malverns, the Chilterns and the Fens, but also with many extensions to the north, south, east and west. In these areas, the basic field system was that which is generally known as the open-field system. However, in one sense, the term 'open fields' is a misnomer in that most of them were not, technically speaking, 'open', as their external boundaries were surrounded by fences or hedges. Moreover, the term has sometimes been used as a synonym for common fields, that is fields subject to common rights or communal management, and sometimes as a description of fields, which although divided into strips, were not communally farmed. For these reasons, it has been suggested that the term 'subdivided field' rather than 'open field' would be more appropriate,[2] in that it could be applied to both types. However, because it has been widely used for a long time and because it is more generally understood, by the layman if not the academic historical geographer, the term 'open field' will be used in this book, to connote both of the meanings described above.

The landscape of the open fields was entirely different from the field system which we see today over much of central England, the regular hedged and fenced fields which are largely the product of the period of parliamentary enclosure in the eighteenth and nineteenth centuries. The older medieval system still shows through the contemporary landscape and substantial fossilised remains of its characteristic ridge and furrow (Plate 1) have been, and are being, identified and mapped all over the country. In the late Middle Ages, much cultivation was still being carried out in great fields, often several hundred acres in extent. They were unbroken by hedges, walls or fences, except where the fields abutted on a road or any areas from which animals might stray. In the latter case, fences of wooden stakes interlaced with tree branches would be erected between seed-time and harvest to contain the animals. Once the harvesting was completed, the livestock would be released from their pounds to feed on the stubble.

The major characteristics of these great fields were the high ridges and furrows, formed by centuries of ploughing along the same lines, and the pattern of 'strips' or lands into which they were divided. These were plainly visible at most times of the year but, in late summer when the crops were high, the open fields were like an undulating sea of waving golden corn. It was for the most part a 'busy' landscape, like a Breughel painting, peopled with peasants at work in the fields and richly endowed with flora and fauna. In these as in most other parts of the country, the characteristic unit of social organisation was the manor. The manor was an essential unit of landholding with legal, political, social and economic connotations. It was an estate held by a lord, who might be the crown at one extreme or a simple knight at the other. It might be small or large, it might be part of a large holding of many manors held by a great landowner or it might be the sole possession of a single landowner, and it could comprise several villages or only one. It consisted of the lord's demesne land, that is the area traditionally reserved for his own occupation, and a variety of customary holdings, freeholdings and tenancies. The lord's demesne typically occupied about one-third of the whole

Plate 1 Brassington in Derbyshire: the fossilised remains of the ridge and furrow of the open fields, which stand out clearly under a light coating of snow. The older pattern of ridges runs through the later rectangular fields superimposed on them by enclosure

cultivated area and comprised strips in the open fields and an area around the manor house. The lord of the manor also held the residual ownership of woodland, pasture and fisheries, the use of which was shared with the tenants. Beyond the open fields lay the common waste land on which the manorial peasants grazed their animals. Rights to use the common were carefully regulated and only 'commonable beasts' – oxen and horses used to pull the plough and sheep whose manure was highly valued – were normally allowed there. The manorial meadow land also made an important contribution to the agricultural economy; normally, it was fenced off in separate lots and each peasant had a share of the valuable hay crop to feed his animals. Animals were indispensable to the peasant. His horses and oxen went with him to the plough and drew his carts, his cows provided him with milk, butter, and cheese, his sheep with wool for his clothes, and his swine with meat.

In a typical medieval manor, there were three great open fields, though two, four, five or even six or more fields were not uncommon. The peasants held strips of land scattered over the big fields, sharing areas of good and poor soil alike, forming a complex pattern of holdings made up of blocks which might follow some minor topographical feature or be based upon agreement between earlier settlers. In some parts of the country, the boundaries of the strips were marked either by narrow turf 'baulks' or tradeways, which have survived in places as green ways or just by wooden posts and stones, but these seem to have been the exception rather than the rule. The strips themselves were grouped into furlongs, known also as 'shots', 'flatts' or 'wongs' in some parts of the country. Technically, the furlong was not a standard unit of length, but merely a 'furrow long', and consequently varied considerably in size even in a single manor. The fields were communally farmed insofar as they were treated as one unit, subject to the same rotation, ploughed as one piece with teams of oxen or horses, sown at one time and harvested at the same time. However within the communal system, each peasant and his family worked his own strips, more or less efficiently than his neighbour, and the harrowing and sowing, weeding and tending of his strips, collectively known as his 'shot', were his own responsibility.

The chief crops grown in the great fields were wheat; peas, beans and vetches; barley; and oats and rye. Modern root crops were unknown so that the only way of maintaining the fertility of the land, in addition to the application of the modest quantities of animal manure that were available, was a primitive form of crop rotation. In a typical three-field manor, in any given year one field might be sown with winter wheat, one with barley planted in the early spring, and one left fallow. Fallowing was important for another reason, namely because it was one of the effective methods of cleansing land of weed growth. Except for certain areas near large markets, such as London, very little agricultural specialisation occurred and the invariable crop was grain for consumption in the villages and for sale in local markets. This lack of regional specialisation was probably because roads were inadequate and the cost of transportation was too high.

The centre of settlement, indeed the only settlement, within the typical manor was the village, consisting of little more than a single street of small timber-framed, wattle-and-daub houses or crude huts in which lived the peasant families who worked the land and from which they set out the short distance to the fields each morning and to which they returned each evening. The only substantial buildings were the church, built of stone, and the manor house, timber framed or where freestone was easily available, also built of stone. The village might vary in size from 50 to perhaps 500 people and in the fielden parts of the country was usually 'nucleated', that is of a compact design.

The full extent of the manorial system described above has been, and remains, the subject of much research, but in 1400 was certainly widely established in central England, especially in Berkshire and Oxfordshire, Warwickshire and Northamptonshire, Middlesex and Buckinghamshire, and Leicestershire and Nottinghamshire. The most famous contemporary relic of this system is at Laxton in Nottinghamshire where a virtually complete open-field system still operates (Plate 2).

This 'classical' system of open-field farming was also to be found in other parts of England, such as the Welsh marshes. It was well

Plate 2 Laxton in Nottinghamshire: a ground-level view of part of one of the great open fields

developed in Shropshire, for example, where every hamlet in the Hundreds of Ford and Condover, respectively west and south of Shrewsbury, had its own set of open fields.[3] In this part of the country, as in Midland England, the open fields formed islands of cultivation surrounded by extensive stretches of waste and woodland. Indeed, the only part of Shropshire where no open fields were to be found was in the north-west of the country near Oswestry where the settlements consisted of isolated farmsteads rather than nucleated villages.

In other parts of the country, marked regional variations of the 'classic' open-field system existed. In parts of western England, for example, where Celtic or Romano-British fields and boundaries had survived into post-Roman times, these had been adapted to the open-field system. These Celtic fields were rectangular and normally smaller than the Midland open fields because of the different physical and soil conditions which led to their creation. Consequently, when they were subdivided into blocks or strips, the resulting furlongs were of a different size and shape. Similarly, in the upland parts of central England where pastoral farming predominated, such as the Cotswolds, in the chalk downlands of south-east England, in the uplands of northern England, and also in areas such as Essex, Hertfordshire, Cambridgeshire, Staffordshire, Cornwall and Herefordshire, terraces known as *strip lynchets* (Plate 3) were commonly found on the steep hillsides. These terraces represent an extension of the open-field system on to steep ground at a time when the more easily worked land was in short supply, as in the thirteenth century.

The normal method of land inheritance in England was, and remains, by primogeniture, that is the succession of the eldest son on the death of his father. In parts of south-east England and East Anglia, however, a system known as partible inheritance was common during the Middle Ages. This involved dividing the land

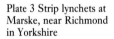

Plate 3 Strip lynchets at Marske, near Richmond in Yorkshire

equally between all the male heirs and, in parts of Kent and Suffolk, for example, resulted in a curious pattern of small block strips, not always cultivated or grazed communally, mixed up with areas of enclosed fields.

Another variant on the 'classical' open-field layout was that which was found in the East Riding of Yorkshire, in the Holderness area. Here the manors normally consisted only of two open fields and many of the strips within the fields were very long, often extending for more than a mile, from one field boundary to another. There were fewer furlongs than in the normal open field and the strips lay parallel throughout the larger part of the field. In parts of south-west England, on the other hand, the open fields presented quite a different appearance. In the uplands of west Somerset and in mid-Devon for example, the arable land lay in strips within a multiplicity of irregular, small fields which were determined largely by the uneven nature of the terrain. The fields were often bounded by massive hedge banks which provided both shelter from wind and rain for crops and livestock, and timber for building and fuel. By contrast, the Fenlands of Cambridgeshire presented yet another pattern of fields. Here, especially in the early Middle Ages, there was a substantial reclamation of agricultural land, both in the peat fens of the south and the silt fens of the north of the county. Large areas of land were reclaimed and enclosed and it seems that the pattern of communal strips was often inextricably mixed up with another pattern of scattered hamlets and farmsteads.

Another important variation of the open-field system was the 'run-rig' or 'infield-outfield' system which was common in areas of poorer land in north-west England. Here, the custom had developed of intensively and permanently cultivating one field, the 'infield', close to the village or farmstead, while less intensively using a second field, the 'outfield', which was further away. The latter was commonly divided into two parts, one being cultivated for several years and then being passed over, the other being left largely uncultivated. Alternatively, the 'outfield' could be abandoned when its yield declined and another one opened up nearby. A form of 'infield-outfield' farming was also practised on the hungry soils of the Breckland in Suffolk; here, large flocks of sheep which were folded on the adjacent pastures provided essential manure for the cultivated fields.

Whatever particular form the open fields might take in a given region, they had in common certain inherent major disadvantages. The peasants had to trudge out from their village homes to the fields in the morning and back again in the evening and, once in the fields, they had to move between their various strips, all time-wasting endeavours. The communal nature of the farming meant that it had to proceed at a measured pace, with an agreed date for ploughing, another for sowing and another for harvesting, to which all had to conform irrespective of individual speed and efficiency.

If a given peasant neglected his strips, the weeds would blow on to those of his neighbours, the careless villager might walk over another man's land or allow his animals to stray and trample down growing crops, and in a system where animals were commoned together, unhealthy beasts infected all the rest. Last, but not least, farming relied as it had done for centuries on primitive technology. In Gregg's words,

> Rejuvenating crops like clover were unknown, seed was wastefully sown, implements were crude, and lack of winter feed for the animals meant a constant straining of resources to keep any animals alive at all for draught, for manure or for providing next year's stock.[4]

However, the general picture of late medieval agriculture as being one of primitive farming methods and relatively low output is relieved by some 'oases' of high productivity. In parts of eastern Norfolk, Huntingdonshire, Cambridgeshire and Sussex, where soils were light and fertile and local urban markets created a demand for food, a system of cultivation had developed which resulted in high yields per acre. It combined the minimum of land under fallow with the use of heavy fertilisation from animal manure, marl and lime. In addition, it seems likely that commercial crops, such as flax, madder, teasels and hemp were grown, principally for use in the manufacture of textiles. Progressive agriculture of this nature was, however, very much the exception and, generally speaking, productivity was low.

The marked shortcomings of traditional open-field, communal farming, together with other considerations, had by 1400 led to a considerable degree of enclosure whereby the large, undivided fields were replaced by a proliferation of small closes, surrounded by hedgerows, each farmed by peasants on an individual basis. This process occurred at different speeds and to different degrees in the various parts of the country and, indeed, within individual counties. In east Devon, for example, enclosure began as early as the middle of the thirteenth century and was virtually complete by the mid-fifteenth, whereas in south Devon it did not begin on some manors until the late fourteenth century and on others not until the sixteenth or seventeenth centuries. A similar process was at work in many other parts of the country and generally took place by the exchange of strips by tenants and their amalgamation into small fields which from about 1300 onwards began to become a regular feature of the landscape. Enterprising tenants would also buy strips adjacent to their own and accumulate them into larger enclosed units. However, the major forms of enclosure which were designed to convert arable land into sheep pastures did not occur on a large scale until the fifteenth and sixteenth centuries and are described in detail in the next chapter.

Although open-field arable farming in its various forms was still characteristic of large parts of lowland England in 1400, as we have seen there existed alongside it another form of agricultural economy, namely pastoral farming which predominated in the 'forest' or wood-pasture areas and in the uplands. Forests were numerous both in lowland England and upland England, north and west of the Exe-Tees line. In the early Middle Ages, substantial parts of the country were designated as 'forests': that is royal hunting grounds to which the 'forest law' applied. This was a body of law designed to protect the beasts of the hunt, especially the deer, and so was very restrictive of cultivation. Although the forests were not necessarily heavily wooded, in practice this was frequently the case as the deer ideally needed tree cover, or covert, in which to flourish. In addition to the royal forests which at their zenith in the twelfth century numbered more than 70 and occupied about one-third of the country, there were at least 26 chases, which were private hunting grounds belonging to great nobles but in which restrictions were enforced similar to those in the forest. The forests were Norman creations and the great majority were in the poorer parts of the country where arable farming was little developed. As the population grew in the early Middle Ages and the demand for land increased, so the forests came under pressure. What has been called 'the journey to the margin of cultivation' developed and poorer, marginal lands were colonised, including the forests from which, for a financial consideration, the Crown was constrained to remove the forest laws.

However, the very nature of the terrain and soils of these areas resulted in a very different agricultural economy and landscape pattern from those of open-field arable farming. The clearing of the forest was itself an arduous task and was frequently undertaken by pioneering individuals. As a result, a pattern of small arable fields developed as part of a mixed farming economy in which livestock rearing was, if anything, more important than crop raising. The most common form of settlement was the isolated farmstead, or croft, rather than the nucleated village of the open-field economy. This landscape pattern was to be found in such areas as Arden in north Warwickshire; in the Chiltern and Cotswold uplands; in the Northamptonshire forests of Rockingham, Salcey and Whittlewood; and in Melchet Forest in Wiltshire and Blackmoor Forest in Dorset, to name but a few. Aspects of the forest landscape can still be identified in some places today, including the evidence of place-name endings indicative of woodland clearance, such as *-rydding, -lea, -wood, -hurst, -dene* and *-holt*; and a mosaic of small, irregularly shaped fields, winding lanes and scattered settlements.

As we have seen in the case of the Fens, marshland reclamation had, by 1400, also added much new land to the agricultural economy. The Fens in eastern England and the Levels of central Somerset in the west were the two largest reclaimed marshlands, but others included the Norfolk Broads; the Essex Marshes; Romney Marsh in Kent and Pevensey Levels in Sussex; the Isle of

Axholme in Lincolnshire; the Vale of York; and the Lancashire Mosses. Although these areas each had distinctive characteristics, they nevertheless were put to very similar uses. Generally speaking, they contained large areas of swampy land, usually under water for a limited period in autumn and winter but dotted with permanent pools and meres. These areas provided very valuable common grazing and sustained large numbers of livestock, especially sheep. Moreover, once reclaimed, they became new meadows which allowed the grazing season to be extended, a very important consideration in an age when winter fodder, or more often its absence, was so crucial to livestock farming. In areas like the Fens where good silt soils and a relatively dry climate were to be found, reclamation was frequently designed to increase the areas of new arable land. In the reclaimed swampy areas, which were still extensive in 1400, other forms of land-use prevailed. Fishing weirs and fisheries were common and fish and eels formed an important part of the local diet, as did wild fowl. Salt pans and rush and sedge collection were important in places and, around the Norfolk Broads, for example, large areas of peat fen were dug for fuel.

Finally, the areas which perhaps contrasted most markedly with the arable open fields of lowland England were the upland pastures on which sheep reigned supreme. These areas consisted mainly of the Yorkshire Dales; the Lincolnshire Wolds; the Cotswolds; the limestone area of North Oxfordshire; much of the Welsh Marches especially in Shropshire and Herefordshire; the chalk downlands of Wiltshire, Hampshire and south-east England; the moors of Devon and Cornwall; and the lower Pennine slopes. These areas, which had been colonised in the early Middle Ages, were thinly settled by lowland standards and for the most part had never been under the plough. Indeed, the only cultivated areas were those close to the settlements which provided food for the farmers and farm labourers. The sheep farms were of two main types: small, individually owned farms, the product of the piecemeal colonisation of the uplands, run mainly by peasants who held their land freehold; and large estates run both by great lay farmers such as the Dukes of Lancaster whose estates were scattered over much of the country and also by religious orders, notably the Cistercians, from their great houses such as Fountains, Rievaulx, Jervaulx, Byland, Kirkstall and Sallay which were all established in remote places in the valleys which bit into the Pennines and the North York Moors.

The small farms were to be found over much of upland England in very substantial numbers and combined sheep rearing with crop raising. The settlement pattern was a scattered one consisting of farmsteads or crofts, which were commonly run by tenant sheep-farmers who managed their flocks as family concerns, sending the wool to the wool market in the nearby town. Occasionally, farmhouses would be grouped into hamlets made up of a few households. More dramatic perhaps in landscaping terms were the large estates run in a highly professional manner by their owners, whether noblemen or monks, and containing very large numbers of sheep. In both cases, the pastoral economy was essentially based on transhumance, with the sheep being moved up to the upland pastures in the late spring and down again to the farmsteads in the autumn, though in some more favoured areas permanent upland pastures were developed. It was as a result of these developments that many upland areas were demarcated by the stone walls which are still today so characteristic a feature of the landscape. English wool was of a very high quality and much prized for its fineness and high felting quality. Among the best of English wools were those from the short fleeces of the sheep in the Welsh Marches, the longer-haired Lincolnshire sheep and especially the Cotswold sheep which by 1400 were becoming the chief source of fine wool.

In addition to sheep, however, the uplands were also the home of cattle farms or vaccaries. They were numerous, for example, either side of the Pennines: the Cistercians had established them in Wyesdale, Nidderdale and Wensleydale in Yorkshire and both religious orders and individual landowners held them in the Forest of Rossendale in Lancashire. Many of these vaccaries, especially those established by the Cistercians in the north of England, were set up as out-stations of the mother house to colonise the upland areas. There were also numerous royal vaccaries, many of them located in the royal forests.

Throughout the Middle Ages, an important and diagnostic feature of the English landscape was its woodland, which in most areas was 'farmed' and managed as carefully as the cultivated lands and the pasture. Wood was an absolutely indispensable element in medieval life. It was the material from which the medieval Englishman fashioned his agricultural implements and building tools, it was used for his furniture, his houses, his carts and carriages, and his fences, and it provided most of his fuel. Tree bark was used for tanning, sap from the bark was used for pitch and tar, wood ash was used for potash, soap, glass and saltpetre, and lime-burners, metal smelters and iron-workers all used wood in the form of charcoal. Animals, especially pigs, were fed upon acorns and beech-mast. The trees that comprised the natural woodland cover were principally the oak, birch and alder. The oak, which was common throughout the country, was the most highly prized tree, for in John Evelyn's words, 'Houses, and Ships, Cities and Navies are built with it.' Other relatively common species included the ash, field maple and lime. Less common was the beech, which was largely restricted to southern England, and the elm and pine, which did not become widespread until long after the Middle Ages. On many manors and farms, the woodland was carefully managed by means of a cropping rotation which ensured that felled timber was replaced. This generally took the form of 'coppice with standards', that is standard trees and underwood. The former consisted typically of oak, ash, hazel, maple, lime and crab apple and yielded timber at regular, if often quite lengthy, intervals. This wood was used for buildings and fashioning implements and furniture. The latter, the underwood, consisted of whole or split sallow, or hazel rods or laths left over from oak timber and were tied together with young sallow shoots or string for use as wattle and daub and for making hurdles and fences.[5] There were, in 1400, still very large areas of woodland and the prospect of a shortage of wood was, with few exceptions, not yet contemplated.

Another important and common feature of the English medieval landscape was the hunting park. Usually fairly small, being perhaps between 100 and 200 acres in size, it was stocked with deer and securely enclosed with a substantial earth bank topped by a fence of cleft oak stakes. The park, which belonged to the lord of the manor and was part of his demesne lands, consisted typically of wooded land beyond the open fields and on the edge of the manor. Its main functions were to provide hunting for the lord of the manor and a source of meat. The hunting parks were at their zenith between 1200 and 1350; numbering at least 1,900, they were to be found all over the country. However, by 1400, they were substantially in decline and many had fallen out of use. Shortage of labour made it increasingly difficult to maintain them properly, many had been disparked or existed in name only and, increasingly, pasture within them was leased out for long periods. However, as we shall see, the fifteenth century was to witness the creation of new parks from tracts of arable and pasture land which had fallen into disuse because of the decline in population. Unlike the hunting parks of the early Middle Ages, they were often quite large, running to hundreds of acres, were probably never securely enclosed, and were conceived from the beginning as amenity parks.

In attempting to paint a picture of the English countryside as it was in the year 1400, we must not overlook the fact that, then as now, the landscape was in the process of change, albeit at a slower rate. Indeed, the previous century had witnessed momentous changes and developments which were still greatly affecting the landscape in 1400.

Perhaps the most dramatic occurrences in the fifty years or so before 1400, and certainly the most terrifying for those who experienced them, were the outbreaks of plague and pestilence. The most celebrated was the so-called Black Death of 1348 and 1349, which it is generally concluded caused the death of one-third of the then population, amounting to over a million persons. The Black Death was a bubonic plague, generally accepted to have been transmitted by the fleas on black rats, though a recent book attributes its cause to anthrax. It was also pneumonic, in that it was spread by direct contagion. Pestilences struck the country again, in

1361, 1369, and 1379 and their combined mortality was such that by 1400 the population of England was probably half of what it had been in 1300. The precise consequences of this enormous rate of mortality on the agricultural economy and, therefore, on the countryside are a matter of considerable discussion and some dispute among historians and historical geographers. It used to be thought that until 1348 both the population and the economy were expanding and that the pestilence brought a sudden stop to this expansion. However, recent research has demonstrated that demographic and economic growth were already in decline by the middle of the fourteenth century and that the Black Death hastened existing developments rather than initiated them.

One major change in the agricultural economy already well under way by 1350 was the decline in 'demesne farming' by manorial landlords. Instead of farming their lands with the customary labour of their peasants, they were increasingly commuting these services for money rents. They were also giving up the cultivation of their home farms entirely; instead they preferred to let their lands to free tenants, becoming *rentiers* in the process, or in some cases to sell them.

Both these trends were accentuated by the plagues, as the resulting sharp drop in population brought about an acute shortage of labour. Thus, there was a growing class of rural yeoman farmers who leased or owned their land, composed of the more intelligent, forceful or lucky peasants who became independent farmers in their own right. This change to tenant farming and a cash economy has been described by Thomson as 'one of the most marked steps in the transition from the traditional medieval economy to the modern.' The shortage of labour in relation to the available land also led to an increase in real wages and a decline in rents for land, with the result that the peasantry who had survived the plague were by 1400 probably enjoying a higher standard of living than during the previous century.

The *Paston Letters* paint a vivid picture of the agricultural landscape in a part of Norfolk at the beginning of the fifteenth century and show how the yeoman farmer, if he was fortunate enough to cultivate fertile land, was in a strong economic position.[6] He grew his corn and other crops on his land, he fed his cattle on the commons or his untilled fields, his dairy supplied him with milk, butter and cheese, and his oxen and his sheep with occasional meat. Wood for repairing his buildings and for fuel was in plentiful supply on the edge of nearby woodlands, and thatch for his house was obtained from reeds in the rivers and ponds or from the long straw stubble of the fields.

The shortage of labour also accelerated the 'retreat from the margin'. Early in the fourteenth century, a deterioration in climate had affected harvests and caused murrain in stock. Pressure of population on marginal land was also causing soil exhaustion and the combined effect of these changes led to a gradual withdrawal

15

from many upland areas and newly reclaimed marshlands. As a result, cultivation ceased in these areas and the land reverted to grass, as for example on the high chalk downlands of Dorset. Much of this grassland has remained unploughed to this day, leaving only the slight undulations of ridge and furrow as evidence of early medieval ploughing. Similarly, many of the strip lynchets carved laboriously out of the hillsides in previous centuries were now abandoned and reverted to grassland, leaving their fossilised remains still to be seen in places in the contemporary landscape. These developments which were accelerated by the plagues of the second half of the fourteenth century, were still in train in 1400.

Perhaps the most marked effect of these changes upon the landscape was the abandonment and contraction of many of the existing settlements. All over the country, villages and hamlets had shrunk and suffered a measure of depopulation as a result of the peasant mortality caused by the plagues. Nor was this shrinkage confined solely to villages and hamlets, as many outlying farmsteads in marginal areas must have been similarly affected. Some settlements disappeared entirely at this time or were substantially reduced. In Oxfordshire, for example, the Black Death caused the village of Steeple Barton to lose 32 of its 36 customary tenants and more than 1,200 acres to fall out of cultivation, while at Tilgarsley in Eynsham the whole population of perhaps 50 families disappeared.[7] However, few settlements were hit as hard as this and most of them struggled with reduced populations. Nevertheless, the evidence of decay was still clearly to be seen in 1400 in the form of deserted farmsteads in the outlying areas and a general air of dilapidation in many villages. In the Bishop of Worcester's manors in Worcestershire, Warwickshire and Gloucestershire, for example, decayed mills and ruinous buildings in need of repair were common.[8] Moreover, as we shall see in Chapter 2, the calamitous events of the fourteenth century were to have longer-term effects and many of the large desertions of settlements which occurred in the fifteenth and sixteenth centuries were probably the culmination of the decline which had set in much earlier.

The only substantial buildings in the medieval countryside, apart from the parish churches and the manor houses in the villages, were the castles owned by the Crown and some of the greater magnates, fortified houses and moated homesteads belonging mainly to lesser lords, and the monastic buildings. By 1400, the great period of castle-building which had seen some 400 castles come into existence since the Norman Conquest was over. There were many reasons for the decline in the English castle and they mirror the changes in society which were taking place in the later Middle Ages. The Norman feudal system which had brought the castle into being was now in decline, a decline accelerated by the mortality engendered by the fourteenth-century plagues and pestilences. The Crown, which owned the majority of castles in

1400, and the great nobles were finding them expensive to maintain properly. The royal administration had become more complex and therefore more sedentary and was settling down in and around London rather than perambulating round the country from castle to castle. By the beginning of the fifteenth century, the true castle was becoming increasingly obsolete as warfare changed and, finally, the aristocracy were increasingly becoming accustomed to higher standards of comfort than the castle could provide. Although the next century was to witness the building of a number of large and substantial residences called 'castles', these were much more in the nature of fortified houses. The fortified house, smaller and less formidably defended than the castle, had co-existed with it for centuries, a splendid and relatively early example being Stokesay Castle in Shropshire. They were to be found all over the country, in somewhat similar numbers to castles, though, like them, construction had tailed off substantially by 1400.

Moated homesteads were considerably more numerous and at their apogee exceeded 5000 in number. Usually the homes of lesser lords, the great majority of them were built in the thirteenth century and the first quarter of the fourteenth century and they served numerous functions. The moat provided an element of protection and a ready supply of water in case of fire, an ever-present hazard in the Middle Ages when timber and thatch were the usual building materials. It also facilitated drainage, especially in lowlying areas like the clay belts of the Midlands, and could be stocked with fish. By 1400, however, many fewer were being constructed. Nevertheless, many remained in use at this time and they still constituted a common and characteristic feature of the English landscape.

Among the most striking and spectacular buildings in the English countryside at the beginning of the fifteenth century were the monastic houses. Of various sizes, the larger ones were usually known as abbeys and the smaller ones were classed as priories. Though they were scattered throughout the country, they were particularly numerous in the Fenlands, in the Severn Valley, and in the southern counties of Somerset, Wiltshire, Dorset and Hampshire. Many were richly endowed and at their zenith in the early Middle Ages they possessed about one-sixth of the land of England. By 1400, however, they had fallen on much harder times. The number of men and women coming forward to be monks was already declining in 1348, when the decline was made catastrophic by the arrival of the Black Death which roughly halved the numbers of people in the religious orders. Although monasticism revived somewhat in the later part of the fourteenth century, by 1400 the number of monks was still only some two-thirds of what it had been a century earlier. Like landlords almost everywhere, the bishops and the Cistercian abbots in the north of England had had to divide up their large farms into smaller ones,

17

which they farmed out on short leases. Finally, the growth of nationalism and anti-papal feeling had by 1400 led to the confiscation of many priories, especially those owing their allegiance to mother houses on the Continent. As a result, many small monasteries and nunneries had fallen into decay and many others had greatly reduced numbers of inmates. Nevertheless, the influence of the Church on the English landscape remained a substantial one.

However, the traumatic changes of the fourteenth century were not all harmful. One result of the decline in population and the consequent fall in land values and the rise in wages was the stimulation of sheep farming. Sheep were immune from plague, the labour needed to look after them was considerably less than for arable farming and there was a substantial demand for wool, the most widely used textile in the Middle Ages, and especially for woollen cloth for export to the Continent. As a consequence, one of the most important industrial developments during the late Middle Ages was the growth of the textile industry. The basis of this industry was the fulling mill which, unlike its continental counterparts in Flanders and Italy, was predominantly located in the countryside. The process of fulling, which consists of the beating and compressing of woven cloth to clean and thicken it, had in earlier times been undertaken by craftsmen: in Langland's words, the cloth was 'trodden under foot in water', in fulling pits or vats filled with water and fuller's earth, a clay still used today as an absorbent of the grease and oil of cloth. The introduction of the fulling mill, a simple mechanism driven by water, revolutionised the process and from the thirteenth century onwards many were built throughout the country by manorial landlords in search of profit. Because they needed access to swiftly running water, the mills were usually sited on hilly ground in the countryside.

Different parts of England were noted for their different qualities of wool and, by 1400, the major cloth-producing regions included Wiltshire and Gloucestershire, where broad cloth was produced for export, the West Riding of Yorkshire, where a lower grade of cloth was produced for the home market, the worsted region of Norwich, the traditional cloth regions of Essex and Suffolk, and the cloth-producing region of Devon and Somerset. The second half of the fourteenth century had witnessed a considerable growth in cloth production both for export and for use at home.

Another important rural industry was the manufacture of iron products, which was located in the woodland areas, principally the Weald of Surrey, Sussex and Kent, the Forest of Dean and the Cleveland Hills, where both iron ore and wood were available. Smelting, which was carried on in small furnaces, required vast quantities of charcoal produced in and from the woodland areas by charcoal burners. The ore and charcoal were heated by ironsmiths in a furnace with the aid of bellows until the impurities in the ore liquefied and separated to form slag and a porous lump of iron, the 'bloom'. The next stage was the heating up of the bloom in a bloomery hearth and the hammering out of as much as possible of the residual slag to obtain relatively pure iron. During most of the Middle Ages all these processes were done by hand. Iron smelting was carried on commercially as well as being found in monastic and lay manors where it supplied immediate domestic needs. A major technological advance in iron smelting occurred in England in the fourteenth century with the increasing use of water power to drive the hammers in the bloomery hearths. For this purpose, ponds and pools would be damned up, and relics of these late medieval 'hammer ponds' are still to be found in the Sussex Weald today. Within the domestic agricultural economy, the smith, or 'blacksmith' to distinguish him from the 'bloomsmith who made the iron', was a key figure who fashioned the iron artefacts so essential to the medieval economy. The smithing hearth, which was to be found virtually everywhere, provided a means of reheating pieces of iron so that they could be shaped efficiently and, for this purpose, very large quantities of charcoal were required. On the whole, the smiths did not make their own iron, which was supplied by bloomsmiths who worked it into standard bars. The medieval blacksmith then produced the many tools and fittings required in medieval England as well as more specialised products such as church doors and screens, weapons and armour.

Among the extractive industries, the most important were the mining of coal, tin, lead and zinc, and the extraction of salt. The extraction of coal was never highly developed in the Middle Ages and the demand for it was fairly small. Most pits were relatively shallow 'bell-pits' and there was some outcrop mining from surface deposits. The main coal-mining centre was the Tyne Valley of Northumberland, but coal was also mined in other parts of the country including Yorkshire, the Midlands, Lancashire and Shropshire. Lead and zinc-mining and smelting also operated on a small scale and the principal centres were the Mendips, the area between Weardale and the upper reaches of Teesdale in Durham, Wharfedale and Wensleydale in North Yorkshire and the Low Peak of Derbyshire. The most important centres of medieval tin mining were Devon and Cornwall, the output of Cornish stanneries alone exceeding a million and a quarter pounds in 1400. Salt extraction was centred in Cheshire, in Nantwich, Middlewich and Northwich; and in Worcestershire, at Droitwich. The industry was relatively small and the salt-workings formed miniature industrial enclaves in the middle of agricultural districts.

Of all the extractive industries, however, the most ubiquitous was the quarrying of stone for building, including limestone, marble, alabaster, chalk and clay. As they commonly occurred near the surface, they could be quarried relatively easily. Except when used for great buildings like cathedrals and palaces, stone was carried only short distances and used locally so that churches and other stone buildings reflected the nature of the local stone, from the honey-coloured Ham Hill stone of Somerset to the pale golden limestone of the Cotswolds, to the grey Barnack stone of Northamptonshire and the dark Millstone Grit of parts of northern England. Marble, as a hard stone and one capable of taking a high polish, was used in churches for making columns, tombs and effigies: the most famous was Purbeck marble, based on the flourishing centre of Corfe. Alabaster, extracted in Chellaston in Derbyshire, in parts of Nottinghamshire and at Tutbury in Staffordshire, was also used in churches and cathedrals.

Other important medieval industries which were essentially craft-based included the making of leather, pottery, glass and pewter. Leather, which was made by curing and tanning the hides of cattle and sheep, was used for innumerable articles including boots, coats, hats, buckets, boxes and chests, bags and purses, and harness and saddles. Leather tanning was widely practised on an individual basis all over the country but there were also a few areas where leather making was carried on on a commercial basis, including Leicestershire and Northamptonshire which were important centres for raising cattle and sheep. Pottery and tile making was also very common. It seems that almost without exception it was carried on in the country where it was probably a seasonal pursuit practised by peasant farmers who were also craftsmen supplementing their income. Pottery kilns were widespread, as clay suitable for making pottery occurs in many parts of the country and their most common products were jugs, bowls and cooking pots. Cups and plates were unknown in the great majority of households and most peasants ate and drank out of wooden vessels. The production of floor-tiles and roof-tiles, although quite widespread, was more specialised and kilns were either built on the sites of palaces, churches or monasteries where their products were to be used, or were constructed in a few places as part of small-scale commercial enterprises.

The use of glass increased considerably during the Middle Ages and by 1400 was being used in windows in cathedrals and large churches and in a few secular buildings. The use of glass vessels as tableware also increased, though in 1400 they were only to be found in the greater houses. Very little documentary or other evidence exists to pinpoint the centres of glass manufacture, but it was certainly made in the Weald of Surrey and Sussex and was no doubt also to be found where other suitable glass-making sands were available. In any case, the glass-makers were probably semi-nomadic and few permanent glass-making furnaces have survived. Pewter, an alloy made up of varying amounts of tin and lead, was traditionally cast in moulds and then turned out and hammered. It seems to have been highly regarded in the Middle Ages and was widely used by the churches and religious houses for such things as chalices and cups. By 1400, it was also being used in an increasing number of the wealthier households for cooking and eating utensils. Although London was by far the most important centre of the English pewter industry at this time, there were centres in other parts of the country, including Cornwall where plentiful quantities of tin were readily available.[9]

It is impossible to say to what extent industrial development in the Middle Ages was hampered by poor communications. Certainly, it seems likely that the medieval road system, which was the principal means of communication, was inadequate for the volume of traffic, especially in winter. Part of the network of Roman roads radiating from London had survived and was still in use. In addition, many other secondary roads had come into existence, serving manor, village and town. However, unlike the Roman roads, they were not 'made' with solid foundations but were rather cross-country tracks of varying width and sizes, being little more than the legal right of way from one place to another. Judging by the limited amount of documentary evidence available, the general condition of the roads in the early fifteenth century was deplorable. It is unlikely that any new roads had been made since the Black Death of 1348 and many of the existing roads must have fallen into disrepair. Nevertheless, they carried a great deal of traffic, including merchandise carried by trains of pack-horses and by carts drawn by horses or occasionally oxen. Moreover, in Stenton's words,

> with all its defects the road system of medieval England provided
> alternate routes between many pairs of distant towns, united port and
> inland market, permitted regular if not always easy communication
> between the villages of a shire and county town . . . and brought every
> part of the country within a fortnight's ride of London.[10]

Next to the roads, the rivers were also of great importance, especially for the transportation of heavy goods. Where possible, heavier loads and those brought from farther away would be carried by water, in river barges drawn by teams of horses, or sometimes oxen, plodding along the towpaths. The major arteries of river traffic were the Severn, the Thames, the Trent, the Great Ouse and its tributaries, and the Yorkshire Ouse. This method of transportation, which was cheaper than packhorse, brought building stone from Northamptonshire along the Welland and Nene, iron ore from the Forest of Dean up the Severn, and timber from the Forests of Needwood and Sherwood along the Trent, to name but three examples. River transportation, however, was not without its difficulties and hazards and these are discussed in detail in Chapter 7.

The picture that emerges from this analysis of the English countryside in 1400 is of a thinly peopled landscape, with most of the population and cultivation concentrated in lowland England, south and east of the Exe-Tees line. Within the latter areas,

Midland England was characterised by its cultivated open fields and nucleated villages, its meadows and commonable waste, beyond which spread the woodland and heathland which were the natural vegetation of the countryside. In downland areas such as Lincolnshire, the Cotswolds, the South Downs, and in parts of the upland areas of the Pennines and the North York Moors, innumerable sheep grazed. In the Fenlands to the east and the Somerset Levels of the south-west, areas of marsh and fen had been reclaimed from the sea, although by 1400 much of it still remained to be reclaimed or was returning to its natural state.

The past 50 years had seen calamitous changes and, as we have seen, the plagues and pestilences of the second half of the fourteenth century had carried away more than a million people. The resulting shrinkage of settlements and dereliction of buildings was evident throughout the country. For the surviving peasants, however, the consequent shortage of labour and rise in wages meant they probably enjoyed a higher standard of living at the beginning of the fifteenth century than had previously been the case. Moreover, some parts of the country, notably the centres of cloth production such as East Anglia and the West Country, were benefiting from a considerable degree of economic prosperity. Everywhere, though, the scene was set for major changes in agricultural techniques and practices which over the next three hundred years were to transform the English countryside and leave a rich legacy of relict features.

CHAPTER 2

Sheep or men?
The cultivated landscape in the fifteenth and sixteenth centuries

The history of the English cultivated landscape in the years between 1400 and 1700 is one of enormous and complex changes which considerably altered the appearance of the countryside. In broad terms, these changes, which accelerated towards the end of the period, may be summarised under four main headings. Firstly, the cultivated area itself gradually expanded as a result of the bringing under the plough of former areas of forest and park, of reclaiming marshland and fen and, towards the end of the period, of the arable cultivation of the thin soils of the chalk and limestone uplands and the sandy heathlands. Secondly, agricultural productivity was substantially increased, partly as a result of the enclosure of the open fields, but more especially because of improvements in agricultural techniques and the introduction of new crops. The introduction of new fodder crops was particularly significant in that it enabled more livestock to be kept so that more manure became available to increase the fertility of the soil. Thirdly, agriculture increasingly became a commercial undertaking dominated by landowners of varying degrees of substance and inevitably accompanied by the retreat of peasant farming of a largely subsistence character. Fourthly, areas of regional agricultural specialisation developed throughout the country. The background to these developments and to a large extent the motive force behind them was that the population of England more than doubled during the period, from about 2¼ million people in 1400 to approximately 5 million in 1700.[1] It was the major achievement of English agriculture over these three hundred years that it succeeded not only in providing the population of the country with almost all its food and drink, a few exotic imported luxuries excepted, but also furnished manufacturers with many of their raw materials.

In 1400, however, these developments still lay far in the future. As we have seen, the sharp drop in population resulting from the plagues had brought about an acute shortage of labour which in turn forced many landowners to change their methods of exploiting their estates. This frequently took the form of abandoning direct cultivation of the demesne land by the lord's paid men and leasing it out instead for a cash rent, a gradual process which varied in time and rate of change from one part of the country to another. However, by the early fifteenth century, it seems to have occurred widely throughout the country and, as the century wore on, what often began as piecemeal leasing increasingly took the form of the farming out of larger blocks of land and for longer terms. By 1405, for example, in the great Percy estates of Yorkshire, the lord was only cultivating his demesne in the two manors of Seamer, near Scarborough, and Nafferton, in the East Riding, compared to five manors fifty years earlier. Although at this time the Percies continued to cultivate all their demesne lands in their four Sussex manors of Petworth, Sutton, Duncton, and Heyshott, twenty years later, in all the Percy estates in both Yorkshire and Sussex the demesne lands had been leased to tenant farmers. A similar process was occurring on ecclesiastical estates, such as the Bishop of Worcester's manors in Worcestershire, Warwickshire and Gloucestershire, where by the beginning of the fifteenth century, virtually all the demesnes had been leased out. Similarly, in the Kent manors of the Archbishop of Canterbury, by 1405, all the demesnes were being leased out, usually to single individuals, but occasionally to two or three friends or kinsmen. However, as we shall see, some lords converted their demesnes to sheep pastures, which were retained under direct management.

The leasing of demesne land to peasant farmers resulted in what Dyer has termed 'a downward social distribution of access to the land'.[2] By this process, the lords, particularly those with large estates, leased their lands not only to the peasants, who would have been in the great majority, but also to the gentry, to the lesser clergy, to businessmen, and to their own reeves or bailiffs who would have had a special knowledge of their estates. These fifteenth century tenant farmers constituted 'an upper class of peasantry', who were cultivating an area of 60 to 80 arable acres, whereas the holdings of their great-grandfathers had been 30. This increase in the size of their holdings was achieved by 'engrossing', that is by purchasing or exchanging strips in the open fields adjacent to their own and forming them into compact blocks of land which they then enclosed. They purchased their own draught animals, oxen or horses, and raised crops and grazed livestock. In this way, the appearance of the countryside was, in many parts of the country, undergoing a slow but steady change, from one of large, communal open fields to small, individual holdings surrounded by hedges and cultivated by tenant farmers. In the middle of the fifteenth century, for example, a Bohemian visitor to England was observing that, 'the peasants dig ditches round their fields and meadows and so fence them in that no one can pass on foot or horseback except by the main roads.'[3] This peasant enclosure was often accompanied by the building of isolated single farm settlements on holdings away from the nucleated villages in which the peasants had traditionally lived.

For the great majority of farmers, however, agriculture was still a primitive business and still conducted on traditional unscientific lines. During the fifteenth century, the chief crops remained wheat, oats, barley, rye, peas, beans and vetches. Roots, clover and many types of grasses were as yet unknown in England and their absence made it impossible for the farmer to cultivate his land by any modern form of crop rotation. All he could do to help to maintain soil fertility was what he had always done, namely let each field lie fallow every second or third year. In the autumn, he ploughed his land and sowed wheat, and in the late winter and early spring, oats and peas were planted, followed by barley. In addition, bits and pieces of land were allocated for the provision of livestock feeding, which in many parts of England was seen merely as an adjunct to arable farming. Sheep and cattle were fed upon the stubble of the arable crops and whatever land could be grazed.

During the fifteenth century, however, strips in the open fields, called 'leys', were increasingly set aside specifically for use as pasture and temporarily put down to grass. Moreover, in some restricted parts of the country around the south and east coasts of England where soils were light and fertile and the large market of London was relatively close at hand, some agricultural progress had been made. In these limited areas, a combination of arable and pastoral farming, which later became known as alternate or convertible husbandry was practised, enabling high yields, by late medieval standards, to be obtained. Even in the grain-growing areas like the Midlands, cash crops such as hemp and flax were grown in small enclosures.

During the fifteenth century, as since time immemorial, agriculture was the essential occupation for the great majority of the people, for almost all the food they consumed was homegrown. As few records exist, it is impossible to draw up a detailed and accurate account of the life and economic fortunes of the fifteenth-century tenant farmers. Overall, however, the country-side had not yet recovered from the effects of the Black Death and the plagues which followed and must still have presented a picture of dereliction with marginal land having reverted to waste and scrub, and farm buildings lying abandoned and ruinous. Moreover, farmers were always at the mercy of the weather and such natural disasters as plagues and murrain. In an average decade, possibly one harvest in every four would be deficient and one in six very bad. Farming households were generally quite small and rarely extended to three generations. In most regions of England, primogeniture was the rule of inheritance and, as in parts of the Irish Republic today, eldest sons often deferred marriage until their fathers died or could no longer run the farm. More substantial farmers might employ 'day labourers' or have living-in labourers, but the majority of farmers with smaller holdings, often no more than 15 to 20 acres, both farmed their own land and

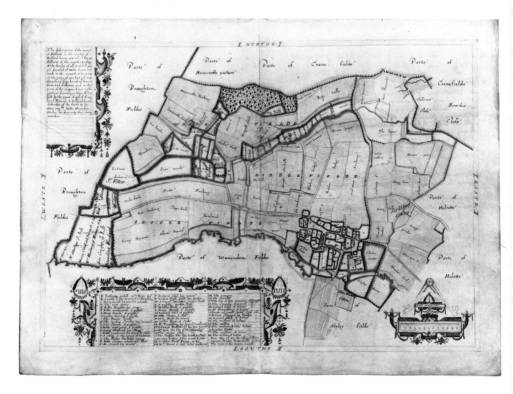

Plate 4 A beautifully drawn map of 1596 of the open fields of the village of Salford in Bedfordshire. The village lies in the south-east corner of the parish and in the north is Salford Wood. The open fields were eventually enclosed by Act of Parliament in 1808

augmented their income by working for other larger farmers or by engaging in small-scale trading such as collecting their food surpluses and those of their neighbours, and taking them off to the nearest market town to sell or exchange for other goods. Whatever the size of their holdings, peasant farmers – known to their contemporaries as husbandmen or yeomen – also kept gardens, in which they grew vegetables, peas and beans, and fruit trees.

Meanwhile, the traditional forms of open-field cultivation continued to dominate large areas of the country, especially within the Midland plain (Plate 4) bounded by the Malvern Hills to the west, the Chiltern ridge to the south and the Fenlands to the east, as well as other parts of the country such as the lighter lands of Wiltshire, Dorset and Hampshire. In these areas, the communal organisation of the manuring, sowing and harvesting of the crops and the regulation of meadows and more permanent pastures continued much as it had for centuries. What is uncertain is how efficiently and profitably these open fields were being farmed. According to some authorities, the fifteenth century witnessed a slow decline in the natural fertility of the arable land in the open fields. The lightly-ploughed soil was seldom manured and so it became exhausted and yields declined. Fitzherbert,[4] writing in the first quarter of the sixteenth century, remarks upon the decline in crop yields and the slovenly methods of husbandry in these areas. Open-field farmers grazed their sheep on the stubble of the crops and relied on them to fertilise the land. Unfortunately, because of lack of winter feed, the livestock became greatly reduced in number in winter and the poor condition of those which remained laid them open to disease. It became commonplace to see the head of an ox impaled on a stake by the highway indicating that the village was infected. This decline in fertility was frequently accompanied by the migration from their home manor of peasants seeking land holdings in other manors, or work in burgeoning industrial villages in such areas as Essex, Wiltshire, and Norfolk, or in London and the larger towns. Given the difficulties of the times, this was probably a sensible thing to do.

As a consequence of this human movement during the fifteenth century, there were changes in the nature and size of peasant landholdings. One of the major effects of the plagues of the second half of the fifteenth century was to create a scarcity of labour and a surplus of land, though there were considerable variations from one part of the country to another. In general terms, however, the average size of peasant holdings grew as increasing numbers of peasants who survived took the opportunity of acquiring vacant land near their own strips and fields, though this often took the form of short-term leasing of land between one and another. According to Butlin,[5] an important feature of the period was the changeover from customary tenure of holdings to leasehold tenure, which was widespread by 1500. In the early Middle Ages, the traditional method of landholding for the peasant was that of customary tenure, or copyhold, by which he held and cultivated strips in the open fields according to the custom of the manor, by copy of the roll originally made by the steward of the lord of the manor. This type of landholding had already begun to change in the early Middle Ages to leasehold, by which the peasant contracted with the lord to rent his land for a fixed term or 'farm'. This movement was greatly accelerated by problems in the land and labour markets created by the plague in the second half of the fifteenth century. However, not only were there considerable variations from one region to another, and indeed within regions, but in some places copyhold tenure was extremely persistent and did not finally disappear until the present century.

In general, tenant farmers, by whatever system of tenure they held their lands, were able to farm them more efficiently than had been the case in the communal agriculture of the open fields. Their holdings were more compact and they had greater and more intimate knowledge of local conditions and markets than their absentee landlords. Moreover, as the land under cereal crops declined in the fifteenth century, so the tenant farmer could devote more acreage to animal production and so produce more farmyard manure with which to fertilise the cultivated land. For

27

many of the 'new farmers' therefore, the fifteenth century was a period of relative prosperity.

During the fifteenth century, and indeed in successive centuries down to the early years of the present one, the character and appearance of the English countryside has been chiefly determined by what is generally described as 'the enclosure movement', a process which had been going on, albeit on a smaller scale, since the twelfth century. The transformation which it has wrought is most apparent in Midland England where the medieval open fields have been wholly replaced by the enclosed, hedged fields of the contemporary landscape. As we have seen, large parts of England were already enclosed by the beginning of the fifteenth century, notably in the woodland and upland regions. This process was gradually to extend to the rest of the country, at varying speeds in different areas, throughout the next five hundred years. In landholding terms, the enclosure of the open fields and the common pasture and waste meant that instead of the land being held and farmed communally, that is by the peasants of the village community, it came into the hands of a single landlord, or sometimes two or three owners, when it was described as being held in severalty.

Before considering the major characteristics of the enclosure movement, it is important to point out that although in practice enclosure nearly always involved the physical demarcation of landholding by hedges, fences, walls and ditches and the appropriation to an individual of whatever common rights attached to the land enclosed, this was not invariably the case. Occasionally, an individual might technically 'enclose' a stretch of open land and remove its common rights but allow it to remain unchanged in appearance. Moreover, as we have seen, the phenomenon of agricultural enclosure long predated the fifteenth and sixteenth centuries, though on a smaller scale. Indeed, the chronology, distribution and causes of enclosure are extremely complex and their study has generated a very considerable literature since the early years of the present century. In parts of southern England and the West Country, enclosure had occurred well before the fifteenth century, in Lincolnshire and the East Riding of Yorkshire it became common in the late fourteenth and fifteenth centuries, in the Midland Plain it became prevalent in the fifteenth century, and in parts of northern England it did not become widespread until the late sixteenth century. Even in individual counties, however, there were considerable variations: in Devon, for example, enclosure was occurring in the eastern part of the county by the middle of the thirteenth century, while in the south it began in some manors in the late fourteenth and early fifteenth centuries and in others it did not take place until the sixteenth and seventeenth centuries. These variations were due as much as anything to the differing nature of the farming in different areas.

As we have seen, one form of enclosure was 'engrossing', or the amalgamation of two or more holdings into one to create larger, more compact units in order to make agriculture more efficient and profitable. This form of enclosure could, and often did, take place by local agreement, with few harmful social consequences. However, another type of enclosure which was widespread by the second half of the fifteenth century was the conversion by lords of both their demesne lands and, more particularly, the communal lands, for sheep farming. This often resulted in the destruction of communities and rural depopulation, occasioning much complaint and social unrest. As we have seen, some shrinkage of cultivated land of agricultural settlement had already occurred by 1400, but there is little evidence of the complete abandonment of the open fields and the desertion of villages. The effects of the plagues in the second half of the fourteenth century had been to cause vacant tenements to remain unfilled and for buildings to become derelict, rather than the total desertion of villages. The recovery of population was very slow and was not helped by the occurrence of further outbreaks of plague in 1413, 1438-9 and 1479. However, there was a gradual take-up of abandoned holdings throughout the fifteenth century and in south-east Durham for example, an area of fertile soils ideal for corn growing, the number of derelict tenements began to decline slowly after about 1420.[6]

The major movement by landlords to enclose cultivated land and put it down to grass for sheep farming occurred from about 1440 to 1520. The chief region where this took place was the Midlands – especially in Oxfordshire, Warwickshire, Buckinghamshire, Leicestershire, Northamptonshire and Nottinghamshire. It also occurred on a substantial scale in eastern England especially in East Yorkshire and the Lincolnshire uplands; in Norfolk where, however, it was largely over by 1485; and in Lancashire. The abandonment of marginal arable land in the fourteenth and the earlier part of the fifteenth centuries, land which tumbled to grass and was used for sheep grazing, was enforced in the sense that it was brought about by declining population and economic pressures. By contrast, the period after about 1440 was one of deliberate enclosure by landlords for profit. The incentive to enclose was the demand for wool for the expanding English cloth industry, at a time when the population had not recovered sufficiently from the plagues to increase substantially the demand for corn. Moreover, pastoral farming required a much smaller labour force than did arable farming, an important consideration in a period when labour was expensive. Furthermore, the decline in the number of tenants during the latter part of the fourteenth century, the tendency to accumulate holdings, and the move towards pastoral farming, had all helped to destroy the cohesion of some of the open field communities and to make it easier for a thrusting landlord to acquire large numbers of holdings and to turn them into pasture. Thus as the number of tenants dwindled and the open fields were gradually abandoned, so the landlord resorted to enclosure in order to recoup his fortune. This process was certainly common in the later fifteenth century in villages in the Midlands, in Warwickshire and Worcestershire, and was probably also taking place in the Yorkshire Wolds.

This enclosure of open fields was necessarily more frequent in the champion districts of arable farming and nucleated villages, for it was here that the open fields were most widespread. During the same period, however, common waste land was also being enclosed, both in the champion areas and in the remainder of the country. In the former districts, especially the Midland counties of Leicestershire, Warwickshire and Northamptonshire, whose heavy arable land was difficult to work and labour intensive, and parts of the Yorkshire Wolds whose thin soils gave relatively poor yields, the degree of enclosure varied from place to place. It was easier for the landlord to accomplish where he was the sole lord of the manor and where the peasants were copyholders and tenants were few. Landholding considerations such as these account in part for the differential distribution of enclosure.

The effect on the landscape was, more often than not, dramatic. In south-east Leicestershire, for example, at Noseley in 1504, an enclosing landlord, Thomas Hazelrigg, was alleged to have 'destroyed 5 messuages, turned six others into pasture. 12 ploughs were put down, 52 persons evicted.'[7] Four years later, seven more messuages were destroyed and 500 acres converted into pasture, thereby making the enclosure complete and bringing about the 'wilful decay' of the whole village. The open fields were then hedged and three large fields were created, called in 1584 Cottons, Mill and Nether Fields, possibly coincident with the former common fields. The first-named was more than 300 acres in size and was grazed by 700 sheep and 100 cattle. At Lowesby, a few miles to the north-west, William Ashby in 1487 seized '3 messuages and 120 acres of arable land and caused the said messuages to be destroyed and the said lands to be enclosed with hedges and converted from tillage into cattle pasture.' The effect of enclosure like this was frequently to cause whole villages to be deserted and depopulated. Indeed, in some cases enclosure took place in stages, often spread over centuries, as at Great Stretton, in Leicestershire (Plate 5). Moreover, changes in the landscape did not necessarily follow immediately upon the desertion of the open-field community and the fields and pasture might be subdivided, or even hedged for the first time, at a later date than that on the original enclosure. Frequently, as we have seen, physical enclosure resulted in the creation of several large fields. More often, perhaps, they were divided up into relatively small, hedged fields or closes which, after being put down to grass, were stocked with different kinds of stock, the animals being moved frequently from one field to another to avoid overgrazing. Unlike later eighteenth- and nineteenth-century parliamentary enclosures, these fifteenth- and early sixteenth-century enclosed fields were not bounded by straight hedges but rather followed sinuous natural boundaries such as streams. The end product was a landscape of irregular fields which can still be seen today in some parts of the country. It was not until a century later that maps became available which show how the enclosed Midland landscape must have looked in the latter part of the sixteenth century, and indeed a century earlier. In Whatborough, Leicestershire, in 1586, for example, the former open fields were divided into eight pasture closes, each surrounded by irregularly shaped hedges. In Radbourne, Warwickshire, by contrast, the Catesby family held the whole parish as a 1000-acre pasture on which they grazed flocks of sheep varying in size from 1,643 animals in 1448 to 2,742 in 1476, not to mention herds of cattle varying from a dozen to 54, and horses from 9 to 17. Radbourne also possessed a rabbit warren, a common enough feature in late medieval manors, with many hundreds of rabbits feeding off the pastures just like the other stock.

Occasionally, the former open fields would be enclosed to form large, new parks or existing parks would be enlarged to take in adjoining areas of cultivated land. Thus the three Kentish parks of Eythorne, Kingsnorth and Tonge were each over 1000 acres in 1474; Eagle in Lincolnshire measured more than 4600 acres in 1446; and Kirby Muxloe in Leicestershire came into existence in 1474, when Lord Hastings imparked 2000 acres there. These parks, unlike their medieval predecessors, were ornamental rather than hunting parks and so were merely enclosed with hedges or fences rather than by high earth banks topped with paling fences. In the high, chalk country of the Yorkshire Wolds, many

Plate 5 Great Stretton, in Leicestershire, a deserted village that was partly enclosed in the fifteenth century, the remainder being enclosed between 1640 and 1670. The church now stands in isolation in the bottom of the photograph and towards the top is a well-defined moated site. Just below the moated site can be seen the indentation of the former manorial fishpond and the village paths and traces of ridge and furrow can also be identified

depopulated parishes were left much as they had always been, grassed over certainly and grazed by livestock, but undivided by walls or hedges. In this region, there was neither the raw material for hedges nor for stone walls so that it was not until considerably later that they were enclosed with hedges and ceased to be an open landscape.

Because of the absence of sufficient documentary evidence it is impossible to assess the true extent of the enclosures which occurred in the period between 1440 and 1520, though generally speaking they represented a relatively small proportion of the total arable land of the counties concerned. For example, Wordie[8] estimates that by 1500 some 45 per cent of the land in England was enclosed and that in the next 100 years only another 2 per cent was added to it. However, in the Midland counties, the rate of enclosure was undoubtedly higher, and Dyer estimates that between 1349 and 1520 about one-third of the arable area of Leicestershire was converted to pasture, and that much enclosure of waste and common pasture land had also taken place. In England as a whole, probably little more than 750,000 acres were subject to enclosure between about 1450 and 1650, a relatively small area by modern standards. However, as it was mostly land converted from arable farming in a country where the cultivated area still occupied a relatively small proportion of the landscape, its significance in terms of agricultural productivity was considerable.

For the peasants farming the open fields, the effects of the enclosure movement were devastating. In place of a busy community of arable farmers, were a few shepherds and their sheep. Villages were depopulated and became deserted, their houses and farm buildings falling into ruin. The regulated and long-established social order of open-field farming was completely disrupted, leaving deep scars not only on the peasants themselves but on society as a whole. The harmful social effects of enclosure, especially the removal of the peasantry from their open-field communities and the resulting desertion of settlements, have been well documented by contemporary writers and later historians. These consequences did not attract serious condemnation and social unrest until towards the end of the fifteenth century. In 1489, for example, in response to growing criticism, the Crown introduced its first measure dealing with the problem of enclosure, a largely ineffective Husbandry Act relating to the Isle of Wight. The Act arose not so much from concern with the social consequences of enclosure, but rather a fear that the depopulation it brought about would adversely affect the defence of the realm. As the government stated, 'If hasty remedy be not provided that Isle cannot be long kept and defended, but open and ready to the hands of the king's enemies.' In the following year, a general Act was passed condemning depopulation, asserting that in townships or villages in which previously 200 people were engaged in work, there were now only 2 or 3 herdsmen, the rest being idle. The act of enclosure itself was not made illegal but rather its effect, namely causing the decay of a house of husbandry which had more than 20 acres under the plough. The comparative lack of protest about enclosure in the greater part of the fifteenth century may have been due to the fact that the relatively low level of population meant that if villagers were evicted by the lord they had reasonable prospects of finding land holdings elsewhere. By the beginning of the sixteenth century, however, circumstances had changed. Population was growing again, vacant holdings were being taken up and rents were rising. Consequently, arable land was once more in demand and its enclosure was much more likely to cause depopulation and rural vagrancy and so to occasion social unrest. Thus, although there had been earlier petitions against enclosure – for example, John Rouse, the Warwickshire antiquary claimed that he had presented one to the parliament of 1459 and in his *Historia Regum Anglie* left a list of 58 depopulated places in Warwickshire – the most famous denunciation of the social evils resulting from enclosure is that of Sir Thomas More in his *Utopia* of 1516,

> Your sheep that were wont to be so meek and tame and so small eaters, now, I hear say, be become so great devourers and so wild, that they eat up and swallow down the very men themselves. They consume, destroy and devour whole fields . . . and leave no ground for tillage. They enclose all pastures, they throw down houses; they pluck down towns, and leaving nothing standing but only the church to be made into a sheep-house.

In 1514, a royal proclamation was issued against the engrossing of farms and in the following year another Act of Parliament was passed making it an offence to convert land from tillage to pasture. Two years later, in 1517, Cardinal Wolsey set up the first of a series of royal commissions to enquire what land had been converted from arable to pasture and what parks had been enclosed since Michaelmas 1488. Further Commissions of Enquiry followed, in 1548, 1566, 1607, 1630, 1632 and 1635, and together they assembled a large amount of information on the subject. However, not one of them investigated the whole country and their findings were frequently incomplete and often of doubtful accuracy. The work of the Commissions did, however, often result in Acts of Parliament directed against the conversion of arable land to pasture and by the end of the sixteenth century no fewer than a dozen such Acts had been passed, albeit to very little effect. The Act of 1534, for example, decreed that no man should keep more than 2000 sheep, some indication of the very large numbers of sheep in England at that time. Indeed, a contemporary observed at the beginning of the sixteenth century that there were three sheep for every person in England which, if accurate, meant they must have numbered nearly 7 millions.

However, by about 1520, the rate of enclosure of arable land for sheep farming was beginning to slow down, and by the middle of the sixteenth century, in the view of most writers on the subject, had fallen off considerably, to revive again only towards the end of the century. This decrease in enclosure was due partly to government action occasioned by popular unrest, partly to the growth in population which increased the demand for corn and so led to more land being used for cultivation and less for sheep pasture, and partly to a depression in the cloth trade from about the middle of the sixteenth century which resulted in lower wool prices. Moreover, from about 1550 onwards, the methods of enclosure were undergoing an important change. They were no longer primarily the work of a single manorial lord enclosing land for extensive sheep farming, but instead were predominantly designed to bring about enclosure by agreement between a number of 'improving' landowners in order to promote more productive intensive agriculture, especially in the form of alternate husbandry, namely the alternation of arable farming and grass, as an alternative to the use of arable followed by fallow.

Before examining in detail the work of the sixteenth-century improvers, it is worth reiterating the broad features of the English countryside as they existed in about the year 1550.[9] The open fields of one kind or another were still very widespread, with the greatest concentration occurring in the 'Midland zone' comprising the south coast of England between Devon and Sussex and running north and east across the country to Durham and coastal Northumberland (Figure 2). Within this area, they were notably absent, however, from the wood-pasture region of central Suffolk, from much of Essex, and from virtually the whole of Kent. In the Midland zone, different forms of open field farming had developed, including two-field systems which were common in southern Warwickshire, parts of Lincolnshire and south Northamptonshire; and three-field systems in north Warwickshire, Leicestershire and north Northamptonshire. In order to increase the intensity of cultivation, many peasants had by agreement moved from two- or three-course rotation to a four-field or multiple system, thereby making intensive cropping easier. This was certainly the case in southern Warwickshire, in neighbouring south-east Worcestershire, and in Lincolnshire.

In other parts of lowland England, many variations in agricultural practices were to be found, including the large open fields of the chalk downs and the Cotswolds, the enclosed field landscape of much of Kent, and the small, irregular fields of the wood-pasture districts such as the Weald and the New Forest. A similar variety was to be found in northern and western England including the 'Celtic' fields of Cornwall, which by this time was wholly enclosed, and the irregular, small-scale field pattern of much of the northern uplands where arable farming complemented the predominantly pastoral economy.

As we have seen, at this time probably slightly more than half the land of England was 'open' and slightly less than half enclosed.

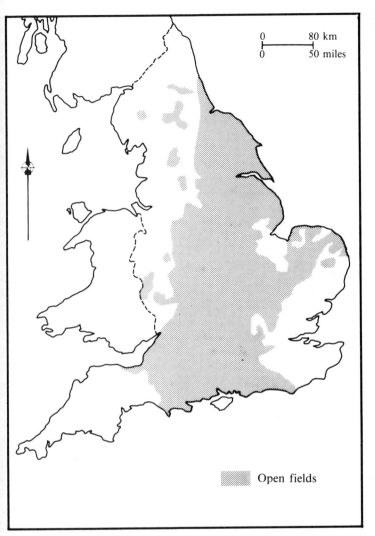

Figure 2 The 'Midland System' of open fields, c.1550

Open fields

Relatively nearby counties often exhibited quite different degrees of enclosure. Berkshire, for example, in the early sixteenth century was mainly a county of small-scale enclosures, with numerous tofts, crofts and small pastures farmed by tenant farmers. In Bedfordshire, on the other hand, open-field agriculture prevailed, grain in the form of barley and wheat remained the principal crop, and the greater part of the population lived in villages and hamlets, with relatively little occurrence of village desertion and depopulation.

In the upland zone, some degree of agricultural specialisation had developed by this time so that in much of Devon and Cornwall, for example, and in the Pennine counties of the north, in addition to sheep being kept for their wool, cattle were reared which were then sent elsewhere to be fattened. In Shropshire and North Staffordshire, on the other hand, cattle were both reared and fattened. In parts of Cheshire, the Vale of Berkeley in Gloucestershire, around Gloucester, and in north and west Dorset, dairying was the main pursuit and in some districts, both in upland and lowland England, horse rearing was important.

In broad terms, the second half of the sixteenth century was a period in which conscious and, on the whole, successful attempts were made to improve agricultural productivity. The most pressing motive for doing so was the sheer necessity of feeding a rapidly increasing population. At this time, there were growing numbers of landowners farming their own enclosed farms on an increasingly commercial basis, who were anxious to maximise profit. Price inflation of a dimension never before experienced gripped the country, there was a far greater increase in the prices of agricultural produce than of other products, and the increase in the cost of grain was greater than that of wool. These developments were inevitably accompanied by a decline in the purchasing power of wages and together they provided the opportunity for some sectors of the population to increase their landholdings and their profitability. The more substantial and energetic peasants consolidated their holdings as the weaker went to the wall and were forced to give up their land so that a class of yeomen and minor gentry emerged, at the expense of an increase in the number of landless who were forced to become wage-labourers or, in some cases, were reduced to poverty and destitution. During the second half of the sixteenth century, this group of lesser landowners and yeoman farmers, benefiting from a general improvement in their standards of living, built houses in large numbers, some of which still survive today.

Another class which benefited from this process was the nobility and greater gentry who were able to take advantage of the release on to the market particularly during the 1540s of the lands held by the Church, following the Dissolution of the Monasteries. During this period, perhaps a quarter of the land of England passed from the Church into private hands, a process which profoundly affected the whole evolution of English landed society until the end of the nineteenth century and later. Many monastic estates were sold to the rising men of the day who, in due course, frequently created parks from them in which they erected splendid mansions.

During the course of the century, a number of landowning families rose to national prominence, largely as the result of profits made from their holdings. Among them were the Northampton-shire Spencers of Althorp, the family of the present Princess of Wales. Their money was largely derived from sheep-breeding and in the later sixteenth century they maintained a permanent flock of about 13,000 sheep, adding at least 4000 lambs to it each spring.

Even larger flocks were owned by Thomas Howard, Duke of Norfolk, whose permanent flocks in 1571 amounted to 17,000 beasts in East Anglia alone. Another great Elizabethan landowner, especially in Staffordshire and Derbyshire, was George Talbot, Earl of Shrewsbury, who, in addition to industrial and commercial interests, exploited both the agricultural and mineral products of his lands. His ambitious wife, Bess of Hardwick, claimed to own 8000 sheep.

As we have seen, both landlords and yeoman farmers were also busy at this time in engrossing and enclosing land by agreement, a process that was to accelerate in the seventeenth century. In the parish of Lydiard Tregoze, for example, a few miles west of Swindon in the grassland region of Wiltshire, the common fields, commons and marshes of the main manor were enclosed by agreement in the second half of the sixteenth century between the lord, freeholders and tenants, only three common pastures being excluded. The task was clearly carried out very carefully with precise records being kept of the allotments awarded. Sometimes enclosure by agreement was concerned with much smaller areas: in Buckinghamshire, in 1551, the owner of the manor of Hartwell, in the northern part of the county, was allowed to enclose 'twenty acres and more' in return for an understanding not to keep a rabbit warren.[10]

As rabbits frequently caused damage, both to grain and pasture, enclosure agreements sometimes included an undertaking not to keep a warren. Nevertheless, by the seventeenth century the keeping of rabbits, or conies, had become very popular among landowners, and their fur and meat could all be sold for profit. In the royal Forest of Leicester, for example, there were four warrens in private hands which had increased greatly in the early seventeenth century when they extended over more than a hundred acres, 'to the oppression of the commoners and to the utter exile of His Majesty's game'.[11] A few years later, they were so common in Suffolk that Robert Reyce wrote:

> there are so many warrens here in every place, which do furnish the
> next marketts, and are carried to London with noe little reckoning,
> from whence it is that there is none who deeme their homes well
> seated, who have nott to the same belonging a commonwealth of
> Conies, neither can wee bee deemed a good house keeper that hath not
> plenty of these at all times to furnish his table.[12]

The keeping of rabbits continued to be very widespread throughout the seventeenth century and towards the end of the period Gregory King estimated that the British Isles contained no fewer than one million of them.

During the second half of the sixteenth century, the major achievement of English agriculture, and particularly of enclosing farmers, was to increase productivity sufficiently to feed the growing population. This self sufficiency was born of the increased agricultural output which resulted in part from the 'improvements' which took place at this time, and more particularly in the seventeenth century. So significant were they that Kerridge has gone so far as to argue that the Agricultural Revolution took place in England not, as is generally accepted, in the eighteenth and nineteenth centuries, but in the sixteenth and seventeenth centuries. While this is probably something of an overstatement, nevertheless there is no doubt that the agricultural developments that occurred, especially between about 1550 and 1700, were extremely significant and, at the very least, laid the foundations for the fundamental changes in agricultural practice which transformed the English landscape after 1700.

The major improvement in agricultural practice which took root after 1550 was the more widespread use of alternate husbandry, which was also known as convertible husbandry, up-and-down husbandry, or ley farming. This was a method of farming by which, instead of land being kept either under cultivation with occasional fallows or under permanent pasture, it alternated between the two. Thus, it would be cultivated as arable land for a few years, laid down to grass for a year or two, then once more ploughed up for cultivation, and so on. The advantage of such alternation was that it improved the quality and therefore the productivity of both the cultivated land and the grassland and, perhaps more important, by providing more pasture it enabled the farmer to keep more livestock. Although the sown acreage was necessarily smaller than previously, this was more than compensated for by the fact that the increased quantities of manure available from the larger herds of livestock enabled higher yields to be obtained from the cultivated fields. The new system also enabled the farmer of enclosed fields to respond more flexibly to market conditions as he could shift much more quickly from arable to pastoral farming and vice versa as prices and circumstances demanded.

Although alternate husbandry had been practised in the open fields in some parts of the country for centuries before 1550, it was only on a relatively small scale and, by this date, was most commonly found in Norfolk, parts of the Midlands, Devon and Cornwall, and the North. Just how fast and how far the practice spread thereafter is uncertain, given the lack of evidence, but Kerridge argues that by 1650 it was in use in about half of the farmland in the Midlands, and to a not dissimilar extent in other parts of the country. This may, however, be something of an overestimate. Alternate husbandry was perhaps most effectively employed on enclosed farms and was, therefore, the cause of some degree of enclosure. However, this caused less controversy than had enclosure for permanent pasture fifty years previously, as it was a relatively labour intensive form of farming and so did not result in depopulation. Alternate husbandry was also employed, to some extent, in the open-field areas of the country. However, as it required the agreement of all the peasants concerned and a rather complicated form of rotation whereby certain groups of strips had to be fenced in and laid down to grass, it seems to have been much less common here than on enclosed farms.

The cause of agricultural productivity was championed by a number of agricultural writers, especially during the last part of the sixteenth century. However, the first book of its kind on farming printed in England appeared as early as 1523. It was *The Book of Husbandry* by Sir Anthony Fitzherbert, or possibly his brother John, and was followed in the same year by his book, *Surveying*. Both books were popular until the end of the sixteenth century and were reprinted several times.[13] Although one cannot assume from a reading of Fitzherbert and the works of his successors that the picture they paint of English agriculture accurately describes the situation as it then existed on the ground, nevertheless they do give an indication of current thinking among the more progressive farmers of the day. Fitzherbert, himself, was a strong advocate of enclosure and went so far as to recommend that each open-field farmer should be given a compact holding near his house, together with a share of the common pasture and waste. He considered that enclosures were particularly advantageous for the keeping of livestock which he insisted thrived best and cost least on enclosed land. He also showed a thorough understanding of practical farming and was well aware of the value of manuring, pointing out that 'an housbande cannot well thrive by his corne, without he have other cattell, or by his cattel without corne.' He also recommended that landlords should convert copyhold to leasehold on short-term rents as a means of increasing agricultural output. There is no doubt that, judging by the wide dissemination of his books, Fitzherbert had a significant influence on agricultural practices in the sixteenth century, as did Thomas Tusser, who in 1557 published his *A Hundreth Good Pointes of Husbandrie*. This book, which was written in doggerel verse, presumably to make it more attractive to its public, contained a variety of useful precepts; as an unsuccesful Suffolk farmer, however, Tusser was presumably unable to follow his own advice. His rhymes, which to some extent must have reflected current farming practice in East Anglia, recommend a three-crop and fallow rotation as being more economical than the prevalent two-crop and fallow. Like Fitzherbert, he was an advocate of enclosure and some flavour of the book is given by the following comparison between 'champion' or open-field land and 'several' or enclosed.

> More profit is quieter found,
> Where pastures in severall bee;
> Of one seelie (good) aker of ground
> Than champion maketh of three.

The book was widely disseminated, an expanded version containing 500 points appearing in 1573, followed by four more editions in the last quarter of the sixteenth century. Numerous other books, both on husbandry in general and on more specialised farming activities such as growing grain, the management of horses, bee-keeping, tree planting, and gardening also appeared during this period.

In addition to books on farming, the student of the sixteenth century landscape is assisted by written evidence of two other kinds. Firstly, there is the contemporary evidence of maps, extents and surveys, and probate inventories. The best-known maps dating from this period are the work of the first great English cartographer, Christopher Saxton, who in 1570 began to compile the first national atlas of county maps, an enterprise which was completed nine years later. A small number of extents and surveys of manors and estates of various kinds had long been in existence before the sixteenth century but, by this time, with the development of the art of surveying, they had become more elaborate and informative. They began to increase in number towards the end of the sixteenth century and occasionally included detailed maps, like the one of Edgware in 1597 (Plate 6). This shows a large number of pasture closures, surrounded by thick belts of trees and interspersed with areas' of woodland. This

Plate 6 A map of Edgware, Middlesex, in 1597. It shows a former woodland area which had by this time been partially cleared to create small fields or closes. Much of the original woodland remains in the form of woods and hedgerow timber

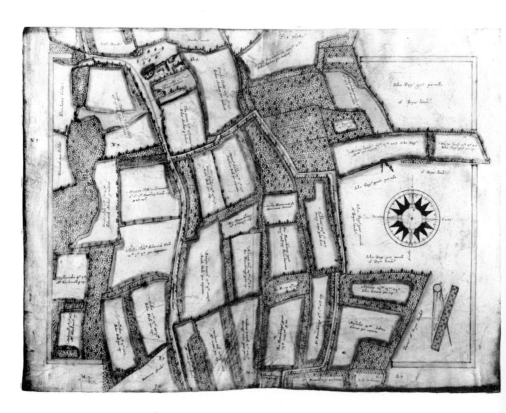

landscape has resulted from the carving out of enclosed fields from an original woodland area, much of which still remained.

Less visual but extremely valuable sources of information, especially for the sixteenth and seventeenth centuries, are the probate inventories. These consist of itemised accounts of the goods and chattels of deceased persons before their estates were distributed among their heirs and, as the great majority related to farmers, they provide detailed information about farming practice in many parts of the country.

Secondly, the growth of patriotism in Tudor times stimulated an interest in England and its geography and topography and as a result there are contemporary descriptions by individuals of the appearance of the landscape. Perhaps the most interesting and informative sixteenth-century example is the work of John Leland. A household official in the court of Henry VIII, he was able by his royal master's laissez-passer to obtain access to every place and building of note in the country and in the years between 1536 and 1543 he explored every county in England and Wales, making notes of what he observed in order to write a full description of the country and a history of its nobility and antiquities. The task proved too great for him and he eventually lapsed into insanity. However, although he never wrote the travel book which he intended, his notes have been preserved in his *Itinerary*.[14] Although this was first printed in the eighteenth century, his manuscript had already been handed around and used with profit by topographical writers. Another national survey, but this time written in elegant Latin, was that of William Camden who like Leland spent years, in the 1570s and 1580s, perambulating the country and collecting material for his *Britannia*, a county-by-county survey, printed for the first time in 1583. The first survey of an individual county, *The Perambulation of Kent*, by William Lambarde, was published in 1576 and contains much useful topographical information. This was followed by Richard Carew's *Survey of Cornwall* which was started in the 1580s but not published until 1602. The example set by these early writers was eagerly followed by others, and many more county surveys were to be published during succeeding centuries.

By the end of the sixteenth century, then, the Tudors had presided over a country, still very largely rural, in which agricultural productivity had managed to keep pace with the rapidly growing population. This was achieved principally by improvements in the output of both the corn growing and the pastoral areas. In some parts of the country, however, types of agricultural specialisation were developing, mainly from the spur of urban growth. This was especially true of London, by far the biggest city in the country, which had long been the largest single market, especially for grain and meat. In the fifteenth century, Kent was already important as a granary of London; by the early sixteenth century the plateaux of Hertfordshire had become the capital's principal granary; and in the Middlesex villages such as Tottenham, there was a change from arable to pastoral farming with the rearing and pasturing of cattle and sheep for the London market becoming increasingly important. The shortcomings of the transport system necessarily restricted this sort of specialisation to within relatively short distances of the principal markets. However, by the sixteenth century, south-east England and East Anglia had both developed a network of road and river transport and coastal shipping which granted them ready access to the London market. Similar specialisation was developing close to other major markets, such as the growing concentration on meat production and dairying on the coastal lowlands of Northumberland and Durham. Nevertheless, these areas of regional specialisation were still very much the exception rather than the rule. Other forms of specialisation which were beginning to take hold at this time were the cultivation of industrial crops such as saffron, rape-seed, woad and madder for dyes, teasels, hemp and flax for linen, and horticulture. In south-east Cambridgeshire, for example, saffron was being grown in the late fifteenth and early sixteenth centuries in small plots and gardens and hemp and flax were becoming increasingly common in the Midlands both in the open fields and on enclosed farms. They were cultivated as cash crops and sold locally to supplement the major arable and pastoral activities. At the beginning of the period horticulture seems to have been restricted very largely to a few specialised monastic and other great gardens and, indeed, the religious houses were virtually the only repositories of horticultural skills, as many monks and nuns were required by the rules of their orders to feed mainly on vegetables and fruits and to grow as much of their own food as possible. With the Dissolution and the passing of many monastic buildings into royal and noble hands, horticulture became more widely disseminated and the Crown began to take a particular interest. Henry VIII, for example, sent his gardener on several missions to the Continent to bring back new plants and seeds for the royal gardens at Fulham, Kensington and Whitehall and, as a consequence, peaches, nectarines and melons are reputed to have been grown for the first time on British soil. Similarly, Henry VIII's chief minister, Thomas Cromwell, introduced three new varieties of plum from France to be cultivated in his gardens at South Kensington. Gradually, the cultivation of fruit and vegetables spread more widely and, by the end of the sixteenth century, their production developed on a not inconsiderable scale in areas adjacent to the London market, such as Middlesex, Kent and Surrey.

This accelerating progress in agricultural specialisation and, more particularly, the impetus to improve agricultural output in the traditional arable and pastoral areas of the country were to gather momentum in the succeeding century. It is the nature of these improvements and their effect on the English countryside that we shall now examine in detail.

CHAPTER 3

Agricultural improvement: the cultivated landscape in the seventeenth century

The seventeenth century, therefore, witnessed considerable progress in both the productivity of English agriculture and also in the extension of the cultivated area. These developments took place against a complex and difficult background. Not only was it a century of social and political upheaval, of which the Civil War of the 1640s was the most obvious and spectacular manifestation, but it also witnessed a considerable rise in population, from just over 4 million in 1600 to just over 5 million in 1700, and a continuation of the price inflation which was characteristic of the previous century. Until about 1650, the demand for grain and consequently its relatively high price tended to encourage farmers to increase grain production rather than their output of livestock products, though circumstances changed thereafter. This was not universally the case, however, even in the earlier period, and for farmers within reach of a large urban market such as London, livestock production was nearly always profitable. This applied to areas as distant from London as the upland region of North Oxfordshire which swarmed with cattle in the seventeenth century and sent meat and dairy products to London down the Thames on barges. As we have seen, at the beginning of the century, there was already a degree of agricultural diversity between one farming region of England and another, a diversity and specialisation that was to increase as regions reacted differently to the challenges thrust upon them. Some areas were able to adapt farming methods to circumstances more effectively than others: the ligher soils of eastern England, for example, lent themselves more easily to alternate husbandry than the heavy clay soils of the Midlands. And the more enterprising farmers were more willing to adopt new methods.

Above all, the seventeenth century was one of growing agricultural innovation and commercialisation, some of it along the lines we have seen developing in the sixteenth century. Innovation was stimulated by the increased demand for food from the rising population and by the example set by farmers in the Low Countries whose agricultural practices became more widely disseminated in England. Alternate husbandry was employed more widely, the 'floating' of water meadows became widespread, new crops and crop rotations were introduced, greater use was made of fertilisers, new and improved methods of livestock breeding were employed, market gardening spread in the vicinity of the towns, and large areas of fen, marsh and waste land were reclaimed. As in the later sixteenth century, these developments were accompanied by a steady spate of literature on farming methods, and the growing national and local patriotism spurred the writing of books of history and topography. The changes in landholding which had taken effect in the 250 years since the Black Death also accelerated, with more and more land, especially in the champion grain-growing areas, coming into fewer and fewer hands. The new class of gentry and yeoman farmers increased in size and wealth and a new aristocracy developed their estates by creating parks and building great houses.

The enclosure movement also gathered momentum, though not without considerable social distress at times. In 1607, for example, the enclosure of arable land in Leicestershire for use as pasture sparked off a popular uprising, the Midlands Revolt, which in turn led to the setting up of the 1607 Commission of Enquiry into enclosures. Nevertheless, the enclosure of open-field arable land, together with substantial areas of common land and waste continued apace. Indeed, it has been suggested that in the light of the evidence now available a strong case can be made out for regarding the seventeenth rather than the eighteenth century as holding the pre-eminent position in the history of English enclosures. The eighteenth and the nineteenth centuries witnessed the heyday of parliamentary enclosure, that is enclosure by means of Acts of Parliament, whereas the great majority of seventeenth century enclosure was achieved by agreement between the parties concerned, without recourse to parliament. However, the first parliamentary enclosure Act, which applied to Radipole, near Poole in Dorset, was passed as early as 1604, and probably another 20 or so Acts were passed in the period up to 1700, applying in all to some 45,000 acres of land. This was relatively small beer compared to the total of 6.8 million acres that were encompassed by parliamentary legislation between 1604 and 1914.

At the beginning of the sixteenth century, probably just under half of England was enclosed, with great variations in the proportion of enclosure from county to county. Thus, Wordie states that seven counties were about 90 per cent enclosed, some a little more, some a little less, – namely Kent, Cornwall, Devon, Essex, Cheshire, Monmouth, and Lancashire – and nine more were between 75 and 30 per cent enclosed – namely Shropshire, Herefordshire, Sussex, Suffolk, Surrey, Somerset, Northumberland, the North Riding of Yorkshire, and Dorset. The conclusion to be derived is that most of the productive, arable land of England, in the Midland counties and in East Anglia and Lincolnshire, was in 1600 still farmed mainly under the open-field system. Some idea of the rate of enclosure in the previous 30 years is given by the 1607 Report of the Commission of Enquiry which stated that very nearly 70,000 acres had been enclosed since 1578 in six Midland counties. This rate was greatly to accelerate during the seventeenth century and it has been suggested that it was during this period that England was to change over from being mainly an open-field country to being mainly an enclosed one. In County Durham, for example, it is probable that from being largely an open-field county in 1600, by 1699 the great majority of parishes were enclosed, of which the greater proportion by far were by agreement. Similarly, Wiltshire was a largely open-field or 'champion' county in 1600, whereas by 1700 it was at least two-thirds enclosed. The effect of this process on the landscape of the north-western part of Wiltshire is vividly described by John Aubrey in his 1685 *Natural History of Wiltshire,*

> About 1595 all between Easton Percy and Castle Coombe was *campania*
> like Cotswold upon which it borders; and then Yatton and Castle
> Coombe did intercommon together. Between these two parishes much
> hath been enclosed in my remembrance, and every day more and more
> I do remember about 1633 but one enclosure in Chippenham
> field . . . and by this time I think it is all enclosed.

However, not only arable land was subject to enclosure during this period, for extensive areas of common wastes and woodland were similarly affected. Indeed, probably as much common and waste land as arable land was enclosed during the seventeenth century, and the majority was probably outside the Midland counties. This often took the form of piecemeal settlement by squatters on the edges of commons. During a time of growing population and land hunger, there were many landless peasants who built themselves huts and cleared pieces of land in the commons or woods, a little way away from the villages, encroachments which like those of today's squatters often attracted the opposition of the villagers. However, in the seventeenth century it seemed to be a common rule that a squatter could establish a right of occupation if he could build his cottage in the night and send out smoke from his chimney in the morning. Another form of enclosure which, as we have seen, was not uncommon in the two previous centuries was the engrossing of large amounts of land by prosperous merchants and farmers in order to build up compact blocks of land on which to establish parks and erect mansions. Land-hungry merchants could, and did, acquire land for this purpose when leases fell in and needed renewing and they were able to outbid the original leaseholder.

Enclosure did not take place solely for agricultural purposes and, during the sixteenth century, many towns enlarged their built-up areas by nibbling away at the open fields which lay just beyond their walls. This process also attracted legislation and, in 1593 for example, an Act designed to stem the growth of the City of London prohibited the enclosure of commons and waste grounds within three miles of the city gates, as interfering with the mustering of soldiers, the practice of archery, and the health of the people of London and Westminster. This piece of legislation, like so many others on the subject, was largely ineffective.

Whatever the purpose of enclosure, the effect on the landscape, both in open-field and wooded areas, was considerable. The newly created seventeenth century fields, like those in the previous century, were more often than not irregularly shaped. Typically, they were bounded by hedges composed of trees. The individual trees were usually elm, hornbeam or hazel and were pollarded to form a strong screen some eight feet tall with prolific top-growth which, cut every few years, provided an important source of poles, stakes, fuels, and animal bedding. In places, where the soil was thinner and less firm, as on the sandy soils north of London, hedges of quick-thorn were common, forming a barrier some five feet high. The size of the fields varied considerably, depending on the wealth of the owner and the purposes to which they were put. Where they were unusually large, they were often lined by belts of well-spaced trees. Walls were sometimes used, but as these were costly they were mainly restricted to areas where freestone was locally available or to the gardens of the richer yeomen and gentry and round nurseries and market gardens where their heat-absorbing qualities were a considerable asset to the growing of fruit trees. Finally, in many parts of the country, fields were bounded by earth banks, without hedge or wall.

One of the main motive forces behind enclosure was the increase of profitability for the individual, enterprising farmer. But enclosure by itself was not sufficient for this purpose, and improved methods of farming had also to be employed. However, it should not be assumed that enclosed farms were all efficiently farmed and that all open-field farming was inefficient, as agricultural improvements could be, and were, undertaken in both farming areas. As we have seen, one important method of increasing productivity which began to be more widespread after 1550 was alternate husbandry, the alternation of arable farming and ley farming in the same fields. This technique spread most rapidly between about 1590 and 1660 and, according to Kerridge, at the end of this period it was in use in half the farmland in the Midlands and in a good proportion of the remainder of the country's farmland by 1700. However, this thesis has been disputed in some quarters and Broad,[1] for example, has suggested that while alternate husbandry spread in the Midlands up to about 1650, thereafter the emphasis shifted to permanent pasture. In the Buckinghamshire parishes of Middle Claydon and Creslow, for example, alternate husbandry was certainly important until the middle of the seventeenth century, but subsequently many fields were laid down to permanent pasture. The main reasons for this change were that population pressure began to slacken after 1650,

47

the demand for foodstuff from urban centres, especially London, grew, the prices of meat and dairy products held up better than grain, and consequently mixed farming systems, with some parts of the land devoted permanently to arable and others to grassland, gave better returns. The expansion of alternate husbandry, at least up to 1650, was at the expense of both the arable land, mainly in open-field champion country, and also of permanent grass, partly in the open fields and partly on enclosed farms. In addition, many parks were disparked at this time and together with some of the very large pastures which had been created a century or more before, were divided up into smaller fields devoted to alternate husbandry. Cattle fattening, dairying and mutton rearing all began to become more important than sheep-rearing for wool and, as they required different farming techniques, generally involving smaller farming units, so they provided the impetus for much seventeenth-century disparking.

Another important development in agricultural practice, which first appeared towards the end of the sixteenth century and took firm root in the seventeenth century, was the 'floating' of water meadows. This was a process of irrigation. which involved the construction of a complicated system of channels, drains and sluices which enabled a stream to be diverted into a meadow thereby covering the whole of the surface with a thin sheet of floating water. Although the process was necessarily an expensive one it more than paid for itself in the form of greatly increased returns. The running water deposited fertile silt on the land and increased its productivity, it protected the grass from frost in winter and ensured that it grew earlier and well in spring and summer. In this way, animal feed became available earlier in the year, grew more profitably, and also provided hay crops during the summer. Larger herds of livestock could be kept on the same area of land and larger quantities of animal manure meant higher yields on the arable land. While the controlled flooding of water meadows alongside streams and rivers had been practised for centuries past, the fully fledged form of 'floating' apparently first appeared in Herefordshire towards the end of the sixteenth century, and then spread to various parts of England during the seventeenth century. Clearly, the use of floated water meadows required suitable physical conditions and was therefore very largely confined to those areas where they were available. During the early seventeenth century, they were to be found in the chalk downlands of southern England and by the end of the century they were widely used along the southern half of the Welsh Marches, and throughout much of Dorset, Wiltshire and Hampshire, where many of them can still be recognised today, albeit in a neglected state (Plate 7). They were also to be found, to a limited extent, in the Chilterns, the Cotswolds, and in the Midlands. Most of the water meadows were devoted to sheep farming and led to a considerable increase in the size of local sheep flocks. By the early

Plate 7 Floated water meadows at Nunton, near Salisbury in Wiltshire. The photograph shows the channels which carried the water over the surface of the meadow, the ridges which kept the water moving, and the drainage ditches by which it was returned to the river

eighteenth century, some of these were so large that Defoe commented that a traveller losing his way on Salisbury Plain, where there were neither clearly defined roads nor sign-posts, would find help from the number of shepherds feeding, or keeping their vast flocks of sheep, which are everywhere in the way, and who, with very little pains, a traveller may always speak with.

The use of alternate husbandry and the floating of water meadows seem to have developed independently in England without recourse to practices on the Continent. The same was not true, however, of the introduction of the new crops which began to gain ground here, especially after about 1650. Although the great majority of these were native to England or already naturalised by the seventeenth century, their use in English agriculture was stimulated both by the growing knowledge of farming practices from abroad, especially in the Low Countries, and by the example of refugees such as the Flemish Protestants who settled in Eastern England. In addition, the seventeenth century witnessed the increasing importation of seeds from Holland. Among the crops which were introduced or whose cultivation spread more widely during the seventeenth century were fodder crops, such as turnips, clover, sainfoin, trefoil and rye-grass; industrial crops such as cole-seed, flax, hemp, woad, weld and madder; herbs and spices such as saffron and liquorice; and tobacco and hops. As we shall see, although some of these crops began to become more widely cultivated in the first half of the 1600s, it was the second half of the century which witnessed a considerable acceleration in their use and introduction. This was partly due to the prevailing economic and social circumstances. After about 1650, England was afflicted by a period of long and intense agricultural depression, more severe and widely felt than any since the end of

49

the fifteenth century. As a result, agriculture was faced with crisis caused by what Thirsk has termed 'the relentlessly fallin prices of grain'. This induced many farmers to concentrate o livestock farming and persuaded them and others to see improved methods of farming. Moreover, by about 1650 innovatio was in the air and more and more farmers, especially the large and wealthier ones, were becoming more interested in improvin farming techniques, partly for profitability and partly for intrins reasons. This growing interest in agricultural practices wa reflected in a greatly increased volume of agricultural literature.

As we have seen, the principal fodder crops prior to th seventeenth century were beans, vetches and oats. In addition, i certain areas some types of grain, especially barley, were fed livestock. The overriding disadvantage facing farmers was th shortage of winter fodder which had long highlighted the need extend the very limited range of fodder crops that were the available. Root crops were virtually unknown, though some carro were grown on the lighter soils of East Anglia from the latter pa of the sixteenth century onwards. However, it was not until abo 1650 that the breakthrough occurred with the introduction turnips as a field crop. Turnips had already been grown in mark gardens and kitchen gardens for the table and they were als cultivated as a cash crop in hop gardens and in hemp gardens, b they appeared as a field crop for the first time in Norfolk, Suffo and in Buckinghamshire in the 1650s. The great advantage turnips, unlike carrots, was that they could be successful cultivated under a wide variety of conditions. In the latter part the seventeenth century their cultivation as a fodder crop sprea throughout much of the country, so that by the early eighteen century Defoe was recording that they were to be found 'ov most of the east and south parts of England'. The turnip provide nutritious feed for livestock during the winter, when the gra stopped growing, though it was probably less important as a sourc of fodder for livestock than clover, sainfoin or rye-grass. Li them, it was frequently grown on land, both in the open fields an on enclosed farms, that would formerly have been left fallow, by process called 'hitching'. In the open fields, initially one or tw furlongs would be temporarily fenced off and sown with turnips, practice which gradually spread until these small tempora 'hitches' were replaced by larger, permanent fields. This was or of the reasons why, in some places, the open fields were bein sub-divided: in seventeenth-century Oxfordshire, for example, th redivision of the traditional two-field system into four or mo fields was occurring throughout the county. The cultivatio turnips brought with it other advantages: being grown on fallow lar meant that its cultivation did not have to be at the expense anything else; the hoeing which they required cleared the land weeds and increased the yield of grain grown in the fields in th following year; and an increased quantity of manure from th

arger herds of livestock that could now be kept also greatly
increased yields.

Cabbages, which had long been grown as a garden vegetable,
were also grown for the first time in the seventeenth century as a
field crop to provide food for stock. Their use in this way has been
attributed to Sir Anthony Ashley of Wimborne St Giles in Dorset,
who introduced the idea from Holland in the first quarter of the
century. He died in 1627 and his elaborate tomb in the church at
Wimborne St Giles has a nine-inch stone sphere at his feet which
is reputed to be the representation of a cabbage.

However, more important both as fodder crops and also for
their influence on farming practice in arable areas were the new
grasses, principally sainfoin, clover, lucerne, trefoil and rye-grass,
which arrived in England from the Low Countries in the middle of
the sixteenth century. The names of all four tended to be used
indiscriminately in contemporary documents and in the literature
of the time so that it is probably simpler to encompass them all
under the generic term of 'clovers'.[2] Credit for the introduction of
clovers into England is generally given to Sir Richard Weston who
was exiled to the Low Countries in the 1640s. On his return to
England in the 1650s he wrote a treatise describing their use there
and also grew them himself on his land in Surrey. The advantages
of these crops quickly became apparent and were spelled out by
Andrew Yarranton[3] in 1663 in these words,

> I can make it appear, six acres of land in *Clover* will keep as many cattle
> as Thirty acres of natural grass: and besides your Land need not now
> be out of tillage, so long as it was wont to do; but once in four or five
> years you may break it up, and it shall be fit for tillage, as though it had
> lain 20 years with natural grass.

The use of the new clovers quickly spread to areas of light soil,
to which they were specially suited, especially in eastern Norfolk
and Suffolk, but also on the Cotswolds in Oxfordshire, in the
chalk country of Wiltshire, in the Chilterns, and in the downlands
of Kent and Sussex. These formerly barren heathlands and sheep-
rearing downlands were greatly improved in soil fertility, enabling
a mixed economy of livestock rearing and corn growing to be
developed. Among the first and most effective users of the new
clovers was the Walpole family on their estates in Norfolk in the
last quarter of the seventeenth century. On the other hand, these
new fodder crops made relatively little impact in areas like the
Midlands, whose heavy ill-drained claylands made the cultivation
of turnips impossible and that of the artificial grasses difficult.
Indeed, it was the introduction of efficient and relatively cheap
methods of drainage of these soils in the nineteenth century that
first made possible their introduction there.

Owing to the lack of detailed evidence, it is impossible to say
how widespread was the use of these fodder crops by the end of
the seventeenth century and how greatly they had by then

benefited English agriculture. While with Clay, it is probably true to say that they 'represented the greatest single source of increased productivity that English agriculture experienced before modern times', it is nevertheless almost certainly the case that it was only the minority of the more progressive farmers in those parts of the country to which they were suited who adopted the new fodder crops. Moreover, as they represented a not inconsiderable capital investment, they were mainly restricted to the wealthier farmers. For the great majority of farmers who farmed relatively small acreages, their farming methods remained virtually as primitive as they had been for centuries. Nevertheless, the innovations of the latter half of the sixteenth century were extremely important not only as a means of increasing productivity, for some at least of the English farming community, but also in providing a firm foundation on which to base the farming improvements associated with the Agricultural Revolution of the later eighteenth century.

In addition to fodder crops, a steadily widening range of other crops became available to the English farmer in the seventeenth century, including such industrial crops as cole-seed, flax, hemp, woad, weld, madder and teasels. From the 1620s onwards, cultivation of these crops was being advocated by writers for two principal reasons: they were labour-intensive and would help to reduce unemployment brought about by economic recession, and they would reduce the need to import expensive hemp and flax for the cloth trade from abroad. Many farmers needed little encouragement and the cultivation of these industrial crops was taken up with alacrity, especially in the arable farming areas such as the Midlands where there was a surplus of labour available, and where they helped to provide an additional source of revenue to that derived from corn. Cole-seed, which was processed to produce an oil used in lamps for lighting and in the manufacture of soap, was grown principally in eastern England from about 1590 onwards and its cultivation increased during the next century. Flax and hemp, which provided fibres from which linen and canvas, rope and netting were manufactured, were grown principally in the corn-growing regions, both by permanent farmers and by itinerant 'flaxmen' who by agreement with landowners would take a single crop of flax and a few subsequent crops of corn before moving on somewhere else. Flax was also cultivated by numerous small farmers and indeed was known as a poor man's crop, being grown by them in their fields in summer and woven in their homes in winter. The growing of flax, in particular, with its light blue flower, gave an attractive appearance to the countryside in summer.

Woad, weld and madder were all cultivated to produce dyes used in the cloth industry. All three of them were mainly grown by larger farmers as they required a substantial capital investment for production on a commercial scale: madder, for example, took three years to mature and to yield its best crop, and the best plants had to be imported from Zealand or purchased in London. Woad was grown extensively in the arable lands of the Midlands and around cloth towns in Surrey and Hampshire, weld grew best on chalk downlands such as those of the North Downs in Kent, and madder, on a smaller scale than the other two, in Wisbech towards the end of the century and around the cloth-working centres. The attractive appearance of growing woad is described by Celia Fiennes as she saw it near Toddington, north Gloucestershire, in 1694:

> ... it rises no higher than lettice, and much in such tuffts; the collour
> of the Leafe is much like Scabins (scabious) and the shape resembling
> that; this they cutt off close to the ground and soe out of the same
> roote springs the Leafe again ... then in a Mill with a horse they grind
> the Leaves into a paste, so make it up in balls and drye them in a
> Penthouse ... this plantation of about 12 acres would employ 2 or 3
> familyes men women and children, and so they generally come and
> make little hutts for themselves for the season to tend it.

She adds, forcefully, 'the smell of the Woade is so strong and offencive you can scarce beare it at the Mill: I could not forse my horse neare it.' Finally, another dye crop which was grown more extensively in the 1660s and 1670s was safflower, or bastard saffron, which yielded a reddish pink dye used by silk dyers. Although imported previously from the Continent, it was native to England and was grown more effectively and commercially around London, in Gloucestershire, and in Oxfordshire. Teasels, which were used in cloth making for raising the nap of the finished product, were grown in a number of places including the Cheddar area of Somerset.

A third category of new crops introduced or more widely used at this time included those that yielded herbs or spices for medicinal and cooking purposes, such as saffron, liquorice, mustard and caraway. Saffron was probably the most important of these, being much in demand, especially for medicinal purposes. A traditional English crop which had been grown here for many years, especially in the Cam and Granta valleys of Cambridgeshire and around Saffron Walden in Essex, by the seventeenth century saffron was also being grown in arable fields in Suffolk and Herefordshire. Liquorice was another specialist crop, whose long sweet root was used in medicine, which was cultivated quite extensively in the seventeenth century. It was grown principally around London, and other towns, including Pontefract where, according to Celia Fiennes in 1697, the outside of the town was 'full of great Gardens walled in all round' which were filled with liquorice plants whose arrangement of branches and leaves she compares to that of Solomon's Seal. Mustard seed and caraway seed were grown as field crops in specific localities. The former was grown in the Norfolk fens and around Tewkesbury, in Gloucestershire, and the latter in Oxfordshire at Clanfield.

Even by the end of the century, none of these new fodder and industrial crops was grown on a really large scale but were mostly restricted to specific regions where their products were used. Nevertheless, together they occupied a very considerable area of agricultural land and Gregory King estimated in 1695 that about 1 million acres were devoted to them out of the total of 11 million acres which he said were used as arable land.

Finally, the seventeenth century also saw an extension of the areas devoted to tobacco and hops. Tobacco, introduced from North America probably by way of Holland, was cultivated in England in about 1571, but the acreage devoted to it was small and it was the early seventeenth century before its cultivation spread to an appreciable extent. The chief areas of production were in Gloucestershire, around the towns of Winchcombe, Tewkesbury and Cheltenham, and on the sandy loams of the central part of the Vale of Evesham in Worcestershire. Despite attempts by the government to suppress its cultivation in order to ensure a home market for the Virginia crop, it continued to flourish here for the greater part of the century. Indeed, had not the government finally succeeded in suppressing its growth, England would probably have become a major producer of tobacco. While it lasted, however, it was quite widely grown by small farmers in their yards and gardens, leading Thirsk[5] to observe that the history of tobacco growing in seventeenth-century England illustrated how well English farmers could respond to a profitable innovation once persuaded of its success. Hops were introduced into England from the Low Countries probably about the time of the Reformation and by the beginning of the seventeenth century were widely cultivated. Prior to that, beer had been brewed from malt barley, and hops at first met with a good deal of opposition from conservative drinkers. By the beginning of the seventeenth century, however, several varieties of hops suited to different terrains had become available and they were being cultivated as widely apart as the Maidstone district of Kent and the Vale of Hereford, which were the two principal areas, as well as in the Vale of Farnham in Surrey and in the chalk country of Salisbury Plain. Their cultivation flourished throughout the century and being labour-intensive and involving considerable initial outlay, was restricted to large farmers many of whom made handsome profits out of it.

However, not only was the seventeenth century a period when a variety of new crops was introduced but, particularly after about 1660, it was notable for the endeavours that were made to secure better seed varieties of wheat and barley. New strains of these traditional crops were experimented with in various parts of the country by progressive farmers to obtain strains more resistant to disease, which ripened earlier, and which gave higher yields. Undoubtedly some successes were recorded and in some parts of the country superior types of wheat and barley were introduced. In addition, routine farming techniques gradually improved, including better methods of tilling the soil and sowing the seed, whose cumulative effect was probably very substantial. Not the least important of improved husbandry practices involved the greater use of fertilisers. The perennial shortage of animal manure could to some extent be ameliorated by the use of other substances and fertilisers, and from about 1550 onwards more progressive and wealthier farmers increasingly turned to them. In various parts of the country, marl, chalk and calcareous sand were locally available. Used to neutralise soil acidity, they made the application of the limited amounts of animal manure more effective. In addition, more lime was processed during the seventeenth century and its application to the land could be particularly effective. Blith, writing in 1652,[6] described it as,

> of most excellent use, yea so great that whole countries . . . that were naturally barren as any in this nation and had formerly (within less than halfe an age) supply with corne out of the Feldon corn country, now is, and long hath been ready to supply them.

Potash from soap boilers was also used as a fertiliser, for example on the Verney estates in north Buckinghamshire from the 1680s onwards, and organic waste products from towns and industries, such as stable manure, malt dust, and pulverised iron slag, were all pressed into use.

Among the important technical innovations in farming practice in the seventeenth century were those concerned with improving the quality of livestock. Although these developments had their effect throughout the country, including the arable areas where cultivation depended upon the application of animal manures, they were most felt in the areas which specialised in rearing livestock. These included a large section of western England extending from Somerset to South Lancashire which was noted for its dairy farming, especially for cheese; the upland areas which traditionally had bred and reared sheep and cattle for fattening in the surrounding lowlands of the Midlands, East Anglia and around London; and the dairying regions of Essex and Suffolk. Although little documentary evidence is available to tell us how stock was selected and cared for and how improved strains were bred, there is no doubt that in the pastoral regions, which were the main breeding grounds for stock, farmers had developed a wide range of different breeds of cattle, sheep and horses, suitable for different farming environments. But it was not only in the pastoral regions of the country that improved varieties of stock were bred: in the arable lands of Leicestershire, for example, ram breeders were prominent in the second half of the seventeenth century. The county was also famous for its horses and Defoe[7] observed that:

> The horses produced here, or rather fed here, are the largest in England, being generally the great black coach horses and dray horses,

of which so great a number are continually brought up to London, that one would think so little a spot as this of Leicestershire could not be able to supply them.

Market gardening was another aspect of English farming which greatly flourished in the seventeenth century. From being the prerogative of the gardeners of the Crown and the wealthy members of the nobility for the greater part of the sixteenth century, it spread far and wide during the last part of the sixteenth century and particularly in the seventeenth century. Horticulture became so successful that instead of having to import fruit and vegetables from the Continent, English markets were supplied by English horticulturalists. Market gardening was essentially a small-scale affair, based on intensively cultivated small plots, and as such was ideally suited to small peasants with little land and capital, but with plenty of family labour and easy access to the towns, which were their markets. Although vegetables were grown both on enclosed farms and also on strips in the common fields, the typical market garden was a small plot which combined both vegetables and fruit, with vegetable beds separated by fruit trees. The chief vegetables were cabbages, carrots, parsnips, beans, asparagus and lettuce and the chief fruit were cherries, apples and pears. Many varieties of fruit trees and vegetable seeds were imported from the Continent but during the seventeenth century were increasingly produced by indigenous market gardeners and nurserymen. Herbs such as saffron and liquorice were also widely grown in gardens. Market gardens were located close to virtually all the main towns, especially in southern England, with London being by far the most important market. In 1635, for example, horticulturists supplying the London market were concentrated in the then rural parishes of Fulham, Chelsea and Kensington on the Thames terrace-gravels west of London, and to a lesser extent in Edmonton and Stoke Newington on the terraces of the River Lea to the north of the city.[8] Many of them owned between 1 and 3 acres on which they grew soft fruits such as strawberries and gooseberries as well as vegetables, culinary herbs and medicinal plants. Many of them also owned strips in the common fields where they grew root vegetables such as carrots and turnips, providing the Cities of London and Westminster and the adjacent villages with 24,000 loads of root crops annually at reasonable prices. After about 1650, a class of wealthy market gardeners emerged who acquired larger holdings whose soil they improved with fertilisers and who employed wage earners to work them. In these ways, a growing volume and variety of fruit and vegetables supplied the London market in the later seventeenth century.

As we have seen, in some parts of the country, fruit farming had developed as a profitable form of farming in the course of the sixteenth century. By 1600, the prominent fruit-growing counties had established themselves, notably Kent, Hertfordshire,

Worcestershire, Gloucestershire, Herefordshire, Somerset and Devon, and the number of orchards increased through the century. The chief fruit trees were apples, pears and cherries and in some parts of Herefordshire, for example, they were to be found in every hedgerow and in the fields. Celia Fiennes when travelling through Herefordshire in 1695 remarked that the county appeared

> like a Country off Gardens and Orchards, the whole Country being very full of fruite trees, etc., it looks like nothing else, the apple pear trees etc., are so thick even in their corn fields and hedgerows.[9]

At the beginning of the seventeenth century there were still very considerable extents of fens, swamps, marshes, and mosses as they were called in the North of England, though it is impossible to say what precise area they covered. Although thinly populated, they were put to good use: reeds and rushes were cut for building materials, their fish and wild fowl provided a source of employment for a few, and in places they constituted summer grazing grounds for cattle, once the winter inundations had receded. Considerable areas of fen and swamp had already been reclaimed during the Middle Ages, notably the Fenlands and the Somerset Levels, and along many parts of the south and east coasts, from Sussex to the East Riding of Yorkshire, piecemeal reclamation had gone on for centuries and continued along traditional lines during the sixteenth and seventeenth centuries. As the shore line slowly receded with the deposition of silt by the sea, so local farmers reclaimed small areas of salt marsh by building protective banks round them. They thus became dry pastures and, in time, they could be planted as arable. In this fashion, thousands of acres were reclaimed in small pieces, especially around the Wash and in the Thames estuary. However, a much more spectacular form of reclamation gathered momentum during the seventeenth century with the large-scale drainage projects of inland fens and swamps. In economic terms, the essential difference between this form of drainage and the piecemeal reclamation described above was that it required professional engineering knowledge and the investment of considerable capital, amounting to as much as several thousand pounds per acre. These requirements largely determined the character and appearance of the landscape which emerged from the marshes. The impetus for this development as in other forms of improvement, was partly profit and partly the prospect of providing more food and more employment for a growing population.

For these reasons, the government passed a General Drainage Act in 1600 which authorised the alienation of land for those who were prepared to put in the substantial investment required of drainage schemes, and thereby ushered in the age of large, speculative ventures. The most important of these schemes was the drainage of some 400,000 acres of inland peat fens, mostly in

Cambridgeshire and Huntingdonshire, known collectively as the Bedford Levels. The professional expertise came from the celebrated Dutch engineer Cornelius Vermuyden and the money was put up mainly by a group of local landowners, headed by the Earl of Bedford. Between them, the latter spent hundreds of thousands of pounds, vast sums of money for the period, and after a chequered history the scheme was eventually declared completed in 1650. Vast engineering works had to be built, including huge new drainage channels such as the so-called Bedford River (Plate 8), which was 21 miles long and 70 feet wide and carried the waters of the Ouse from Erith in Cambridgeshire to Denver in Norfolk, and numerous embankments and sluices. The upheaval for the local peasantry was enormous and, inevitably, a good deal of social unrest resulted, especially in the 1640s. However, the Bedfordshire Levels survived the disorder of this decade, as did some 70,000 acres of reclaimed land in the East Riding of Yorkshire. On the other hand, drainage works which had earlier in the century been completed in Lincolnshire, embracing tens of thousands of acres, did not survive the uprisings there in the

Plate 8 Cornelius Vermuyden's map of the Fens, 1642

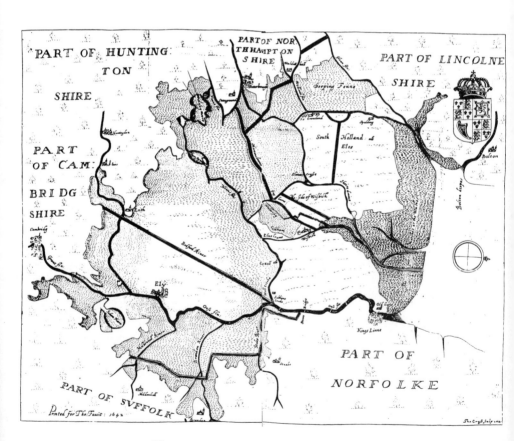

58

1640s, when the embankments were destroyed and the land returned to marshland. Nevertheless, the overall effect of these drainage schemes was greatly to increase the productivity of the areas concerned. Where previously few people obtained a livelihood, now many more were employed in the farms growing grain and thriving new crops, and keeping large numbers of cattle and sheep, so much so that an observer in 1655 commented of the Fens that 'the country thereabouts is now subject to a new drowning, even to a deluge and inundation of plenty'.[10] However, once in operation, the scheme was not without its problems. Completely unforeseen by the engineers was the problem of peat shrinkage, for once the peat marshes were drained their surface quickly lowered, falling by as much as two feet during the dry years of the 1660s. This required the bottom of the main drains to be lowered and the banks to be strengthened. Before 1700, the ground surface had fallen so much that windmills were introduced to raise water into the drains and during the eighteenth century they were found everywhere in the Fens, adding a new and distinctive feature to the landscape. The chief beneficiaries of these schemes were the large landowners who replaced the local inhabitants and who created large farms running into hundreds of acres made up of large, rectangular, level fields.

Another type of land to which arable and pastoral farming was extended in the seventeenth century was that devoted to woodland and forest, and parkland. As the population grew so the demand for land increased. This enabled landowners to charge high rents, making it an economic proposition to divide up for settlement by peasant farmers land which was previously untilled, either because it was relatively infertile or because it was reserved for hunting. Woodland areas, such as the Wealden Vales in south-east England, were substantially cleared of their trees by 1650 and put down to agriculture, the wood being used for constructional timber and for nearby iron, glass and dye-works. The forests, which had been royal hunting preserves, and the deer parks which were owned both by the Crown and by many individual landlords, were frequently, though not necessarily, wooded. Many of them were disafforested and disparked in the late sixteenth and throughout the seventeenth centuries and divided up and turned over to agriculture. Many of these areas of woodland and of former forest and park were of low fertility and required considerable investment, for the clearance of the trees and the application of fertilisers, before they became productive. For these reasons, the new farmlands were often the preserve of the wealthier farmers rather than the peasantry. However, in other woodland areas, such as the Forest of Arden in Warwickshire, the seventeenth century witnessed a rise in the standard of living for all sections of the landed peasantry.[11] The economy in this area, which in the middle of the sixteenth century was largely a pastoral one, had by 1700 changed out of all recognition. In 1695, an observer commented,[12]

... the inhabitants have turned so much of Wood- and Heath-land into Tillage and Pasture, that they produce corn, cattle, cheese, and butter enough, not only for their own use, but also to furnish other Counties, whereas, within the memory of man, they were supplied with Corn, etc, from the *Feldon*.

The total extent of the increase of farmland, for both arable and pasture purposes, during the sixteenth and seventeenth centuries was clearly considerable. As we have seen, sandy heaths were cultivated for the first time, fens and marshes were reclaimed, and forests and parks were broken up and given over to agriculture. The effect of these developments was probably to add several million acres to the country's farmland, amounting in the case of the cultivated area to an increase of the order of about 25 per cent in the two hundred years from 1500 to 1700. If one adds to this the increased productivity in much of the existing farmland, then improved and extended agriculture made it possible to feed the country's growing population.

Two other important agricultural developments were the rise in commercial farming and the increase in regional and local specialisation, both of which accelerated during the seventeenth century. Gradually, the peasant farmer was being eliminated and his land taken over by greater landowners who had both the capital and also the desire for profit and 'improvement' to invest in more efficient agricultural practices. Regional and local agricultural specialisation was also, to a considerable extent, the product of the growing commercialisation of farming, as entrepreneurial landlords turned to the products that were best suited to local conditions of soil and climate and which would bring the best return from the local markets. This was especially true of south-east England and East Anglia, where the London market acted as a huge magnet, but it also applied to other parts of the country, such as the agricultural regions supplying York and Bristol. Thus, by 1700, agricultural specialisation was firmly established. In the coastal lowlands of Northumberland and Durham, for example, sheep and cattle were raised for mutton and beef, and dairy farming was also practised. Dairy farming developed in different ways in different parts of the country and Wensleydale cheese, for example, first appeared towards the end of the seventeenth century. Sheep farming had changed significantly in that, unlike the late fourteenth and early fifteenth centuries, sheep were no longer reared almost exclusively for their wool. Mutton was fast becoming the Englishman's national dish and a different, fatter type of sheep was required to produce good mutton. In parts of the Midlands, such as Leicestershire, Northamptonshire, Bedfordshire and Buckinghamshire, where arable farming still largely prevailed, areas of permanent pasture had developed to raise sheep, cattle and especially horses. Fruit growing had expanded significantly, especially in the orchards of Kent, Herefordshire, Somerset and Devon. Pigs and poultry were being raised in growing numbers, especially near the large towns, and market gardening had also expanded in these areas.

The seventeenth century, like the latter part of the sixteenth century, was notable for an intensification in the growth of both national and local patriotism. A strong sense of county and community evolved, a feeling which climaxed perhaps in the mid-seventeenth century. The county was the strongest focal point of loyalty and affection among many landowners and as a result it became the unit around which manuscript, map and printed records have been arranged. The works of the county historians increased in number including, among the greatest of them, William Burton's *The Description of Leicestershire* in 1622, William Dugdale's *The Antiquities of Warwickshire* in 1659 and Robert Thoroton's *The Antiquities of Nottinghamshire* in 1677. The mapmakers also developed their art in the seventeenth century and, following Saxton's first survey of England and Wales on a county by county basis in the 1570s, other distinguished cartographers followed in his wake. John Norden began a projected series of county histories about 1593 but in the upshot only 5 county maps were published, *Middlesex* appearing in 1593, *Hertfordshire* in 1598 and the other three, *Cornwall, Essex,* and *Northamptonshire*, not until more than a century later. The third distinguished, late Tudor cartographer, in addition to Saxton and Norden, was John Speed whose *The Theatre of the Empire of Great Britaine*, an atlas of the counties of England and Wales, was first published in 1611. It turned out to be an enormously popular work right down to the end of the eighteenth century, though its popularity may have derived more from the coats of arms, inset views of towns, and elaborate cartouches with which the county maps were embellished, than their intrinsic topographical merit. Thereafter, the work of seventeenth-century cartographers was largely derivative, borrowing liberally from the work of Saxton, Norden and Speed, often with less than satisfactory results. However, towards the end of the century, in 1695, Edmund Gibson published a new translation of Camden's *Britannia* for which Robert Morden, described as 'a person of known abilities in these matters', drew a new set of county maps. An important innovation had appeared twenty years earlier, in 1675, with the publication of John Ogilby's road maps in his *Britannia, or an Illustration of the Kingdom of England and Dominion of Wales.* Hitherto, maps had featured few, if any, roads; now Ogilby had produced a book of roads which, though not in the form of maps did, however include a good deal of incidental topographical and other detail alongside the roads he so carefully delineated (Plate 45).

Throughout the seventeenth century, agricultural literature devoted to the dissemination and improvement of farming techniques was very profuse. However, space permits only a brief mention of the more important authors. The first of them was

John Norden, whose travels throughout England in the 1590s and his position as Surveyor of the Crown Woods in the first decades of the seventeenth century enabled him to observe different farming practices and to recommend the best of them. He also succeeded in carrying out some important reforms of the royal estates in 1614 and 1615. His book, *The Surveyor's Dialogue*, which was first published in 1607 and appeared in subsequent editions later in the seventeenth century, was infused with suggestions for improving farming land. The same was true of the voluminous writings of Gervase Markham whose works, some original, some plagiarised and generally less reputable than those of Norden, spanned almost the whole of the first four decades of the seventeenth century. Perhaps his most useful books, both devoted to general farming, were *The Country Farme*, published in 1616, and *The Whole Art of Husbandry*, issued in 1631. Another very influential writer on agricultural practices, whose work appeared at about this time, was Walter Blith, at one time a captain in Cromwell's army. Although he wrote only two volumes, the latter an expansion of the former, they contained eminently practical advice, so much so that he has been termed 'the greatest of the mid-seventeenth century writers'.[13] His *The English Improver; or a new survey of husbandry discovering the Kingdom that some land, both Arable and Pasture, may be advanced Double and Treble, and some Five and Ten-fold*, was printed in 1649, and an expanded version appeared in 1652. Among other things, Blith gave advice on the drainage of fields and on making water-meadows, advocated the use of alternate husbandy, and recommended the careful preservation and use of manures. He also invented a plough which remained in general use for a century or so. He was a strong advocate of enclosure and, consequently, had little good to say of the traditional open-field farmer, of whom he wrote:

> He will toyle all his days himselfe and Family for nothing, in and upon his common arable fielde land; up early and downe late, drudge and moyle and ware out himself and family; rather than he will cast how he may improve his lands of impasturing and enclosing of it.

Also writing about this time was Sir Richard Weston, whose *Discourse on the Husbandrie used in Brabant and Flanders* appeared in 1645. As we have seen, his significance was chiefly as a means of communicating good practice which he had observed in exile in the Low Countries. He was particularly impressed by the well-established system of alternate husbandry in Flanders which alternated a three-course system of corn and fallow with a six-year pasture for the production of meat and manure. Another important figure amid the welter of literature on agrarian practices that appeared in the middle of the seventeenth century was Samuel Hartlib. His best known work was his *Legacy*, published in 1651, which also described and recommended the intensive agricultural practices of the Low Countries. The book, which went through several editions and was very influential, dealt with many aspects of farming, including the cultivation of artificial grasses, the growing of hemp and flax, and the keeping of orchards.

During these middle decades of the seventeenth century, scientific curiosity and innovation were in the air and more and more of the large estate owners and farmers were showing a keen interest in new agricultural methods. For this reason, the newly founded Royal Society commissioned reports on a county-by-county basis of English farming as a means of disseminating new farming methods. Its agricultural committee was particularly active in this regard and in 1662, for example, strongly urged that the potato should be cultivated more extensively as an insurance against famine and to set a good example, recommended that the members of the Society should plant the crop and also encourage their friends to do the same. Just how valuable a contribution the Royal Society made to agricultural progress during the last 40 years of the seventeenth century it is difficult to estimate. However, in 1682 one of its members, John Houghton, a London apothecary and notable writer on agricultural matters, wrote in the following glowing terms,

> . . . since His Majesty's most happy Restoration the whole land hath been fermented and stirred up by the profitable hints it hath received from the Royal Society by which means parks have been disparked, commons inclosed, woods turned into arable, and pasture land, improved by clover, st. foine, turnips, coleseed, parsley, and many other good husbandries, so that the food of cattel is increast as fast, if not faster, than the consumption, and by these means, although some particular lands may fall, I strongly persuade myself that altogether the rent of the kingdom is far greater than ever it was.[14]

In the last third of the seventeenth century, two writers are particularly credited with making notable contributions to agricultural developments, both of whom were strongly influenced by the new spirit of scientific observation and measurement that were becoming influential at the time. They were John Worlidge, a Hampshire farmer, and John Houghton himself. In his *Systema Agriculturae : the mystery of Husbandry discovered*, first published in 1609 and running through five editions in his lifetime, Worlidge was the first to produce a comprehensive and reasonably systematic treatise on agriculture. In it, he aimed to assemble all the written and practical knowledge of the time, including the use of the new grasses and the then novel field crop of turnips. He also invented a drill to replace the traditional methods of broadcast sowing, which both drilled the seed and also dressed it with manure. His book is also interesting in that it describes aspects of farming then being pursued in different parts of the country.

John Houghton's chief claim to fame is that he was the first man to publish what amounted to an agricultural periodical. This consisted of a series of six pamphlets, issued between 1681 and

1683, entitled *A Collection of Letters for the Improvement of Husbandry and Trade.* They included comment and advice, not always firmly rooted in fact, on virtually every aspect of farming as well as on such subjects as the arts of fowling and fishing, and the management of country estates. Then, between 1691 and 1702, he issued a more or less continuous weekly paper which contained, among many other things, short articles on agriculture and much information on the rural economy of the time.

Although the significance of the improvements in agriculture which these publications helped to bring about should not be overestimated, since they were implemented by only a minority of England's farmers, nevertheless the fact remains that by 1700 substantial gains in agricultural productivity had been made as a result of technical advances. This was particularly true of the second half of the seventeenth century so that by the end of our period prosperity was much more widespread than had previously been the case. Moreover, the significance of this situation for the succeeding century was very great in that it was to lead to further and accelerating improvements in agricultural productivity and the more widespread adoption of improved farming methods: the process which was to lead to the Agricultural Revolution of the eighteenth century was, by 1700, well under way. The great achievement of agriculture, especially during the second part of our period, was that, despite a rapidly increasing population, England never ceased to feed her people in normal years. This increase in population also inevitably brought about a greater density of settlement and buildings in the countryside and it is to this aspect of the English landscape that we shall now turn our attention.

CHAPTER 4

Settlements and buildings in the countryside

As we have seen, from 1400 to 1700 the English countryside was, by today's standards, very thinly populated. As the great majority of people throughout these years lived and worked in the countryside, the volume and density of settlements and buildings were both relatively light. Outside the towns, the chief settlements were, of course, the villages and hamlets, the latter being smaller, subsidiary settlements without a parish church. In addition, especially in the upland areas, scattered, isolated farmsteads were widely distributed. More substantial buildings dispersed through the countryside included country houses, monastic settlements, and castles.

Villages

England today contains about 13,000 villages. Located mainly in the lowland areas, many have been continuously settled for up to 1500 years and the great majority certainly existed in 1400. At the beginning of our period, by far the most prominent building in the village was the church, the only one which was generally built of stone. The next most important building, though not all villages had one, was the manor house and this, too, was sometimes built of stone, but more often of timber. At this time, there was almost everywhere still a great abundance of wood so that the great majority of village buildings would have been timber-framed. The preferred and very durable wood, for those who could afford it, was always oak and the wealthier peasants would build for themselves 'cruck houses', with an oak curved timber supporting the roof. The majority of cottages, however, were little more than hovels, consisting in many areas of wattle-and-daub construction. The wattle would have been of an inferior wood to oak, such as elm, willow, ash or hazel, and the daub was dried clay or mud. It is hardly surprising that these primitive dwellings rarely survived for long; indeed, many of them were built of such flimsy materials that they required rebuilding every 25 or 30 years. However, in some parts of the country where local stone was freely available, more

65

lasting cottages were built. In north-west England, for example, various local building stones were used, including sandstone in the Eden Valley, limestone in Lonsdale, blue shale in parts of the Lake District, and rounded cobbles along the Solway shore. Throughout the region, these cottages were rendered with clay daub. The houses and cottages were usually roofed with thatch, made from reeds where obtainable, or from the ubiquitous long straw which was available in every part of the country before the coming of the combine-harvester. In areas where grain could not be grown, as in the uplands, heather would be used as roofing in place of straw. The whole settlement had a temporary, camp-like appearance and seemed almost as much a part of its natural environment as the fields and woods. The approaches to the villages consisted of grassy tracks which became very muddy in winter. At this time, therefore, the principal domestic building materials of the English village were wood, mud and thatch. As yet, stone was little used and brick scarcely at all.

The individual character and relative prosperity of fifteenth-century villages inevitably varied considerably. Those that were near towns which provided a ready market were in a favoured position, as in the case of the Middlesex village of Tottenham,[1] which gained greatly from, and was substantially affected by, its close proximity to London. The very strong influence of the capital city was felt in many ways. Firstly, more and more Londoners purchased land and bought houses in the village, perhaps for investment, to obtain a country residence, as a form of gentleman farming, or even to escape the plague. Other nearby villages such as Edmonton and Enfield were also favourite locations where London citizens bought land and houses. Secondly, it is likely that the centre of the village was moved at some time early in the fifteenth century, from around the parish church to over half-a-mile away along 'Totenhamstrete', the main road into London. This sort of move, which was quite common in the Middle Ages, enabled the villagers to profit from the traffic along the high road and made it easier for them to move their produce into London. The state of the road at this time was parlous and every cart using it had to pay a penny a week and every pack horse a farthing a week to obtain funds for its repair. The village itself grew so that by the middle of the fifteenth century it must have been a bustling place, with lodging houses, six inns, embryonic shops, and even brothels. The economy of the village also changed and its farmers increasingly concentrated on rearing and pasturing cattle and sheep for the London market. These developments were in marked contrast to the majority of English villages, such as neighbouring Hackney, which remained backwaters, much as they had always been.

Moreover, many villages at this time must have witnessed the migration rather than the influx of peasants. One such example was the village of Hampton Lovett,[2] in Worcestershire, about 7

66

miles north of Worcester. A typical nucleated settlement, it lay in the centre of open-field farming, inhabited by peasants most of whom held modest amounts of land of about 60 acres each. As the size of peasant families was increasing, by between 20 and 40 per cent by the early sixteenth century, and as land was handed down from father to the eldest son, other family members sought better prospects in nearby towns. Most of them migrated relatively short distances to such centres as Droitwich, Tewkesbury and Worcester where they could ply a craft, and some as far afield as Bristol. The effect on the village was one of stagnation, and several of the houses were in a dilapidated condition as the peasants were poor and sometimes unable or unwilling to repair them. The sort of migration that occurred in rural Worcestershire in the fifteenth century was being duplicated in many other parts of the country.

Villages, then as now, came in all sorts of shapes and sizes, depending on their history, their location and their economic fortunes. In general, however, they fell into three main categories. The first was the 'street village', with the houses strung in a line along one street. The second can best be described as the 'green village', with a large grassy open space, the village green, dominating the centre of the village. In some of these villages the houses were distributed in an orderly fashion around the village green, while in others they were more higgledy-piggledy with some actually on the green itself. The third category of village can be described as agglomerated, or compact, having no distinct shape and made up of a formless tangle of houses and lanes. This form of village often resulted from a small hamlet having cottages added to it at a later stage. Finally, many villages fell into none of these categories precisely, but thanks to a complex history partook of several of the features described above.

As we have seen, the fifteenth century witnessed the complete disappearance of a substantial number of villages. Although some had been deserted before 1450, the majority of depopulations took place in the seventy years between 1450 and 1520. By this time, many village communities had become debilitated by the combined effects of plague and economic misfortune and landlords then took the final step of removing what peasants were left, allowing the village to tumble into ruin, in order to convert the land to sheep pasture. To a considerable extent, therefore, the occurrence and distribution of villages deserted during this period resulted from the decisions and whims of individual landlords. Just such a one was William Cope of Wormleighton, in Warwickshire. Granted the manor by Henry VII in 1498, for an annual rent of 20 marks, or £13 6s 8d, he promptly set about purchasing all the lands of smaller landlords in the parish. Having thereby gained control of the entire parish, he proceeded in 1499 to remove the occupants of the remaining twelve houses and three cottages, numbering sixty people in all, to destroy the habitations, and to convert the arable land to sheep pasture. Much of the deserted village of Wormleighton can still be seen in the landscape today, as can the traces of many others, especially in the Midlands.

The sites of the former peasant houses are represented by low, regular-shaped mounds and bumps. In the larger villages, where a manor house existed, its site may be denoted by a bigger mound, as in the case of Great Stretton, in Leicestershire (Plate 6). Here, the manor house had another distinguishing feature, namely a rectangular moat, which was quite commonly found in the clay lowlands. Alongside the remains of the moated manor house is a smaller depression marking the site of another common feature of the medieval village, the manorial fishpond. Along with the houses, the village church also fell into decay. Once the village was deserted, the houses tumbled down and became overgrown and the church fell into ruins. Occasionally, if several villages were affected but not all were deserted, then one church might continue in use, as at Great Stretton where it is the only building remaining from the original village and at Wharram Percy in the East Riding of Yorkshire. In many deserted villages, the crofts were enclosed within a single boundary bank, which probably also served as a base for a fence, thereby separating them from the open fields. In the villages the village street gradually became silted up and covered in grass and the latter sometimes formed 'hollow ways', still occasionally to be seen in the modern landscape. Many deserted villages are today represented solely by isolated farmsteads, as for example in the Hundred of Ford in mid-west Shropshire where of 70 medieval hamlets mentioned in the Domesday Book 9 are totally deserted and 33 are single farms.

Many of the deserted medieval villages have been identified thanks to the pioneering work of Beresford and Hurst, work which is being continued by the Medieval Village Research Group. This identification can be achieved either from documentary evidence, or from the landscape, or best still from both. One of the very few maps which exists of a village which subsequently became deserted is that of Boarstall in Buckinghamshire, dating from 1444 (Plate 9). Although crudely drawn and not to scale, it shows the open fields, the village church and manor house, and just to the south of the village the manorial 'dere hide' or enclosure for deer. Occasionally, post-desertion maps of the countryside reveal the disappearance of a village by marking the site of the 'Old Town' or by entering field-names such as 'The Town's Coppice' or 'The Town's Piece'.

Between 1350 and 1500, probably 10 per cent of the settlements of rural England disappeared from the landscape. Among the surviving villages, however, shrinkage was common and individual tenements, once deserted, would often subside into ruin, leaving gaps between the remaining dwellings. On the other hand, a minority of villages, like Tottenham, were more fortunate and grew and prospered. In any case, it would be a mistake to suppose

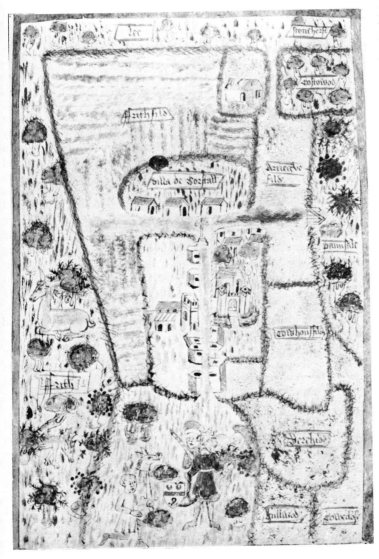

Plate 9 A map of the village of Boarstall in Buckinghamshire in 1444. It shows the village with its church, its manor house, and its open fields

that villages were stable and largely unchanging, either in their economic fortunes or their layout. Throughout the period covered in this book, change occurred at a considerable pace. Some villages moved about and radically altered their layouts, while others declined, became deserted, or were replanned. This process of change was sporadic and uneven and was often a response to such events as the occurrence of plagues, the waxing and waning of sheep farming, the growth of industry, and changes in the structure of society.

69

In the sixteenth and seventeenth centuries, for example, it was not uncommon for parts of villages, or on occasion entire villages, to be removed for the creation of parks around the country houses that were being built or extended at this time. Powerful landlords simply evicted the villagers, demolished their dwellings and turned their fields into parkland. In Staffordshire, for example, among the villages and hamlets that disappeared in this manner were Great Sandon, Wrottesley, Blithfield and Chartley.

However, the vast majority of villages were unaffected by such developments and their centre pieces consisted, as they had long done, of the parish church and manor house or hall. It was not until the seventeenth century that the desire among the wealthier landowners for detachment and splendid isolation led them to abandon their manor houses in the village and to build new ones in isolated sites in the middle of large parks surrounded by high walls.[3] As far as parish churches were concerned, the fifteenth century witnessed the rebuilding, wholly or in part, of almost every other one. This was the period of Perpendicular ecclesiastical architecture which was to flourish without interruption until the Dissolution of the Monasteries in the 1540s. There was a rich harvest of church building and enlargement, especially in the cloth-producing parts of the country where rich wool merchants and landlords sought salvation for their souls by pouring money into the extension and glorification of the parish church. This was especially evident in the shape of the church tower, which reached a state of perfection at this time that made it one of the major English contributions to medieval art. Extraordinary numbers of

Plate 10 The noble parish church of Long Melford, Suffolk, rebuilt in the Perpendicular style between about 1460 and 1495

Perpendicular towers were built. Between 1350 and 1535, about 1100 new church towers were erected and some 2300 churches with towers already in existence either had them made higher or were given new ones. Unlike their Norman predecessors, they were very well constructed; consequently, they nearly all survive, providing us with a marvellous architectural legacy.[4] Using such local building stone as was available, they range from the stone towers of Somerset to the flint towers of East Anglia. The former are noteworthy for their tall pinnacles, elaborately worked parapets, buttresses and large windows, while the East Anglian towers are characterised by their flushwork, a chequerboard combination of knapped flint and stone which shows prominently in such Suffolk towers as those at Eye, Bungay, Lavenham and Monks Eleigh.

In some instances, the whole of the church was rebuilt at this time, as at Lavenham and Long Melford (Plate 10), in Suffolk, and as a result some of the finest Perpendicular churches in England are in what were always small villages. But it was not only

Plate 11 Baddesley Clinton Hall, Warwickshire, a moated manor dating from the fifteenth century

the exterior of the church that was being glorified at this time. Superb fonts, font-covers, tombs, monuments, screens, effigies and stained glass are all part of the rich legacy left to us by fifteenth-century merchants and landlords as tokens of the high priority they accorded to the after-life.

Like the parish church, the manor house also benefited from the greater prosperity of its owners and some splendid examples of fifteenth-century construction still survive, some half-timbered, some in stone, and some combining both. Perhaps the finest examples are in Warwickshire, among them the mid-fifteenth century Baddesley Clinton Hall which, with its grey stone buildings and moat, stands before one as the perfect late medieval house (Plate 11). Some eight miles away to the southeast is Coughton Court, another splendid, slightly later, stone Warwickshire house. It was the home of the Throckmorton family from the early fifteenth century to the present day. They rebuilt the church in the late sixteenth and early seventeenth centuries and slowly erected a new house, from about 1510 onwards, including the gatehouse, the oldest part of the present building (Plate 12).

During the fifteenth century, *dovecotes*, which were also known as pigeon houses or culverys, became increasingly associated with manor houses. Square or circular in shape, built of half-timber, stone or brickwork, and the special prerogative of the lord of the manor, they increased greatly in popularity until in Stuart times

Plate 12 Coughton Court, Warwickshire. The Tudor stone gatehouse in the centre dates from the early sixteenth century. It is flanked on the right by a much-restored timber-framed range also built at about the same time

there were probably 26,000 in existence in England (Plate 13).[5] The pigeons were kept for food and, especially in winter when fresh food was at a premium, they provided a reliable and cheap source of meat. They constituted a significant part of the diet of the lord's household, the old birds being eaten at the turn of the year and the young ones, or squabs, in the spring. Keeping pigeons was also relatively inexpensive, as they lived off the land and, moreover, their droppings provided a valuable source of fertile manure. However, dovecotes declined in importance in the late seventeenth century when root crops became available for winter feed for cattle, so that with fresh meat being on hand at any time, pigeon meat was less important. Although many dovecotes still survive, very few are in use today.

By 1500, many lesser manor houses were essentially farmhouses whose owners were peasants rather than gentry and who farmed relatively small estates. This was especially true of the northern

Plate 13 The dovecote at Dormston in Worcestershire. Built originally in the seventeenth century, it was given a Regency-style roof early in the nineteenth century

part of the country which by this time was already generally less prosperous than the south. In counties like Lincolnshire and those further north, houses were smaller in size and simpler in arrangement than those in the southern half of the country.[6] In both north and south of the country, however, the standard type of early sixteenth-century manor house continued to be the hall-house, that is a house with its hall in the middle, open to the roof, flanked on either side with two-storey wings, one containing living rooms, the other the services. A number of these houses though since much altered, survive today. Many of them were essentially working farms which included dairies among their outbuildings. The dairy usually consisted of a wooden frame filled in with wattle and daub and with a straw-thatched roof. It was frequently a free-standing building, sometimes with an internal partition to separate cows' milk and ewes' milk both of which were in general use at this time. Most of the milk went into cheese making, some into butter, some for treating sheep-scab, some for feeding up ailing livestock, some for human consumption, and the remainder for sale as unprocessed milk.

In some of the larger and more prosperous villages, schools and almshouses were founded at the end of the fifteenth century and during the sixteenth century. Although schools were more frequently established in towns, they were also located in villages: in Shropshire, for example, towns like Shrewsbury, Bridgnorth, Oswestry, Newport, Whitchurch and Market Drayton all had schools by the end of the sixteenth century, as did a few villages like Bitterly, Worfield and Donnington in Wroxeter.[7] A particularly sturdy and long-lived example of a fifteenth-century village school is that at Ewelme in Oxfordshire founded in 1437 by the Earl and Countess of Suffolk and built of brick. At the same time, they built almshouses in the village, also largely of brick, to house thirteen poor men under the care of two chaplains. Although brick was being used in East Anglia at this time, its use at Ewelme is among the earliest examples in Oxfordshire. In the next century, many other notable examples of village schools and almshouses, were erected, usually of local materials and encompassing excellent examples of local craftmanship. Like the Perpendicular towers and chantry chapels of parish churches, they owe their origin to the desire of their wealthy donors to demonstrate their piety and philanthropy. Less worthy features perhaps of most villages were the inns and alehouses which were frequently the cause of excessive drinking, unlawful gaming and other connected offences.[8] Although some were inns providing accommodation and refreshment for travellers, many were little more than private houses selling and competing with one another to see which could brew the strongest ale.

Travellers came to villages, then as now, for a variety of reasons. Some would be passing through, some would be attending the weekly village market and the annual fair, and some would come to the villages to trade. The passing traffic took many forms, including carters and carriers, bearing everything from messages to building materials such as timber, bricks and stone. Markets were not just restricted to towns, but were also found in a number of villages. In south-west England, for example, weekly markets were so numerous that few places, even the most remote, were more than ten miles from one. These village markets were normally very small and served only their immediate locality. Farmers, craftsmen, small-scale traders and entrepreneurs of all sorts took their surplus produce to market, and indeed took anything else which could be bought or sold. There was also frequent movement between peasants living in a particular village and the markets in others nearby, so that the peasant in one village might be a trader in the next and a cottager in one an innkeeper in another. Another feature of some villages was the annual fair which, like the markets, was mainly of local significance. Both markets and fairs served as more than merely centres of trade: they were also a forum for meetings, for the exchange of news, farming methods, and gossip, and an opportunity for social diversion.

With the growth of population during the 1500s, especially during the latter part of the century, villages began to expand though there is little or no evidence of new villages being founded. For example, in 1570 the village or township of Cannock in Staffordshire had 52 dwellings which, together with some others in its dependent hamlets of Hednesford and Leacroft, housed a total population of about 320. By the turn of the century, this had risen to 400.[9] Similarly, Rugeley and its associated hamlet of Brereton had 115 dwellings in 1570 and a population of about 520, which had risen to over 600 by 1600. Both villages had a weekly market and a large number of alehouses, 9 in Cannock and 18 in Rugeley, representing one alehouse for every 20 adults living in the villages.

Villages were not only increasing in size at this time but were also being extensively rebuilt. The more prosperous inhabitants of late Tudor England displayed their wealth by building themselves larger and more substantial houses. Indeed, during the hundred years between about 1540 and 1640 most of England was undergoing the 'Great Rebuilding' or, in Camden's words, 'the great bravery of building which marvellously beautified the realm'. Its most magnificent product was the country house, but it also found expression in village dwellings, including the late Tudor stone houses of Cotswolds villages and the timber-framed farmhouses in many Suffolk and Warwickshire villages (Plate 14). What characterised this building boom, therefore, was that, unlike medieval buildings whose patrons were very largely powerful nobles and ecclesiastics, it was essentially carried out by local craftsmen for local use and enjoyment. In Sussex, for example, the tradition of vernacular timber-framed building found virile

Plate 14 The village of
Kersey in Suffolk with
its timber-framed houses
dating from the sixteenth
and seventeenth
centuries

expression at this time in villages like Lindfield, East Grinstead
and Crawley, which are still incomparably rich in such dwellings.
Moreover, as well as building new houses, many yeomen and
husbandmen substantially improved existing dwellings, often
lavishing their money on a more sumptuous interior, leaving the
outside looking relatively unchanged. As a result, we have
inherited a wealth of stone and oak doorways, linenfold panelling,
moulded beams and timbered ceilings. But it was not only cottages
that were being built at this time; manor houses, farmsteads,
barns, almhouses, schools and dovecotes were all going up in
Elizabethan villages.

Plate 15 Moat
Farmhouse, near
Dormston in
Worcestershire, a
timber-framed building
dating from 1663

This village rebuilding continued through much of the seventeenth century, a period which was notable, among other things, for its wealth of substantial farmhouses (Plate 15). Good examples are to be found today in such villages as Madeley, near Newcastle-Under-Lyme in Staffordshire, whose high-gabled, well-proportioned timber-framed Stuart farmhouses are still to be seen in the centre of the village.[10] A typical Stuart farmhouse, like its Elizabethan predecessor, contained a large hall, which with its open fireplace and heavy oak beams was still the centre of family living, with connecting passages leading to 2 or 3 smaller rooms. Above were 2 or 3 sleeping and storage chambers, at first reached by ladders from the ground floor and later by fixed staircases. In the Cotswolds, numerous stone houses and cottages were going up at this time and among the most picturesque is Arlington Row, in Bibury, Gloucestershire, a row of small stone cottages, dating from the early seventeenth century when they were used as weaver's cottages for supplying cloth to the local fulling mill (Plate 16).

This great rise in secular building activity was paralleled by a steep decline in church building and rebuilding which from the middle of the sixteenth century until the end of the seventeenth century, was notable largely by its absence. The Elizabethan contribution to church architecture was negligible and seems to have been mostly confined to church fittings and monuments,[11] of which there are many splendid examples in churches all over the country. Some of the families who acquired land and wealth from the Dissolution of the Monasteries celebrated their rise by placing fine family tombs in the parish churches, often in chapels which

Plate 16 Arlington Row, Bibury in Gloucestershire, facing a mill leat of the River Coln. The cottages, which are built from local limestone and are roofed with Cotswold slates, date mainly from the seventeenth century

they had built for the purpose. For most of the seventeenth century, there was a similar scarcity of church building and rebuilding, especially during the Commonwealth. A small number of older churches were rebuilt in the first half of the 1600s, still entirely in the Gothic style, including those at Fulmer in Buckinghamshire in 1610, Stowe-Nine-Churches in Northamptonshire in 1620, and Carsington in Derbyshire in 1648. The last-named, which lies 6 miles south-west of Matlock, is typical of churches rebuilt at this time and is a complete example of a Gothic survival church. On its east wall it bears a sundial with the legend 'Re-edified 1648'. The interiors of these churches are, however, frequently anything but medieval in appearance and, like that of the outwardly-Gothic gem of Staunton Harold parish church in Leicestershire, built in 1653 (Plate 17), often contain wooden pulpits, galleries and box pews which are characteristically seventeenth century in appearance.

Plate 17 Staunton Harold parish church, Leicestershire. Dating from 1653, it is one of the very few churches to be built during the Commonwealth

During the first fifty years of the seventeenth century, the fashion for erecting family monuments in parish churches continued to flourish and some superb tombs date from this period. The Midlands are particularly noteworthy in this respect and two splendid examples are the monument to John Spencer

and his wife, dating from the 1620s, in Great Brington church, Northamptonshire, and the collection of funeral monuments to the St John family in Lydiard Tregoze church, near Swindon, in Wiltshire. On the other hand, northern counties tend to be much less well-endowed and north Lancashire, for example, can only boast one seventeenth-century monument of note, that of Edward Weightinton, who died in 1658, at Standish, some five miles south of Chorley. With the coming of the Civil War, the size and sumptuousness of church monuments of this sort declined and never thereafter regained their former glory.

The Restoration of Charles II to the throne of England in 1660 ushered in a new period of English church building in which the traditional Gothic style was largely replaced by a classical one, and in which liturgical changes made the chancel obsolete. This architectural revolution was largely brought about by Sir Christopher Wren with his rebuilding of London churches after the Great Fire of 1666. Although he himself built few, if any, churches in the country, a few delightful village churches of simpler type were built under his influence, including Willen in Buckinghamshire in 1680 and Hopton Cangeford in Shropshire at the end of the century.

The latter part of the seventeenth century was also notable for the arrival in English villages of the starkly simple Nonconformist meeting houses and chapels. Among the earliest examples is the Dissenter's Chapel at Great Houghton in the West Riding of Yorkshire, built about 1656. Later seventeenth-century examples include the Swarthmoor Quaker Meeting House, near Ulverston, in Cumbria, a simple barn converted into a meeting house by George Fox in 1688, and Jordans Quaker Meeting House near Chalfont St Giles in Buckinghamshire, also built in 1688 and of historical importance as the burial ground of William Penn, founder of Pennsylvania. Although the contribution of parish churches to the English scene is extremely well recorded, that of chapels and meeting houses is little recognised.[12] Yet in many villages, these tiny halls built of local stone or brick are characteristic and easily recognisable.

Country houses

The country house is one of the particular glories of the English countryside and we have a richer inheritance than almost any other country in the world. During the fifteenth century, however, as throughout the Middle Ages, most large buildings were either ecclesiastical, like the Perpendicular churches, or military, as instanced by castles and fortified houses. By 1400 the great period of medieval castle building was over and although a small number was built during the next 100 years, they partook more of the character of fortified country houses than true castles. A very important innovation at this time was the revival of building in brick, a material which had been used by the Romans in England and then very largely fell out of use. Its use was revived in the fifteenth century, principally in East Anglia, and a prominent example of a fortified brick house of this period is Tattershall Castle, near Sleaford in Lincolnshire. A stone house had stood on this site and it was rebuilt of brick in 1434-45 by Ralph, Lord Cromwell, who was Treasurer of England under Henry VI and a veteran of Agincourt. Although Tattershall Castle's rectangular tower and turrets rising to 120 feet above the ground are clearly designed to impress, it is essentially a building intended for comfort rather than for defence. The second floor of the south-west turret is lined with wattle and daub, moulded into resting places for hundreds of doves. Similar brick strongholds are Caister Castle, near Yarmouth, in Norfolk, built between 1432 and perhaps 1446; and the Leicestershire castles of Ashby-de-la-Zouch and Kirby Muxloe (Plate 18) built by William Lord Hastings between 1474 and 1483, and 1480 and 1484 respectively. Occasionally, brick buildings of this sort were erected in or near villages and the first buildings of Eton College, in Buckinghamshire, were being put up in brick in the 1440s. Not far away, in Buckden in Bedfordshire, the Bishop of Lincoln built the great brick tower which still dominates the centre of the village, between 1472 and 1480, and the rest of the house, of which only parts survive, was probably completed by his successor between 1480 and 1494.

However, building in brick was probably an expensive luxury which very few could afford and, as a result, the great majority of

Plate 18 The ruins of Kirby Muxloe Castle in Leicestershire, built in brick but never completed, by William Lord Hastings between 1480 and 1484

small manor houses built in the countryside in the latter part of the fifteenth century continued to be timber-framed, with infilling of wattle and daub. Some of them, like Lower Brockhampton, in Herefordshire (Plate 19), or Great Dixter, near Northiam, in Sussex, have proved to be remarkably longlasting. But whether these houses were built of brick or timber, the grandeur of their outward appearance was not accompanied by comfort and hygiene inside. Even as late as the end of the century, Erasmus described the interior of many manor houses thus:[13]

> The floors are commonly of clay, strewed with rushes, so renewed that the substratum may be unmolested for twenty years, with an ancient collection of beer, grease, fragments, bones, spittle and everything that is nasty.

To these unhygienic conditions, he attributed, probably with justice, the frequent plagues that broke out in England. However, the interior comfort and splendour of manor houses were greatly to increase during the sixteenth century.

Indeed, the coming of the sixteenth century confirmed a trend that was already becoming apparent in the previous century, namely that the focus of day-to-day life was shifting from the religious to the secular. Ecclesiastical building, which was in decline by 1500, was dealt a final blow some 40 years later by the Dissolution of the Monasteries. By placing great wealth in secular hands, this traumatic event gave a great impetus to the building of country houses. Powerful merchants, lawyers and magnates, especially those in the courts surrounding the Tudor kings, vied with one another to put up splendid country houses, with more and more luxurious interiors and with rising standards of internal comfort. Moreover, with the end of the Wars of the Roses and the

Plate 19 Lower Brockhampton House, Herefordshire, a moated timber-framed house dating from the late fourteenth and the fifteenth centuries

81

advent of the Tudor dynasty, the country became more secure and the need for defensive buildings was past.

During the reign of Henry VIII (1509-47), the popularity of brick as a building material increased rapidly and a number of houses went up during this period which are among the finest in the country. Eminent among them is Compton Wynyates, in Warwickshire. An old house rebuilt in the early years of the sixteenth century, its nostalgic, picturesque appearance dates from that time. Another brick building of this period is the stupendous gatehouse of Layer Marney in Essex; built in about 1520 by Henry, Lord Marney, Treasurer to Henry VIII, it was intended as the frontispiece to a courtyard house of equal magnificence which was never built. Nor was Henry VIII himself less enthusiastic a builder. Indeed, he was clearly one of the most extravagant builders of all our monarchs and during his lifetime he erected or rebuilt no fewer than ten royal residences, of which the most spectacular was probably Nonsuch Palace, near Cheam in Surrey. Built by the King for his own use, its exterior walls were a frenzy of decoration, and its interior included Renaissance detail like decorative plasterwork executed by imported Italian craftsmen. Unfortunately, Nonsuch, like most of Henry VIII's buildings, has long since disappeared. Of his palaces which remain, perhaps the most spectacular is Hampton Court, Middlesex. Built and planned by Cardinal Wolsey for himself, it was extracted from him by the King, who took it over in 1525 and stamped his own image firmly on it. Hampton Court is notable also for its garden, shaped and patterned by Wolsey and his monarch in turn. At this time, the cult of the formal, artificial garden developed; designed as the antithesis of the natural landscape, it was enclosed and made rigidly geometrical with its straight alleys lined with fruit trees and its clipped box hedges.

Most of Henry VIII's frenetic building took place from about 1538 to the end of his reign and included an extraordinary array of defence works around the coast all the way from the Scottish border to Cornwall, the best known being the chain of coastal forts from Tynemouth to Falmouth.[14] The cost of all this work was enormous; the rebuilding of Hampton Court alone cost more than £60,000, an immense sum by the standards of the day, with much of the money coming from Henry's spoliation of the religious houses. However, as we have seen, the King was not the only one to benefit from the Dissolution of the Monasteries, as during the 1540s and early 1550s perhaps a quarter of the land of England passed from institutional into private hands. Monastic lands were purchased by country gentlemen who in the process substantially increased their power and wealth. Moreover, the physical destruction of the religious houses furnished huge quantities of dressed and rough stone which provided the fabric of a series of magnificent mansions which sprang up either in the immediate neighbourhood of the ruins or within easy reach of them. In some cases, the religious houses were wholly or, in part, converted into private houses, among the most notable being Newstead and Lacock Abbeys. Newstead, near Nottingham, which became famous for its associations with Byron who lived there for a short time, was originally remodelled soon after the Dissolution from an Augustinian priory into a magnificent private house incorporating the west front of the priory church and the abbey's cloister. Lacock Abbey, in Wiltshire, one of the last religious houses to be suppressed in England, in 1539, was purchased by Sir William Sharrington, who kept much of the original building, including the cloister, sacristy, chapter house and warming room and incorporated them into his new timber-framed house which he built with a large courtyard and octagonal tower.

This vast transfer of church lands into private hands was one of the major reasons for 'the Great Rebuilding', the building boom which accelerated during the reign of Elizabeth. A period of rapid upward social mobility, its rising families like the Cavendishes, the Cecils, the Harveys and the Thynnes first appear on the national scene at this time. Determined to demonstrate their new-found wealth in secular fashion, they set about erecting magnificent country houses, which represented a flowering of great house-building that has never been equalled since. The details of these houses are to be found in books like Olive Cook's excellent *The English Country House*, upon which this chapter draws. Although their owners were thrusting, and in many cases flamboyant, the houses they built were generally restrained, sharing a plain symmetry and order which the Tudor gentry sought to give to a turbulent society. Their characteristics were, by this time, well developed and included two principal structural features, a staircase and a long gallery. The staircases were usually of oak and richly carved, while the long galleries were uniquely English and ran the whole length of the top floor of the house. Typical of these Elizabethan mansions is Cowdray House near Midhurst in West Sussex, built mainly in the 1540s. Though long deserted, its ruins still constitute what Nairn and Pevsner describe as 'an absolutely consistent epitome of Tudor architecture at its plainest and most sober, very English in its understatement, its dignity and concern for volumes and solidity.'[15] Another splendid example of a late Tudor mansion, fortunately in excellent condition, is Hardwick Hall, near Chesterfield in Derbyshire (Plate 20). With its overwhelming expanse of windows, so that it appears to have been constructed more of glass than stone, and its enormous long gallery, Hardwick is a monument to the formidable Countess of Shrewsbury, Bess of Hardwick, who began its construction in 1591 at the age of 71 and whose huge initials 'ES' rise above its parapets. Perhaps the most flamboyant of all the Elizabethan prodigy houses, and therefore somewhat uncharacteristic, is Burghley House, just off the A1 near Stamford in Lincolnshire. Built mainly of Barnack stone from a quarry in the village of that

Plate 20 Hardwick Hall in Derbyshire, now in the possession of the National Trust. Built for 'Bess of Hardwick', the Countess of Shrewsbury, at the end of the sixteenth century, its parapets ostentatiously display her initials 'ES'

name a few miles south-east of the house, it was constructed for William Cecil, Lord Burghley, the greatest of Elizabeth's statesmen. A four-sided courtyard palace of stone, set in a vast deer park, it is a monument to Tudor England, with its huge five-storied gatehouse, its rounded frontispiece adorned with classical columns and its roof-tops filled with pepper-pot domes and clustered chimneyshafts.

But if the great Elizabethan houses were built of stone, the

84

tradition of timber-framed building continued in many parts of the country, especially in Cheshire and Lancashire, Sussex and East Anglia, where it was particularly popular and where it continued to be common well into the seventeenth century. Perhaps the finest and most exuberant specimens are to be found in the northern counties, none more so than Little Moreton Hall, near Congleton in Cheshire (Plate 21). A black-and-white half-timbered moated manor house, built by William Moreton and his son probably about the middle of the sixteenth century, it is so picturesque that Crowl[16] compares it to a stage set for Verdi's opera *Falstaff*. A similar black-and-white, timbered house is Speke Hall, about eight miles south-east of Liverpool in Lancashire. Built by the Norris family during the second half of the sixteenth century round a square courtyard, it occupies a rural setting close to the River Mersey.

Most of the great Elizabethan houses were built on a simple E-plan or U-plan, but by the beginning of the seventeenth century, these began to give way to an H-plan which allowed both the front and back elevations to assume a grander and more elegant appearance. Perhaps the greatest of Jacobean houses to be built

Plate 21 Little Moreton Hall, Cheshire, a gem of a black-and-white timber-framed manor house, built about 1559

along these lines is Knole, near Sevenoaks in Kent. One of the largest houses in England, with no fewer than 365 rooms, it is set in a magnificent deer park of 1000 acres. A house was already in existence on the site when Thomas Sackville, the first Earl of Dorset, rebuilt it between 1603 and 1608 into essentially its present shape and appearance. It became increasingly fashionable at this time to build taller and taller houses and two splendid Yorkshire examples are Burton Agnes and Fountains Hall. Burton Agnes Hall, which lies six miles south-west of Bridlington, in Humberside, was constructed of mellow red brick between 1601 and 1610 for Sir Henry Griffiths, with three lofty floors of rooms and graceful semi-circular bow windows on the end faces of short projecting wings. Fountains Hall, which lies south-west of Ripon, was built in 1611 on the land of the former huge Cistercian house of Fountains Abbey by Sir Stephen Proctor. Constructed from the materials of the ruined abbey, and set into a steep hillside, it rises to no fewer than five storeys.

By the time of the accession of Charles I in 1625, the parvenu exuberance of Elizabethan country-house building was coming gradually to be replaced by classical propriety, a trend reinforced by Inigo Jones, who was the first to introduce the classical Italian styles of building into England. Although relatively little of his work has survived, his influence on English architecture was nevertheless profound. Among the most influential buildings he designed was the Queen's House, Greenwich, begun in 1617 during the lifetime of Queen Anne and eventually completed for Charles I between 1629 and 1635; a comparison with other houses built at this time reveals the boldness and novelty of its conception. To this single building has been ascribed much of the credit for bringing to an end the architecture of the Middle Ages and ushering in the English Renaissance. Inigo Jones also had a large hand in the restoration of Wilton House, near Salisbury in Wiltshire, for his patron, the Earl of Pembroke. This building, which was rebuilt after a fire in 1647, is perhaps most celebrated for its sumptuous interior and in particular its seven magnificent state rooms, including the remarkable double and single cube rooms.

Inevitably, the outbreak of the Civil War put an effective stop to the building of country houses as did the puritanical atmosphere of the Commonwealth. Consequently, it was not until after the Restoration that country-house architecture revived, to usher in a period dominated by Sir Christopher Wren, an architect ideally fitted to continue the work started by Inigo Jones a generation earlier. The exile of the King and his court abroad had led to the introduction of foreign, particularly Dutch and French styles of classical architecture which quickly established themselves. Although Wren himself built no country houses, his influence was profound and in Sacheverell Sitwell's words,[17] he was 'the first to elevate the red brick vernacular into great architecture'. A fine example of the subdued, reticent and urbane style characteristic of this period is Ham House, a palatial red-brick mansion rebuilt in the 1670s from a modest Jacobean manor house, near the attractive village of Petersham in Surrey on the south bank of the Thames. Similarly sophisticated classical houses built or rebuilt at this time include Honington, near Shipston-on-Stour in Warwickshire; Ranbury, east of Marlborough in Wiltshire; and Belton House, near Grantham in Lincolnshire (Plate 22), frequently but erroneously attributed to Wren himself. Belton, built of rich grey-golden Ancaster stone instead of brick, has been described by Pevsner as perhaps the most satisfying among the later seventeenth-century houses in England.

During the last decade of the seventeenth century, Wren was at work on Hampton Court Palace, where his building for William and Mary was extensive. However, only a fragment is left today, consisting of the Park and Privy Garden façades and the Fountain Court in the angle between the two. Two other notable houses under alteration and construction as the seventeenth century faded away were Chatsworth and Dyrham Park, by the same under-estimated Dutch architect, William Talman, who had also assisted Wren at Hampton Court. At Chatsworth, in Derbyshire, he demolished the south range of the existing Elizabethan building and erected in its place an Italianate classical façade of local stone (Plate 23) and at Dyrham, in Gloucestershire, he built the entire house of pale gold Bath limestone.

Plate 22 Belton House, near Grantham, in Lincolnshire

87

Monastic settlements

During their heyday in the early Middle Ages, there were more than 1000 monastic settlements scattered the length and breadth of England and Wales, both in towns and in the country. Indeed, almost every large building in the English landscape that was not a manor house or a castle was certain to be a religious house of some kind. Of various sizes, the large monasteries were usually known as abbeys and other houses were classed as priories. Among the religious orders who founded and ran monastic houses in England the most prominent were the Benedictines and the Cistercians. Benedictine foundations were scattered throughout the country but were particularly concentrated in three main areas: the Fenlands, including the great abbeys of Peterborough, Ely, Ramsey, Thorney and Crowland; in the Severn Valley around Gloucester, Tewkesbury and Pershore; and in the southern counties of Wiltshire, Dorset and Hampshire. Nearly all the Benedictine houses were richly endowed and by the twelfth century they possessed about one-sixth of the land of England[18] which they farmed in a similar fashion to other medieval landlords. The Cistercians, or White Monks, came to England during the twelfth century and adopted a rule that the sites of their abbeys should be far from the habitation of man. Consequently, they colonised remote and unpopulated areas in the Midlands and the north and west of the country, founding abbeys in places like Bordesley in Worcestershire and Stoneleigh in Warwickshire, or the edges of the Forests of Feckenham and Arden and, above all at Fountains, Rievaulx and Kirkstall in Yorkshire. The Cistercians flourished greatly and by the end of the twelfth century had established more than 230 abbeys and priories. Their growth was due in large part to their successful farming practices: although their houses were located in remote parts of the country, through their dedicted labour they made the land bloom; they introduced profitable agricultural practices such as sheep farming; and they welcomed illiterate and humble followers who became the field workers upon whom their material prosperity depended.

By the fourteenth century, however, many monasteries had begun to decline, partly because of fewer benefactors and greater taxation, partly because fewer men and women were joining the religious houses as the opportunities for literate men and women outside the monasteries increased in a more sophisticated society. This decline became catastrophic with the arrival of the plagues in the middle of the fourteenth century. They halved the number of monks and visited the principal monastic centres of the Benedictines and Cistercians with extreme severity. Although the religious orders recovered somewhat after 1360, the numbers of monks in 1400 were still only about two-thirds of what they had been in the thirteenth century. As farm labour became scarcer during the fifteenth century, so Cistercian and Benedictine abbots, like other great landowners, had to divide up their large farms into smaller ones that could be leased out. However, some of the surviving monastic settlements profited from the wool trade and were prosperous enough to repair and extend their buildings: thus, Fountains Abbey, the most picturesque of Cistercian houses, situated near Ripon in the West Riding of Yorkshire, was able to build an imposing North Tower not very long before the Dissolution (Plate 24). More generally, the growth of nationalism and anti-Papal feeling in fifteenth-century England had led to the confiscation by the Crown of a number of smaller monasteries and the cumulative effect of these developments was such that by the time of the Dissolution probably only about 650 religious houses still remained in England and Wales.

With the Dissolution of the Monasteries, which began in earnest in 1536 and was entirely completed in 1540, monasticism in England came to a sudden end. The suppression of a number of smaller houses had already occurred, but the general dissolution began with Henry VIII's Act of 1536 which decreed that all religious houses of fewer than 12 monks or nuns and with revenues of less than £200 a year should be closed and that 'His Majesty should have and enjoy' all their possessions. At this stage, neither Henry VIII nor Thomas Cromwell, the King's Vicar-General or deputy in spiritual affairs, may have clearly intended the dissolution of all the monasteries and, indeed, as late as 1538 the majority of them, including nearly all the greater abbeys, were still in existence. Within a period of 18 months, however, from the last quarter of 1538 to the first quarter of 1540, Cromwell set about systematically obtaining the surrender of all the surviving houses with the result that, in the words of one of the King's ministers, 'The great abbeys go down as fast as they may.' We are not here concerned with the religious, political and dynastic reasons for the Dissolution, but rather with its effect on the landscape, both at the time and in the longer term.

Plate 24 Abbot Huby's
tower at Fountains
Abbey, near Ripon in
Yorkshire. About 160
feet high, it was built in
the late fifteenth and
early sixteenth centuries

By 1539, the King was making it clear that all the monastic
buildings were to be destroyed and, as a result, once a monastery
was surrendered, the lead was to be stripped off the roof and the
walls were to be razed to the ground. However, the total
demolition of churches and conventual buildings of this sort was
neither cheap nor easy and the degree of ruination varied from
house to house. Overall, it has been calculated that of all the
monasteries suppressed in England, about one-third have left no
trace at all, and that of the remainder rather less than one-third
are represented by substantial remains of buildings.[19] In any case,
destruction continued over a long period, as throughout the
second half of the sixteenth century, local builders used deserted
monasteries as easily worked quarries for stone. In some parts of
the country where there was little building stone available, as in
East Anglia, sites were more intensively plundered. In other sites
like the remote Yorkshire dales where the great Cistercian abbeys
were located, less stone was removed and more substantial ruins
remain. However, the demand for lead from roofs was great
everywhere. Fortunately, some of the monastic buildings were
preserved and put to other uses after 1540. As we have seen, some
were purchased by lay owners and converted into private
dwellings; former abbot's houses and gatehouses seemed to have
been highly regarded for conversion into desirable country
residences, as at Beaulieu and Titchfield in Hampshire, and
Woburn in Bedfordshire. At nearly a hundred places, monastic

churches continued to be used as places of worship, many of them being converted into parish churches, as in Cartmel in Lancashire, Dorchester-on-Thames in Oxfordshire and Christchurch in Hampshire. The manorial agricultural buildings of ecclesiastical estates, such as home farms and tithe barns, were also often left intact.

The variation and quality of the ruins that remain today can be illustrated from the Thames valley, in Oxfordshire, a favourite location for monastic foundations.[20] They range from the once-great Benedictine abbey at Eynsham, where only some doorways and a piece of arcade remain; through the Augustinian abbey at Dorchester, where the magnificent monastic church is still in use as the parish church; to the large abbey of Osney, originally just outside the city walls at Oxford and now in the city, where the only depressing remains are a small oblong fifteenth-century building with one window.

Castles and moated homesteads

Like the monastic settlements, castles were most numerous in the early Middle Ages, reaching their zenith about 1150. By 1200, there were probably 400 castles in existence in England and Wales, and they remained at about that figure until the beginning of the fifteenth century, when the true castle began to decline. From 1400 onwards, as we have seen, a number of 'tower houses', or fortified houses was built, frequently of brick, such as Tattershall Castle in Lincolnshire, Caister Castle in Norfolk, and the Leicestershire castles of Ashby-de-la-Zouch and Kirby Muxloe. These so-called castles were more residential extravagances than true castles and lacked the formidable defensive strength of their predecessors. Instead, the emphasis was increasingly being placed on domestic comfort; even their warlike features like crenellations and machicolations were for show rather than defence. Tattershall Castle, for example, has the appearance of a powerful keep, but its numerous windows would scarcely have allowed it to withstand a siege.

During the fifteenth century, the majority of true castles belonged to the Lancastrian kings whose resources were inadequate to maintain them all. Moreover, their military value was reduced because of changes in methods of war which was being waged increasingly by larger, more professional armies which conducted battles in the field. Finally, as the country prospered and the ruling classes became more sophisticated, so they sought higher standards of comfort and residence than a castle could provide. In one part of the country, however, namely along the Scottish border, the troubled conditions of the fifteenth century continued to favour castle-building. These were built by the greater landowners, who were few in number, while the lesser gentry built stout tower houses known as 'peles'. The latter also made fortified additions to their farms, known as 'Bastles', the same word as 'bastille'. Peles normally consisted of little more than a simple square or rectangular structure, with one room placed upon another. While the great majority of peles and bastles have disappeared altogether, or have become ruinous, a few have been tastefully converted into private houses and put to other uses. In Northumberland, for example, the vicar's pele at Elsdon, now a private house, dates from the fifteenth century, while that at Alnham, now a youth hostel, was also a vicar's pele in 1541. Notable bastles include a fifteenth-century one at Akeld and two late sixteenth- or early seventeenth-century examples at Gatehouse.[21]

Moated homesteads were another form of defensive residence commonly found in the English countryside. Far more numerous than castles, at their zenith they numbered well over 5100 and were to be found in every county in England. They were essentially manor houses, surrounded by an encircling ditch, their owners being more often than not small landowners. The moat served a variety of functions: it provided a measure of protection at times of lawlessness; it made available a copious supply of water in case of fire, an ever-present hazard at a time when buildings were mainly composed of timber and thatch; it provided a degree of protection against wild animals that might carry off young livestock; it could be stocked with fish and used to water livestock; and, last but not least, in some parts of the country like the heavy clay lowlands of the Midlands, it facilitated drainage. Moated homesteads, though numerous almost everywhere, were particularly concentrated in three areas: the tract of country between Chelmsford and Harlow in Essex and Bishop's Stortford in Hertfordshire; an area extending from Suffolk into north Essex, with a particular concentration north of Framlingham; and the Birmingham area extending south into Warwickshire and Worcestershire. By the end of the Middle Ages, however, they were becoming less common as growing prosperity enabled the local gentry to build new, larger houses away from the damp, unsanitary sites occupied by many moated homesteads. Nevertheless, a number of splendid examples remain in the English countryside, including Baddesley Clinton Hall in Warwickshire (Plate 17), Lower Brockhampton House in Herefordshire (Plate 25), and Ightham Mote in Kent.

With the advent of the Tudor dynasty to the throne of England in 1485 and the growing centralisation of power that ensued, the Crown set about acquiring as many private castles as it could lay its hands on. As a consequence, by the time that Henry VIII had reigned for a decade or two he owned far more castles than he could possibly use or maintain. Some of them degenerated into county goals, the keep being used for that purpose, and the others were demolished or allowed to decay. Leland during his tours of the country between 1534 and 1542 made frequent references to castles being 'far gone into decay' or 'once a great thing but now a pound for cattle'. On the other hand, between 1539 and 1543 Henry VIII himself built a chain of new fortresses along the south and east coasts to protect the shores from French attack by sea, using materials from recently suppressed nearby monasteries for at least five of them. They took varying forms, but typically they were low-lying semi-circular bastions with a tower at the centre. Although they were never used for their original purpose, some are still in good condition such as those at Deal in Kent, Camber in Sussex and, perhaps the most romantic looking of them all, St Mawes in Cornwall.

When Elizabeth came to the throne she continued her father's work, including the rebuilding of the fort at Tilbury; the construction of the remarkable little fort at Upnor on the Medway, built in the early 1560s to protect shipping lying at anchor; the strengthening of Carisbrooke Castle on the Isle of Wight in 1587; and some modest additions to Windsor Castle. During the latter part of the sixteenth century, a small number of castles was given by the Crown to private individuals who turned them into private residences. In 1563, for example, Elizabeth gave Kenilworth Castle to Robert Dudley, Earl of Leicester, who erected a substantial block of buildings there; and in 1600 she presented Wallingford Castle, in Berkshire, to the Earl of Northampton. The latter was razed to the ground during the Civil War and only fragments of it still remain. In addition, a few private owners of old castles modernised and extended them, including Broughton Castle in Oxfordshire, the ancestral home of Lord Saye and Sele; and Dunster Castle, in Somerset, the home of the Luttrell family.

By the turn of the century, however, the great majority of castles were being allowed to decay, though even then an interest in preservation rescued a few castles like Pontefract, in Yorkshire, which was saved 'to prevent the ruin of a monument of such antiquity and goodly building'. It was not until the outbreak of the Civil War in the 1640s that castles once more became the focus of attention. Although at first most of the important fighting took place in the open between two relatively untrained armies, groups of men on both sides locked themselves up in castles, some of which were held by Royalists and some by Parliamentarians, and held up their enemies by means of prolonged sieges. This eventually led Cromwell to adopt the policy of 'slighting' castles, that is once acquired he ordered them to be blown up so that they could not be used again. Although some wealthy owners of parliamentary castles, such as Warwick Castle and Broughton Castle, saved their residences from destruction, many castles were 'slighted' at this time. However, the stoutness of massive stone castle walls often prevented their total destruction and to this fact we owe the spectacular ruins of Corfe Castle in Dorset (Plate 25) and Tutbury Castle in Staffordshire (Figure 3), to name but two

Plate 25 The spectacular ruins of Corfe Castle, Dorset. Built of Purbeck Stone from the time of William the Conqueror to the fourteenth century, it was slighted after the Civil War, much of the stone being used to build houses in the village which can be seen in the background

examples. A few castles, despite being 'slighted' by one side or another, were restored by their owners after the Civil War, including Arundel Castle in Sussex, but the great majority simply fell into decay and ruin, partly as a result of natural erosion by the elements and partly because they provided a useful supply of local building material.

Thus, during the period covered by this book, the total number of buildings in the countryside increased considerably. The doubling of the population was mainly accommodated by the considerable growth in the size of towns, especially London, but villages also expanded. In addition, numerous splendid country houses were built and, in response to changing fashions, were placed away from the villages and located in their own parklands. On the other hand, there were also considerable losses, notably with the ruination of the great majority of monastic buildings, following the Dissolution.

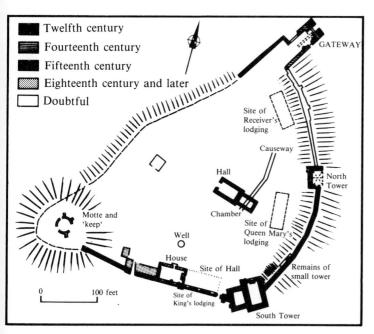

Figure 3 The remains of
Tutbury Castle,
Staffordshire. Built
originally shortly after
the Conquest, it has
been rebuilt several
times, before being
finally reduced in the
Civil War. In the
eighteenth century, a
mock ruin was erected
on the motte

Moreover, with the coming of the Tudor state and a measure of
national security, the need for fortified castles was past and, of
those that remained, many were reduced to ruins immediately
after the Civil War.

On balance, however, England in 1700 was incomparably richer
in buildings, and especially in country houses, than it had been in
1400. Hand in hand with this building went the demand for
timber and with it the gradual decline of many of England's woods
and forests. In the Middle Ages, the numerous hunting parks that
existed had also been generally well-wooded, but these too
changed their functions in our period. It is to these features of the
English landscape – the woods, forests and parks – that we shall
now turn our attention.

CHAPTER 5

Woodland:
forests, chases, parks and gardens

England in 1400 was a very well-wooded country, though even at this date there were great variations in the amount of woodland to be found from manor to manor and region to region. During the course of the next 300 years the wooded nature of the English countryside was greatly reduced, a reduction due to many causes. As we have seen, the population doubled during this period and, as a consequence, agriculture expanded, woodland was cleared away and trees were cut down to enable more land to be cultivated. The increase in population also led to an expansion in the size of towns and villages – London, for example, more than doubled its population during the seventeenth century alone, from 200,000 in 1600 to about 575,000 in 1700 – which required very large amounts of timber for building purposes. During the 'Great Rebuilding' from 1540 to 1640 and the rebuilding of London after the Great Fire of 1666, enormous amounts of timber were used, both in the buildings themselves and as charcoal to provide fuel for brick making. A rise in the standard of living, at least for the more prosperous section of the population, placed added pressure on sources of wood which was the prime material for the great majority of products used during this period. The increase in shipbuilding, especially during Henry VIII's reign, was also very consumptive of timber: many more and larger ships were built than during the previous century and each one required large quantities of oak. Following the Dissolution of the Monasteries, the new owners of the former monastic lands often sold off the woodland and timber on their estates to help pay for the houses they were so busy erecting. During the sixteenth century, changes occurred in the way in which timber was prepared: it became the practice to cut logs lengthwise into several timbers, which required large trees and made it more difficult to use trees that were not straight. The use of wood for industrial fuel, particularly for making iron and glass, increased in such areas as the Weald and the Forest of Dean though, as we shall see, such demands did not necessarily result in the long-term denudation of woodland. Finally, the rise of hop-growing in the seventeenth century led to a demand for large wooden poles.

In the early fifteenth century, however, these pressures on woodlands were still a relatively long way off. England still possessed much timber, both in the form of woodland and in a wealth of hedgerow trees. Virtually every manor possessed woods in common use by manorial tenants for collecting deadwood and grazing animals; and 'outwoods', woodland usually reserved for the landlord's use, were also quite common. In addition, substantial areas of land, much of it wooded, were devoted principally to hunting. These were the royal forests, the chases which were in fact private 'forests', and parks, securely enclosed areas belonging to the lord of the manor. Within these hunting grounds, as in the private woodlands, the timber was an important part of the agricultural economy. The natural English woodland consisted principally of oak, birch and alder. Oak, which was to be found virtually throughout the country, was the most common and most valuable timber tree and its bark was also stripped for tanning, as was that of birch and alder. Other fairly common species included the ash, field maple and lime. Less common was the beech which was native only to the southern half of England, being found in such areas as on the flinty clay loams of the Kent downlands, in parts of High Suffolk and in the Chilterns. Elm and sweet chestnut were also to be found in places, but coniferous trees which had existed in England in Roman times had virtually disappeared and were not widely reintroduced until the eighteenth century.

As wood was a valuable and much-prized commodity, woodland was for the most part carefully and intensively managed. Typically, a cropping rotation was used to ensure that felled timber was replaced. This commonly took the form of 'coppice with standards', that is standard trees and underwood. The former, consisting principally of oak, ash, hazel, lime, and crab apple, yielded timber at regular, if quite lengthy, intervals which was used principally for the construction of buildings and agricultural implements. The underwood consisted of whole or split sallow, or hazel rods or laths left from oak timber, which were tied together with young sallow shoots or string, and used for wattle and daub for making hurdles and fences. This form of woodland management created a very different appearance from that of today. This was true, for example, of the Chiltern beechwoods during the period. Although they were similar in extent and occupied similar geographical locations to those of today, they were maintained as coppice woodland and, therefore, not allowed to attain their full height, as is the case today. The wood they supplied was an important source of fuel both for London and the Vale of Aylesbury and was also used by small local industries such as brickmaking, charcoal burning and glassmaking, and by local carpenters making carriages, carts and furniture. Although the chalk soils of the Chilterns were almost as favourable to oak as to beech, the latter predominated here because it was preferred for coppicing and, as a consequence, was extensively planted, especially on the open land of the former grazing commons.[1]

The careful management of woodlands and the consequent sale of timber brought in substantial sums of money to their owners. In the early sixteenth century, for example, the farms and manors of the estates of the Dukes of Buckingham in the Midlands, Home Counties and the South West, brought in more than £413 between 1513 and 1515 alone, while in 1521, reserves on the English estates as a whole were worth at least £5,200, an enormous sum of money by contemporary standards.[2] To an economically inclined landlord, the possession of woodland was a form of credit which he could realise quickly when he needed to raise money in a hurry, while at other, less demanding, times, he could lease it out to contractors or use it for building. Not all woodlands were properly and efficiently managed, however, and by the end of the fifteenth century the government were increasingly concerned that woodlands were being decimated by felling and that, in the absence of replanting, the supply of timber would rapidly decline. From 1483 onwards, therefore, it made successive legislative attempts to control the management of woodland. The most important of these was the Statute of Woods of 1543, the 'Acte for the preservacion of woods' which, among other things, required woods to contain a minimum of twelve standard trees per acre, forbade the felling of trees that were not of a respectable size, and ordered the replantation of trees 'to cure the spoils and devestations that have been made in the woods'. Unlike much other legislation of the time, this Act seems to have been reasonably effective, largely because it made obligatory a practice that was already beginning to take root.

During the sixteenth century England still gave the visitor an abiding impression of its well-wooded character. One foreign traveller visiting England in 1558 described it thus:

> The country is well wooded and shady, for the fields are all enclosed
> with hedges and oak trees, and several others sorts of trees, to such an
> extent that in travelling you think you are in a continuous wood.[3]

The woodlands and forests were still extensive, even within relatively close proximity to London, and as late as 1594 John Norden described Hertfordshire as 'most inclined to woods and coppices' and areas in Essex as 'for the most part woods and woody grounds and forests, as the most part of Essex in time past hath been.'

In the course of the seventeenth century, the amount of woodland declined further, principally as trees were cleared in order to bring land under the plough to feed the growing population. In addition, there was a greater demand for wood for ordinary domestic purposes, for use in house-building, for building ships and to provide fuel for industrial purposes. As a result, the price of wood rose steeply, especially in the early decades of the seventeenth century, and increasing numbers of landlords took to selling timber on their land, both in the form of standing trees and also fallen wood. Unfortunately, relatively few of them adopted a policy of re-afforestation and England's woodland cover inexorably declined. The Crown, in particular, was desperately short of money, especially during the years from 1625 to 1640, and sold off considerable amounts of Crown woodland.

On the other hand, the shortage of wood fuel forced the iron industry to rely more and more on wood from coppices which by the middle of the century were increasingly being planted for this purpose. Around 1660, for example, the extension of coppice woods in the Weald of Kent, Surrey and Sussex was estimated at more than 200,000 acres and, at about the same time, the Forest of Dean and the Forest of Wyre, in Shropshire, were described by Yarranton as containing 'many thousands of acres of copses' newly planted.[4] Over the country as a whole, however, the depletion of the woodland cover continued and, by the end of the century, the shortage of English timber came to be accepted, at least by some economists who comforted themselves with the thought that wood could be easily imported from the Continent. The areas most affected by clearance were those most accessible to navigable waterways. Because of the difficulty and expense of transport, the remoter parts of the royal forests still frequently remained well-wooded. From a regional standpoint, major arable areas such as East Anglia were already largely cleared of trees, even by 1600, while in the course of the seventeenth century, some counties such as Warwickshire and Staffordshire lost much woodland to feed the ironworks of a burgeoning industry. Elsewhere, away from industrial areas and where soils were infertile and of no great agricultural value, particularly in parts of south and central England, large extents of woodland were preserved. Indeed, over the country as a whole, even by 1700, many woods and coppices remained, managed by landlords in the same way as they had been for centuries, and hedgerow timber was plentiful and varied.

Throughout the whole period from 1400 to 1700, much of this timber was located in royal forests, in chases and in parks and we shall now turn our attention to these specific features of the landscape.

Forests and chases

As we have seen, the royal forests and private chases were among the principal areas of woodland in the country. The forests which belonged to the Crown were not technically, or necessarily, wooded but were areas outside the common law of the land and under special laws and regulations, known as the 'forest law', designed to protect the King's hunting. The principal beast of the chase was the fallow deer which ideally required woodland, or 'covert', in which to flourish. The precise extent to which the royal forests were covered with woodland is unknown: some in the upland areas of the country, like Exmoor, Dartmoor, and the High Peak, were almost entirely upland and moorland, while lowland forests like the New Forest and the Forest of Dean were thickly wooded.

The concept of the royal forest was introduced into England by the Norman kings whose love of hunting led them to place large areas of the country under the forest law. These reached their greatest extent in the twelfth century when they were at least 70 in number and covered more than one-fifth of the country. For the most part, they were concentrated in the south-central counties, the east and west Midlands, the Peak District, and parts of Lancashire, Yorkshire, Cumberland and Northumberland. Apart from providing the King with hunting, the forests were also put to other uses. Their prime function was probably as a source of timber used for repairing royal castles and houses, fitting ships for the navy and making weapons for the king's armies as well as supplying wood for charcoal-making and as a source of fuel for heating. In addition, oak and beech mast provided pannage for pigs and, in places, herbage was available for domestic animals. The deer provided large quantities of venison and some forests contained vaccaries, or cattle farms, and horses were raised. Finally, royal forges for the working of iron ore, in the Forest of Dean, for example, and lead-smelting in the Forest of High Peak in Derbyshire were typical of the industrial activities of some of the forests.

By 1400, however, many of the royal forests had disappeared and others had diminished in extent. Moreover, during the greater part of the fifteenth century the policy of the Lancastrian kings and the anarchic conditions which existed over much of the country resulted in an increasingly ineffective application of the forest law so that many areas became 'forests' in name only. This in turn led local landowners and peasants to nibble away at the edges of the forest woodlands, to cut down and clear timber and to poach the royal deer and other game. In the Forest of Dean, for example, trees remained dense only in the more inaccessible places; elsewhere poorly stocked woods were common, with the trees being increasingly thinned out by the action of man and beast. Game became scarce and only remnants of the herds of previous centuries remained.[5] In some forests, such as Needwood in Staffordshire, the woodlands were over-exploited and by 1500 timber sales were greatly reduced as large areas of woodland were sold to charcoal-burners. In Ashdown Forest, in Sussex, by 1520, tenants complained that 'much of the King's woods were cut down and coled for the iron mills and the Forest digged for Irne by which man and beast be in jeopardy.'[6] The decline continued through the sixteenth century, even though the value of timber was increasing due to the growing national need for fuel, arms, vehicles, bridges and ships.

The combination of declining woodland and increasing demand for timber led the Crown to attempt some form of conservation policy and the first major, if ineffective, attempt was made by Henry VII with the Act of 1483. As we have seen, sixty years later, the passing of the Statute of Woods of 1543 had rather more effect partly because interest in woodland conservation was growing. This interest is shown by John Fitzherbert's *Book of Husbandry* in 1523 which had much advice to give on the subject of arboriculture, and by Raphael Holinshed's *Chronicle of England, Scotland and Irelande*, published in 1577, in which he drew attention to 'the great sales yearly made of wood, whereby an infinite quantity had been destroyed within these few years.' Much anxiety was expressed about the scarcity of wood and growing cost of fuel and timber. However, much of this shortage was probably due more to a decline in readily accessible timber than to a widespread denudation of woodland. In many of the royal forests, many timber-trees remained but the costs and difficulties of transport mitigated against their exploitation. In 1559, Elizabeth made another attempt to conserve the shrinking woodland by means of an Act which prohibited the felling of timber-trees of oak, beech, and ash to make charcoal for the iron industry, if the trees were within fourteen miles of the sea or a navigable river. Because of the difficulty of transporting trees which were any great distance from navigable waters, it was thought necessary to restrict the felling of trees only to the more accessible supplies. Two similar Acts, in 1581 and 1585, also attempted to restrict the felling of certain trees by the iron industry, but applied only to south-east England and to the neighbourhood of navigable waters. Like previous legislation, they were of doubtful efficacy. In the earlier part of her reign, Elizabeth adopted a policy of attempting to obtain more revenue from her forests and appointed surveyor-generals of her woods, charged with conserving them. Among the most important of these was Roger Taverner who, in 1565, drew up a *Book of Survey* of all the Crown forests and woods south of the river Trent, in which he gave acreages, numbers of timber-trees and details of underwood: at that time, twenty English counties contained a total of 53,000 acres of Crown woods, of which almost one-fifth, or 9980 acres, were in the Forest of Dean. The position in the northern half of England seems to have been considerably worse and a report of 1564 describes the northern forests in the following terms,

> . . . we now be informed that as well the woods and deer of all our forests and chases and also of all our parks by the north Trent be much spoilt, wasted and destroyed both by the inordinate taking, felling and browsing of the woods and also by the killing of the game and deer without restraint or correction.[7]

However, it seems quite likely that the extent of woodland depletion was exaggerated. It is doubtful, for example, if the felling of trees for fuel, particularly for the iron and glass industries, was as destructive as contemporary witnesses thought. As Rackham points out,[8] industrialists had an interest in conserving fuel supplies and by the latter part of the sixteenth century many landowners were replanting their woods. Indeed, industry may well have been more protective of woodland than the farmers who cleared the trees for cultivation. Nor was shipbuilding quite the villain of the piece it has sometimes been made out to be. Most of the naval timber in the sixteenth century came from woodlands within easy reach of the dockyards which were generally located in south-east England. Consequently, it was Surrey, Sussex, Kent and the Upper Thames Valley which supplied the wood for building ships. In any case, shortages of oak, which was the wood most favoured by naval shipwrights, were due to lack of funds, organisation and transport rather than to shortage of trees. Certainly, by modern standards even by the end of the sixteenth century, much woodland remained and a traveller journeying, say, from Southampton to the East Midlands would have ridden most of the way through woodland: he would have traversed the Forests of Bere and Alice Holt in Hampshire, Windsor Forest in Berkshire, Bernwood and Shotover Forests in Buckinghamshire, and Whittlewood, Salcey and Rockingham Forests in Northamptonshire. Moreover, in former forest areas such as Purbeck in Dorset (Plate 26), there were still extents of woodland and deer were plentiful.

On the accession of James I, sales began to be made of Crown woodlands and, as with his predecessor, he ordered that surveys should be made of royal forests, parks and chases. A survey of 1608, which for some inexplicable reason left out the Forests of Dean in Gloucestershire and Wychwood in Oxfordshire, lists both the number of sound timber trees and decaying trees.[9] In all, it records that royal forests, parks and chases contained over 580,000 timber trees and some 490,000 decaying ones. The forests listed include Windsor Forest in Berkshire; Bernwood in Buckinghamshire; High Peak in Derbyshire; Gillingham in Dorset; Leicester Forest; Sherwood Forest in Nottinghamshire; various forests in Northamptonshire, Shropshire, Surrey and Hampshire; Leighfield Forest in Rutland; Wyre Forest in Worcestershire; Pensham and Braden Forests in Wiltshire; and Galtres, Knaresborough, Pickering and Hatfield Forests in Yorkshire (Figure 4). Even though the survey may not have been complete, it reveals that only a small proportion of the once-great medieval forests remained. Moreover, the policy of James I, which was also followed by Charles I, was soon further to reduce the Crown woodlands by grants of disafforestation, for a consideration. In the 1630s, for example, the Forest of Bernwood in north Buckinghamshire was disafforested. The bounds of this forest had

The Boundes of the said Ilande goeth and doth extende from a waye lyenge betwixt Flowerthery and a wood called whitwaye, and from thence to Ludgeford and from thence to Warham bridge and so still from thence by the sea syde towrd the castle to a place called Studland Castle And from thence commonially by the sea coastes vnto Sainct Aldeomes chaple And so still by the sea coastes west ward vntyll you come againe to the said place of Flowry burye aforsaid.

SEPTENTRIO.

OCCIDENS

ORIENS

THE ISLE OF PVRBECK

MERIDIES

been fixed in the thirteenth century and had then remained unchanged until disafforestation. Although well-wooded, like all the royal forests, it had long contained a number of villages, each with its cultivated fields, and in the sixteenth century had been the subject of much enclosure and clearing. Once disafforestation was finally agreed, by 1635, the surviving woods were quite rapidly felled, the tree roots grubbed up and the land divided up into closes by means of hedges and ditches and then put down to pasture or cultivated for crops. By the end of the century, the old landscape had virtually gone and new isolated farmsteads had begun to appear.

Charles I, in his desperate search for money, continued James' policy of selling Crown woodlands, sometimes to court favourites, so that in the fifteen years from 1625 to 1640, the decline of the forests continued. He approved, for payment, the disafforestation of the small remaining forest left in Surrey, agreed that the High Peak be disafforested and the surviving deer be destroyed, and in 1628 sold Leicester Forest for the comparatively small sum of £7000. He also sold large numbers of oak trees from the remaining Crown woodlands. Moreover, Charles went further by

Plate 26 The Isle of Purbeck, Dorset about 1585–6, a map drawn by Ralph Treswell

103

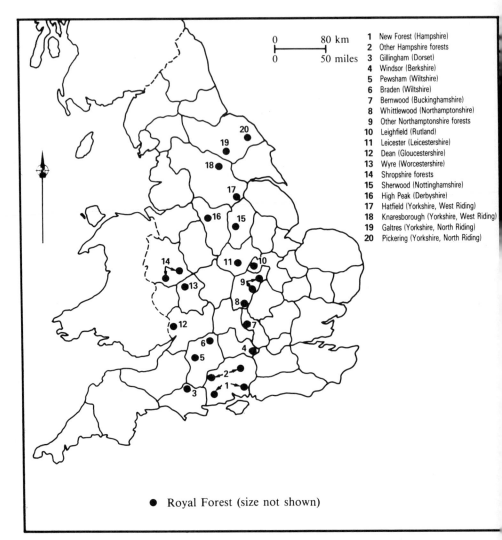

1	New Forest (Hampshire)
2	Other Hampshire forests
3	Gillingham (Dorset)
4	Windsor (Berkshire)
5	Pewsham (Wiltshire)
6	Braden (Wiltshire)
7	Bernwood (Buckinghamshire)
8	Whittlewood (Northamptonshire)
9	Other Northamptonshire forests
10	Leighfield (Rutland)
11	Leicester (Leicestershire)
12	Dean (Gloucestershire)
13	Wyre (Worcestershire)
14	Shropshire forests
15	Sherwood (Nottinghamshire)
16	High Peak (Derbyshire)
17	Hatfield (Yorkshire, West Riding)
18	Knaresborough (Yorkshire, West Riding)
19	Galtres (Yorkshire, North Riding)
20	Pickering (Yorkshire, North Riding)

● Royal Forest (size not shown)

Figure 4 The Royal
Forests of England, 1608

trying to resuscitate the forest laws which had fallen into disuse, ir
order to make his subjects pay money to contract out of them
This move aroused great opposition and his arbitrary behaviour
was largely responsible for the 1640 Act for the Limitation of the
Forests which virtually did away with the application of the fores
laws and accelerated the demise of the royal forests.

During the Civil War, the care of the royal woodlands inevitably
took a back seat but once the fighting was over Parliament turned
its attention to them. In 1651, it vested all the royal forests in
trustees, intending eventually to sell them. A few years later, a
survey was made of the royal woodlands, a relatively low value was

attached to them, and their disafforestation and sale were authorised. However, the process was a very slow one and, in any case, Cromwell himself had other ideas and was more concerned with improving the forests and using them for the benefit of the Commonwealth. As a result, some forests disappeared during the Commonwealth while others survived, to be saved by the Restoration. In those that remained, however, much destruction of timber had occurred: in the Forest of Dean, for example, more than 40,000 trees had been cut down during the Commonwealth by order of the House of Commons so that by 1660 fewer than 30,000 were still standing.

With the accession of Charles II to the throne, attempts were made once more to arrest the decline of England's woodland, particularly as there was a scarcity of oak-timber for the navy, for which the King had a particular regard. The newly founded Royal Society was asked to suggest a remedy and as a result John Evelyn, the Society's reporter, prepared his famous treatise, *Sylva; or, A discourse of Forest Trees and the Propagation of Timber in His Majestie's Dominions*, published in 1664. It recorded the destruction of timber that had taken place in the past twenty years or so and urged replanting and conservation. However, this sound advice was scarcely heeded and, by the end of the seventeenth century the destruction of England's forests was virtually complete, even though in some cases legal disafforestation was much longer in coming. Even those few that remained were much depleted and, according to two contemporary sources, the number of sound timber trees in the New Forest, for example, fell from about 124,000 in 1608 to under 12,500 by the end of the century. Something was saved from the wreckage, however, and during the latter part of the century, deliberate tree-planting did take place both in the New Forest and in the Forest of Dean.

Moreover, much royal time was devoted to beautifying Windsor Forest in Berkshire, in the Crown lands surrounding Windsor Castle. In the early seventeenth century, the Forest consisted of sixteen walks, surrounded by woodland, and numerous empark-ments, which are commemorated today in Windsor Great Park and Home Park. In the 1680s, Charles II added to its scenic features by planting the Long Walk, a three-mile-long double avenue of elms, most of which lasted for 250 years. It is still a notable avenue today, although since the end of the last war it has been replanted alternately with plane and horse chestnut trees. Today, Windsor Great Park extends over 4,800 acres and contains some of the oldest relics which still exist of broadleaved woodland in Europe, with an accompanying variety of indigenous life and flora.

Of the once-great medieval forests of England, only a few now remain and, of these, perhaps only the New Forest, the Forest of Dean and Epping Forest give some idea of how they must have looked in their heyday. Of the great majority which have vanished, varying traces are to be found on the contemporary landscape. For example, of those which proliferated in central England, Wychwood, in Oxfordshire, is represented mainly by some 1400 acres of woodland incorporated into the Cornbury Park estate and by a wealth of forest place-names; Whittlewood forest, near Towcester in Northamptonshire, has dwindled to a number of woods and a large park dotted with oaks and surrounded by copses; Rockingham Forest, also in Northamptonshire, still contains large woods, mainly in private hands, one of the largest belonging to the present owners of Rockingham Castle; Braden Forest in Wiltshire is similarly recalled by scattered copses and place names; while another Wiltshire forest, Savernake near Marlborough, has substantial remains, including 5000 acres of woodland and famous beech avenues and woodland glades.

The history of the English chases has been very similar to that of the forests, namely one of reduction and eventual disappearance. In strictly legal terms, the chase differed from the forest in that it belonged to a private individual instead of the Crown and was an area of land, often quite extensive, over which local magnates, usually nobles or great ecclesiastics, were given rights of hunting by the king. Although the chase was normally subject to common law rather than forest law, for the peasants who lived in it the restrictions imposed upon them by the great lord's officials were little different from those which obtained in the royal forests. In any case, both during the Middle Ages and when they were at their height, and indeed since, the terms 'chase' and 'forest' have been sometimes used interchangeably. Indeed, some areas such as Cranborne Chase have been at various times in private hands and therefore chases, and subsequently in the hands of the Crown and technically forests.[10]

At various times during the Middle Ages, there were at least twenty-six chases in existence although by 1400 relatively few still remained. The greatest owners of chases were probably the Earls, later Dukes, of Lancaster, who during the fourteenth century controlled the chases of Bowland and Blackburn in Lancashire, Duffield Frith in Derbyshire, Needwood in Staffordshire, and Leicester in the western part of Leicestershire. However, when the Lancastrian dynasty began with the accession of Henry IV to the throne in 1399, the Duchy of Lancaster became Crown land and the Lancastrian chases became royal forests. Of those chases which still remained in private hands subsequent to 1400, the history of Cannock Chase is fairly typical. It came into being in 1290 when the Bishop of Coventry and Lichfield was given permission to turn his manors of Cannock and Rugeley into a private forest. At this time, it enclosed an area of about forty square miles and, although chases were not normally enclosed by earthworks, part of the western edge of Cannock Chase was delimited by a boundary bank, which can still be seen today at Huntington a few miles north of Cannock. It was probably erected because no other topographical feature was available to mark the bounds of the chase. Cannock Chase remained in the Bishop's hands throughout the Middle Ages until the Dissolution of the Monasteries. Leland, passing this way in the 1540s, described the Chase as being formerly very barren but 'now waxithe metely good' and its woodland 'be in many places so cut downe that no token is that ever any were there'. In 1546, the Chase was sold to Sir William Paget, who was created Lord Paget in 1549. It remained in Paget hands only a relatively short time and reverted to the Crown in 1583 when a later Lord Paget fled the country. The wood and timber on the Chase was valued at £20,000 in 1588 and in the following year it was leased out, thereby marking its virtual disafforestation.[11] More than three hundred years later, after 1920, a large part of the former chase was leased by the Marquess of Anglesey and other local landowners to the Forestry Commission who created the new State Forest of Cannock Chase. As a result, it is today once more heavily timbered, although for the most part the place of the medieval oak has been taken by the coniferous tree.

Parks and gardens

The English landscape is particularly fortunate in its rich inheritance of parks and gardens, having perhaps a greater wealth and variety of them than any other country of its size. However, during their long history, the character and appearance of English parks have undergone many transformations, not least during the period under review.

In the Middle Ages, their function, and therefore their appearance, was quite different from that of their modern successors. The medieval park was essentially a hunting ground and, in order to retain the deer which was the principal beast of the chase, it was securely enclosed, commonly by means of a combination of a substantial earth bank, topped by a fence of cleft oak stakes, with an inside ditch which together constituted a formidable barrier to the deer inside the park. In some areas, where freestone was easily available, the wooden fence might be replaced by a stone wall, and occasionally a quickset hedge would serve in place of a fence. The medieval hunting park was normally fairly small, being usually between 100 and 200 acres in size, though some parks, especially royal ones, were very much larger: Woodstock in Oxfordshire, and Clarendon in Wiltshire, for example, were both seven miles in circuit. The park, which was usually elliptical in shape for ease of construction, was owned by the lord of the manor and was part of his demesne lands. Typically, it lay on the edge of the manor away from the cultivated fields and consisted of 'unimproved' land, including woodland. Woodland was an essential part of the park for as John Manwood,

107

the Elizabethan authority on hunting and the forest wrote, 'it must be stored with great woods or coverts for the secret abode of wild beasts and also with fruitful pastures for their communal feed.'[12] Thus, it was quite different in appearance from the later 'amenity' parks which developed in substantial numbers from the sixteenth century onwards. Moreover, it contained no manor house which, at this time, was normally situated in the village itself.

In the course of the Middle Ages there were at least 1900 deer-parks in existence in England, scattered throughout the country but with particular concentrations in wooded counties such as Essex and Staffordshire.[13] As carefully managed as other parts of the lord's demesne lands, the medieval park in addition to providing hunting for the lord also furnished venison for his table, particularly welcome in winter when other meat had to be salted down. As in the royal forests, it was a valuable source of timber, and also provided pannage for pigs and, in some cases, pasture for cattle. Fish-ponds were also frequently to be found in parks and were, indeed, a not uncommon feature of the medieval landscape, both within and without parks. They were usually constructed by means of an earth bank across the line of a stream and although the great majority of medieval fishponds have since lost their water, traces of banks and dams can often still be found in the modern landscape.

Being both more numerous and more extensive than fishponds, the medieval parks have left substantially more traces of their existence. In many places today, evidence can still be found in the form of the earth bank which constituted the perimeter of the park (Plate 27), field-names and farm-names, and curving hedge lines which mark the line of the former park boundary (Figure 5). Regrettably, as with other intimate features of the English landscape, modern farming methods, road construction, and urban sprawl have removed many of the traces of banks.

As with other major features of the medieval landscape, the plagues of the middle of the fourteenth century marked a watershed in the fortunes of the park. Although many were still nominally in existence in 1400, by this time they were already in decline. The labour was no longer available to maintain them properly, the herds dwindled, many were leased out for pasture and other agricultural uses, and others simply fell out of use altogether. On the other hand, in the course of the fifteenth century, a number of parks were being created in various parts of the country and others were being considerably extended. However, they differed from their predecessors in being generally substantially larger and consisting often of tracts of arable land, common pasture or woodland which could no longer be properly farmed because of shortage of labour. Typical of these were Eastnor, in Herefordshire, created in 1460, and the three Kentish parks of Eythorne, Kingsworth and Tonge also created in 1460, each of which was over 1000 acres. Exceptionally, they could be

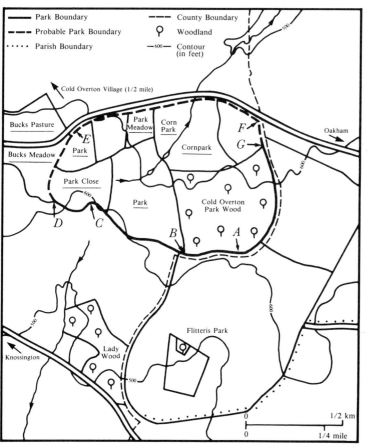

Plate 27 Cold Overton Park, Leicestershire. This aerial photograph shows the imprint of a medieval park on the contemporary landscape, which can be compared with Figure 5. The elliptical outline of the park boundary shows up clearly as does Cold Overton Park Wood in the south-east corner of the park.

Figure 5 Cold Overton Park, Leicestershire. The field names which are underlined are derived from the Victorian tithe map. Just across the former Leicestershire-Rutland boundary is 'Flitter's Park', the farm named after the former royal park in the Manor of Oakham

109

even larger as in the case of Ashby de la Zouch in Leicestershire in 1474 and Eagle in Lincolnshire in 1446, the former consisting of 3000 acres and the latter of 4600 acres. However, these parks no longer functioned as hunting parks and so were not enclosed by high earth banks, but probably by hedges or merely paling fences. Moreover, being much larger than the hunting parks, they were more constrained by existing field and property boundaries and as a result they tended to be more irregular and rectilinear in outline than the earlier parks cut out of the waste. Once circumscribed in this way, they provided a source of timber to be exploited by the lord and also pasture for his cattle and pannage for his pigs.

In addition, the later part of the fifteenth century witnessed the creation of the first amenity parks which were intended to provide an appropriate backcloth to the new and grandiose manor houses that were beginning to go up in various parts of the country. Examples include Kirby Muxloe in Leicestershire where Lord Hastings built his unfinished fortified house in the 1480s; Chamberhouse in Hatcham in Berkshire, where John Pury enclosed 344 acres to form a park in 1446 and at the same time extended his manor house, now long since gone; and Great Hampden in Buckinghamshire where John Hampden enclosed 500 acres of land and 100 acres of wood to form a park which remained in the hands of the Hampden family until modern times.

Some of these fifteenth-century emparkments, as was the case in the following centuries, were encompassed at the expense of the local peasantry. For example, at Wilstrop in Yorkshire, near the junction of the rivers Nidd and Ouse a few miles northwest of York, in about 1490 the Wilstrop family enclosed the common fields of the village and evicted the villagers in order to build their park.[14] Despite repeated attacks on the park pale by villagers and local gentry who in 1497 and 1498 'riotously pulled and beat down rails and pales', the village and its cornfields went for ever and the park remained.

In the course of the next century, the general pattern of the decline of the hunting park and the creation of the amenity park continued. Particularly from about 1540 onwards, the number of gentry families increased considerably and with them the desire to build more comfortable and gracious homes surrounded by parkland. The majority of lords of the manor wanted to have a park, partly to proclaim their status and partly to ensure a supply of fresh meat and fish. As a result, by the end of the sixteenth century, probably every manor house with any pretension was in a park dotted with clumps of trees, at various stages of growth, the whole being enclosed by a high wooden pale. By far the larger part of the typical sixteenth-century park was still used as a deer-park, though for the most part the deer were not hunted but kept for food and ornamental purposes. The landscape of the park had not greatly changed, therefore, from that of its predecessors, and the only 'artificial' section was the formal garden by the house.

The inspiration for the garden came principally from the example set by Henry VIII at Hampton Court. He developed the site of more than 2000 acres which had been walled in by Cardinal Wolsey with dark crimson bricks with chequered lines and crosses of glazed black bricks, many of which are still to be seen today. Within the walls were two deer-parks where Henry was able to indulge his passion for outdoor sports, and especially his favourite sport of stag-hunting. There was also a great complex of gardens, developed principally between 1535 and 1538, including herb and vegetable gardens and a 'knot' garden consisting of small, clipped box hedges and topiary laid out in geometric shapes, with flower beds of roses, lilies, sunflowers, violets, poppies, daffodils and hyacinths. Within these gardens were arbours with shaded seats and dovecotes. The fashion for these formal pleasure gardens, which owed their origins to Renaissance Italy and France, spread to country houses throughout Tudor and Stuart England, where they became an essential attribute. Their basic features consisted of a series of square enclosed knots, elaborate patterns made up of plants or of coloured earths, the whole encompassed by interconnecting galleries.[15] In addition, they made much use of running water in the form of fountains, moats, which served as fences, springs and fishponds. The mount, an artificial hillock usually pyramidal in shape, was another important feature of most Tudor gardens; with a building on the top, it provided a view of the garden, the park, and the surrounding countryside. Henry VIII followed his work at Hampton Court by creating similar gardens at Whitehall, which were completed by 1545, and at his palace at Nonsuch, between 1538 and 1547. The influence of Hampton Court, in particular, was evident also in the number of great houses which during the sixteenth century assumed the name of 'Court': in south-east Oxfordshire alone, for example, they included Blount's Court, Greys Court, Phillis Court and Wyfold Court.

The formal gardens occupied the foreground of the new parks and were placed immediately below the windows of the great houses so that the pattern could be looked down upon. However, they were not just restricted to the great houses and a steady stream of gardening literature appeared from the 1550s onwards, which testified to the fact that the pleasure garden with its decorative knot was becoming common even in quite small manor houses. For example, the earliest comprehensive gardening book in English, *The Gardeners' Labyrinth* by Thomas Hill, published in 1571, contains much advice on the construction of knot gardens. Unfortunately, none of the original sixteenth- and seventeenth-century knot gardens still survive intact today, partly because they demanded a great deal of labour and partly because by the time of the reign of Charles II the parterre had become more fashionable. However, in recent years, a number of them have been created anew, including that at Little Moreton Hall in Cheshire, where the National Trust laid out a knot garden with yew tunnel in 1975 (Plate 28). Based on a design in *The English Gardener*, published by Leonard Meager in 1688 which was itself probably Elizabethan in origin, it takes the form of an 'open knot', that is with gravel used in the spaces between the bands of dwarf box which form the pattern. Other recently created knot gardens include those at Barnsley House, near Cirencester in Gloucestershire, made by Rosemary Verey in 1975, and at Ham House, near Petersham in Surrey, which is based on a map of the original garden dating from 1670.

Although the typical medieval hunting park declined during the sixteenth century with deer being frequently replaced by cattle, the Crown at least could afford to maintain some and, indeed, create a few new ones. Henry VIII, for example, adopted a policy both of disparking and renting out his more distant parks, as opportunity offered, and also of creating new ones close to his principal palace of Westminster, in London. In Cornwall, for example, he disparked some parks of the Duchy of Cornwall, though, if Carew is to be believed, to no great profit,

> Cornwall was stored not long since with many parks of fallow deer, but King Henry the Eighth, being persuaded (as it is said) by Sir Richard Pollard that those belonging to the Duke could stead him with little pleasure in so remote a part, and would yield him good profit if they were leased out at an improved rent, did condescend to their disparking. So four of them took a fall together, viz. Cary Bullock, Liskeard, Restormel and Lanteglos. Howbeit, this good husbandry came short of the deviser's promise and the King's expectation . . . [16]

However, other landowners, partly for profit and partly in emulation of the King, followed Henry's example and in Carew's words,

Plate 28 The knot garden at Little Moreton Hall, Cheshire. In the background can be seen the yew tunnel with the mount beyond it

... most of the Cornish gentlemen, preferring gain to delight, or making gain their delight, shortly after followed the like practice, and made their deer leap over the pale to give the bullocks place ...

Henry VIII adopted a similar policy of renting out his parks on Cranborne Chase, where he disparked Alderholt in Dorset, Breamore and Burgate in Hampshire, and Faulston in Wiltshire. Alderholt Park was described as comprising 154 acres 'within the ditch and containing a herd of deer which were destroyed at the time of disparking'.[17] Another great Dorset royal hunting park of more than 1000 acres, also on Cranborne Chase a few miles north of Cranborne, was Blagdon which had been in existence since 1321 and was disparked by Elizabeth in about 1570. In his survey of 1605, John Norden describes the park as being formerly full of large timber trees and wood for burning but now bare of both, and containing only some scanty coppices and thinly growing under-wood. Once full of fallow deer, it had been turned into six holdings of arable and pasture land and contained a long-established rabbit warren in its south-west corner.

Earlier, Henry VIII had enclosed as hunting parks both Hyde Park and St James's Park, then on the edge of London, in 1536 and 1532 respectively. Hyde Park comprised about 600 acres and was often used by Henry and later Tudor monarchs to provide sport for important foreign guests. St James's Park, extending over 93 acres, was also liberally stocked with deer and provided hunting for the king and his courtiers.

By the second half of the sixteenth century, both in the new parks that were being created and in the longer established ones, the vogue for stocking them with deer was passing and more and more were put to more profitable use for cattle grazing, though frequently herds of deer were kept for their meat or as an amenity, rather than for hunting. Some idea of the very large number of parks in existence at this time is given by Saxton's county maps of the 1570s and 1580s, which record no fewer than 817 parks in England and Wales, not including the county of Norfolk and parts of Wales which were not mapped.[18] Saxton adopted the conventional symbol for a park, one copied by many later cartographers, of a small circle ringed by palings (Plate 10). This symbol was clearly based on the appearance of the medieval hunting park, even though its function had very largely changed by Saxton's time. Saxton, like John Norden, who adopted the same symbol to represent parks in his few county maps, was probably selective in his indication of parks and probably rather more than 817 were in existence at the end of the seventeenth century. Certainly, their creation had transformed large sections of the rural landscape. In 1577, William Harrison in describing the English countryside was affirming that, 'The twentieth part of the realm is employed upon Deere and Conies already... the owners still desirous to enlarge those groundes do not let daily to take in more.'

During the seventeenth century, the decline in the number of traditional hunting parks continued while, at the same time, new amenity parks were being created all over the country. In many instances, the two processes were telescoped into one as hunting parks which had fallen into disuse were enlarged and converted into amenity parks. As in previous centuries, these emparkments were sometimes accomplished at the expense of peasants and other people living in the neighbourhood. In 1618, for example Lord Audley purchased the manor of Stalbridge, about 6 miles east of Sherborne in Dorset, and built himself a house, which was eventually demolished in 1822, and surrounded it with parkland which at that time consisted of 'a great pasture and waste and wooddy ground', traditionally used as grazing land by tenants of the manor. The farmers objected so strongly to the emparkment that they brought a case against him in the Court of Chancery but to no avail and Lord Audley's success in appropriating the land is symbolised by the great wall, more than five miles in length and more than six feet high, with which he surrounded his park and much of which survives today. A few miles away, just to the south-east of the town of Sherborne, lay Sherborne Park. It was originally a manor of the Bishop of Salisbury, who in the twelfth century built himself a fortified palace here and created a hunting park nearby. By the end of the sixteenth century it had come into the hands of the Crown. Queen Elizabeth leased it to Sir Walter Raleigh in 1592 and allowed him to buy it outright in 1599. Raleigh proceeded to build himself a new house a short distance from the ruins of the Bishop's castle and carved out a large new park round it which included the area formerly covered by the small medieval park. The park which we see today is, however largely the creation of Capability Brown who landscaped it in the prevailing fashion in 1756 and again between 1776 and 1779.

During the early seventeenth century, it became fashionable to create terraced gardens within the park, close to the house, and indeed the terrace remained the most important ornamental feature throughout the century. Typically, the house was built on a high plane and below its front a series of terraces fell away with parterres and knots on the upper terraces and vegetables and fruit below. Steps descended from the house to the gate which was often quite elaborate, with stone posts, an archway and armorial bearings. At the side of the terraces there might be a bowling green. A spectacular terraced garden of this kind was built by Robert Cecil, Lord Salisbury, at Hatfield in Hertfordshire between 1607 and 1612. A few miles away at Gorhambury, in about 1608 Francis Bacon was constructing an elaborate water garden with islands including a large central one with a house on it. Perhaps the most celebrated garden prior to the Civil War was the Hortus Pembrochianus, the garden of the Earl of Pembroke at Wilton, in Wiltshire. Created between 1632 and 1635, its shape was a huge rectangle with a broad alley running from the middle to the centre of the house. The garden itself was divided into three sections; the first consisting of a group of four embroidered parterres, with fountains and statues; the second a wilderness with more statues and fountains; and the third an area laid out as formal walks. Described as 'the supreme expression of English renaissance garden design and a vivid reflection of the ideals of the court of Charles I',[19] the garden was derived from those of Venetian villas on the mainland opposite Venice and reflected the strong desire for order in the gardens of this period, as expressed in rational ideas of pattern and symmetry.

Topiary, the art of sculpting hedges into unusual shapes, also flourished greatly at this time. Although it had long been practised in England, it achieved its greatest expression and extravagance in the seventeenth century, when close-clipped box and yew were used to construct forms both fanciful and geometric. The oldest surviving topiary garden in England is at Packwood House in Warwickshire (Plate 29). Created in 1650, it consists of tall

Plate 29 The topiary garden at Packwood House in Warwickshire

columns of yew arranged in a loose formation in a rectangular enclosure at the head of which is a huge cone of yew set in a conical mount. It seems that the popularity of such gardens in the seventeenth century may have been due to the fact that they strengthened man's belief in his ability to control nature and offered country gentlemen ordered refuges from political and religious turmoil, and from civil war. However, not all landowners allowed themselves to be governed by the aesthetic appearance of their parks and gardens. Especially during the hundred years from 1540 to 1640, some landlords were mercenary and others were improvident; for example, if coal lay under their parks, they would allow coal-pits to be dug, even in front of the windows of their mansions.

By the outbreak of the Civil War, the number of parks in some counties had probably never been greater: in Staffordshire, for example, there were at least 79 of them, of which 49 were stocked with deer.[20] However, the disorders of the Civil War and the Commonwealth which followed brought about the despoliation of some parks, especially royal ones, and the confiscation of much parkland property. Stands of timber were cut down and the deer were killed. Many of the celebrated gardens characteristic of the courts of James I and Charles I lapsed into decay following

Plate 30 The gardens of Doddington Hall in Lincolnshire as they appeared in Kip's engraving of 1707

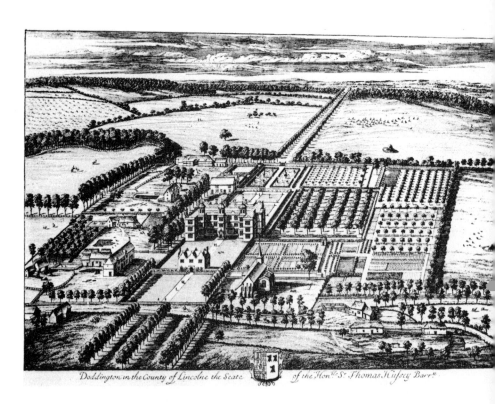

Doddington in the County of Lincolne the Seate of the Hon.ᵇˡᵉ Sʳ Thomas Hussey Barrᵗ

116

sequestration by Parliament. However, once Charles II and his court returned from the Continent in 1660, the great era of the formal landscaped gardens was ushered in. Much influenced by the great French landscape gardener, Le Nôtre, English gardens modelled themselves on those of France with their great avenues and masses of foliage and broad expanses of grass and water. In these ways, the formal concepts were spreading from the garden into the park and, for a period of 50 years or so from 1660, the grounds of English country houses were laid out on a much bigger scale than ever before. The typical garden of this period is well

Plate 31 Part of the extensive formal garden, with its yew hedges and wide avenues at Melbourne Hall in Derbyshire

shown in the numerous engravings from the drawings begun in about 1694 by Leonard Knyff and also by those of his engraver, Johannes Kip. However, it must be borne in mind that these engravings were sometimes idealised and, on occasion, showed their owners' intentions rather than their actual achievements. Among the great gardens laid out in this manner were Longleat in Wiltshire, which was replanned in the 1680s, Ragley in Warwickshire, Wimpole in Cambridgeshire and Doddington Hall in Lincolnshire (Plate 30).

Unfortunately, very few examples of seventeenth-century gardens remain and then only in fragmentary fashion. At Castle Abbey in Northamptonshire, for example, the grand avenues in the park which were laid out in 1695 immediately after the visit there of William III may still be seen. At Charlecote in Warwickshire, only the avenue from the road is left of the once great formal garden; and the elms which lined it were devastated by Dutch elm disease a few years ago and have been replaced by young Turkey oaks. The disappearance of the formal seventeenth-century garden and parkland was due to changes in fashion, especially the coming of the eighteenth-century English landscape park. However, one of the few examples of the formal garden to survive relatively intact, albeit dating from the early eighteenth century, is that of Melbourne in Derbyshire (Plate 31). On a much smaller scale is the garden of Moseley Old Hall in Staffordshire, laid out by the National Trust as it might have looked when Charles II took refuge there after the battle of Worcester in 1651.

While our magnificent inheritance of parkland and garden owes much to the entrepreneurial activities of the great sixteenth and seventeenth century landowners, it is perhaps as well to remember that their ruthlessness exacted a considerable social price and in R.H. Tawney's words, the parks were created 'for those motives of social amenity and ostentation which have done so much to make the English countryside the admiration of travellers, and so much to ruin the English peasantry.'

CHAPTER 6

Industries in the countryside

England in 1400 was an industrial backwater, lagging behind her European neighbours both in industrial techniques and in her range of industry. Indeed, apart from the production of woollen cloth, she possessed little industry of note. During the sixteenth and seventeenth centuries, however, a substantial increase took place in both the scale and diversity of industrial production so that by 1700 it accounted for more of the national income than ever before and employed a greater proportion of the population. This industrial development took many forms, including the introduction of new industries from the Continent, such as the manufacture of brass, copperas, gunpowder, sugar and paper; a very considerable increase in the size of previously small-scale industries such as the production of iron, soap, and glass; and the growth of long-established staple industries like textiles, mining, building, salt-production and leather-working.

The transformation of English industry during this period had many causes, but particularly important was the demographic factor: the doubling of the population between 1500 and 1700 created an internal market for industrial products which greatly stimulated the production of a wide range of manufactured products. Moreover, the growth of population in rural areas, especially those with a pastoral economy, imposed acute pressure on land-holding and led many people to turn away from the land, either partly or wholly, to seek a living in industry. In addition, the role of the entrepreneurs, especially the great landowners who invested large sums of money in industrial experiments, was extremely significant.

During the 300 years under review, as in the preceding centuries, most industry was based upon the towns. However, some industrial development naturally took place in the country-side and in mineral-yielding areas, for example, agriculture and industry were ancient bedfellows. Indeed, in such places it is difficult to ascertain whether the development of settled agriculture preceded or followed the mining of such minerals as tin, lead, copper, iron, stone and chalk. Certainly, by 1400, the two occupations of farming and mineral extraction had long since dovetailed together; this was especially true of the western half of England where pastoral farming predominated and, since it required less labour than arable farming, left the peasant free to engage in mining while his family looked after the land and the animals. Thus, most industries in a rural setting were there because their location was based on the particular natural resources being exploited. These were often carried out in remote and thinly populated parts of the country such as the valleys and moorlands of Cornwall and neighbouring parts of Devon which produced tin; and the hillsides of the Peak District, the Mendips and the northern fells where lead was produced. Other mainly rural industries were the smelting of iron, lime burning, and the making of pottery and glass using raw materials which were locally available in various parts of the country but which required very large amounts of fuel which were very expensive to transport. In addition, other rural-based industries included the quarrying of stone and the production of salt either from the inland brine springs of Cheshire and Droitwich or from sea-water.

The only important industry located in the country which was not directly based on local resources and which by 1400 had begun to develop a national market was the manufacture of woollen cloth and it is to this industry that we shall first turn our attention.

Woollen cloth-making

Many of the major English cities including London, Norwich, Bristol and York were engaged in the manufacture of woollen cloth in the later Middle Ages. In these cities the medieval craft guilds, which organised urban craftsmen and supervised their standards of workmanship, had become extremely strong and in the process had imposed irksome restrictions which held back production and maintained high prices. As a consequence, producers and merchants increasingly turned to the countryside and by 1400, cloth-making had spread in both the villages and the small market towns in various parts of the country, especially in parts of south-west England, East Anglia, in the Weald of Kent, the West Riding of Yorkshire, and Westmorland. In these areas, the putting-out or domestic system prevailed and by the sixteenth century the spare hours of at least one quarter of the cottage-farming population in England were spent in spinning and carding wool, in knitting stockings, and in weaving cloth. In countless parishes in Tudor England – in parts of the country such as Dorset, Somerset, Gloucester, East Anglia, the Pennines and the Weald of Kent – travellers would hear the sound of turning spinning-wheels, and see the distaff, the stick that held the bunch of wool, twirling in innumerable farm labourers' cottages.[1] None of these rural cloth-producing areas relied solely on local supplies

Figure 6 The main areas of woollen cloth manufacture, c.1550

of raw material but imported them from some of the most prolific wool-producing counties, such as Lincolnshire, Northumberland, Sussex, Northamptonshire, Herefordshire and Shropshire, none of which had a major textile industry of its own.

Typical of these rural cloth-producing areas at this time was the Wiltshire broadcloth area, situated in the north-west of the county between Malmesbury and Westbury and to the south-west around Mere. It was part of a larger region stretching in an arc from the Windrush valley of Oxfordshire, along the edge of the Gloucestershire Cotswolds, and south through eastern Somerset and western Wiltshire to Salisbury (Figure 6). Its chief and most

121

valued product, like that of the other important west countr
cloth-making area, around Cullompton and Tiverton in Eastern
Devon, was the heavy, warm and relatively expensive broadcloth
Broadcloth was much in demand on the Continent and by the late
fifteenth century large quantities were being exported, much of i
undyed and undressed. The cloth-making areas of Wiltshire, like
most of the other areas, were pastoral country supporting dair
farmers who were also cloth workers in their spare time. Wiltshire
had long been a centre for the making of fine broadcloth
especially in the town of Salisbury, but it was not until the late
fourteenth century that its production spread into the countryside
The introduction of fulling mills required a supply of fast-flowing
water to drive them and so they were built on the banks of stream
in rural areas. With them went dyers, fullers and weavers so that
soon, the pastoral areas were called upon to provide reserves o
labour for cloth-making, a very labour-intensive industry. And
here cloth-making remained, on a domestic basis, throughout the
period covered by this book.

The same process occurred in East Anglia concentrated
especially in the pastoral region of southern Suffolk where the
fast-flowing waters of the Stour, the Orwell and the Deben and
their tributaries provided power for the fulling mills. Similarly, in
the Weald of Kent, cloth-making was established by the
fourteenth century in the parishes of Cranbrook, Goudhurst
Tenterden, Hawkhurst, Headcorn and neighbourhood where
supplies of fullers' earth were to be found and where narrow
valleys enabled streams to be dammed up to provide power for the
fulling mills. The Kentish wool-making industry eventually died a
mysterious death in the seventeenth century. In the West Riding
of Yorkshire and stretching over the Pennines into Lancashire, the
rural cloth-industry was located in the Pennine valleys, the mos
sparsely inhabited areas where pressure on land was least intense
and where the fast-flowing streams provided ample power. Finally
the manufacture of woollen cloth in the Lake Counties was also
well established by 1400 around the town of Kendal, which was
well-known for its coarser and cheaper cloth. During the fifteenth
century, the industry spread out into the neighbouring countryside
so that by the sixteenth century there were 18 fulling mills in the
neighbourhood of Ambleside and Grasmere alone.[2] However, fo:
various reasons, one of which may have been that Kendal cloth fel
out of favour with London tradesmen, the Westmorland cloth
industry did not survive the reign of Elizabeth.

As has been indicated, the making of woollen cloth, the larges
and most important of England's industries, expanded greatly
during the later Middle Ages in response to a growing oversea:
market. This expansion continued, if at varying rates, in the
sixteenth and early seventeenth centuries and increasing quantities
of cloth were shipped abroad, mainly through Antwerp, to markets
in north-west, central and eastern Europe. About 56,000 cloths a

year were being despatched around 1490, rising to almost 126,000 a year in the 1540s. For the rest of the sixteenth century, overseas demand was steady, to increase again for a short period in the early seventeenth century, only to decline irregularly but continuously for the rest of the century. One of the reasons for this decline was the deterioration in the quality of English broadcloth; as the English pastures were improved, with enclosure, so the wool staple was becoming coarser and longer and less suitable for manufacture into high quality woollens. Moreover, with prosperity, there was a growing preference for lighter varieties of textiles, 'the New Draperies', so that the home market did not expand to compensate for falling exports. However, our concern is not with the ups and downs of the export trade in this commodity but rather with the effects on the home industry, especially that based in the countryside. Clearly, however, those parts of the country which specialised in producing heavier cloth were particularly badly affected in this regard so that by about 1700 the textile industry had almost completely collapsed in some parts of Gloucestershire, in most of Suffolk, and in the Weald.

On the other hand, other parts of the country reacted to the changing circumstances by developing new cloth products which were lighter and cheaper and in greater demand. Indeed, by using different types of wool and mixing them with other fibres such as cotton, linen, silk and mohair, manufacturers produced new varieties of cloth which became so popular that their production more than compensated for the decline in the manufacture of the traditional broadcloths. In East Anglia, for example, in parts of Suffolk and in Essex around Colchester, coarser part-woollen and part-worsted fabrics, known as bays and says, were being made by the early seventeenth century. Similarly, at the same period, in parts of Wiltshire and Somerset, a lightweight product known as Spanish cloth became increasingly important and resulted in the area enjoying a reasonable degree of prosperity which lasted throughout the century. Further west in Devonshire, a range of lighter cloths, described generically as kerseys and dozens, was also being produced and successfully exported by the early seventeenth century. Finally, in the middle and later decades of the century, a similar and better quality product known as serges, or perpetuanas, became increasingly popular. Indeed, these became the most successful of all the new textiles and resulted in considerably increased exports, particularly in the last third of the seventeenth century. As a consequence, the areas where they were produced, such as east Devonshire, flourished considerably and the main urban centres, Exeter and Tiverton, grew considerably in size. The home market was also increasing about this time and was supplied with kerseys and dozens in large quantities by the West Riding of Yorkshire in particular.

As a result of these developments, the production of woollen cloth in 1700 was more varied than it had ever been and probably was also greater in volume. Much of the production remained in the countryside, as had been the case for at least 200 years.

During this long period the woollen textile industry produced what Muir calls, 'quite different landscapes of spectacular success and grinding soul-destroying failure',[3] representing many stages of growth and desertion. As we have seen, among the growth areas towards the end of the seventeenth century was South Devon, so that when Celia Fiennes visited the Exeter area in 1698 she found

> the whole town and country is employ'd for at least 20 mile round in spinning, weaving, dressing, and scouring, fulling and drying of serge, it turns out the most money in a weeke of anything in England. . . . The carryers I met going with it as thick all entring into town, with their loaded horses, they bring them all just from the loome and soe they are put into the fulling-mills . . . [4]

Another of the prosperous areas of textile-manufacture was East Anglia and here in such villages as Sudbury, Kersey (Plate 20), Clare, Long Melford and Stoke-by-Nayland, evidence of their former prosperity is to be found in the wealth of massive timber-framed houses of sixteenth- and seventeenth-century cloth merchants and dyers. More modest were the cottages of the Yorkshire handloom weavers, whose short rows of terraced houses were grouped round a hall where the pieces of woven cloth were gathered together for sale to dealers. They would often have a common loft where combing and weaving were undertaken collectively and a feature of these cottages is still the long mullioned 'weaving windows' in the top storey, with between five and twelve lights each against which the handlooms were set.[5] In places like Heptonstall and Hebden Bridge situated on the banks of fast-flowing streams in the Pennine valleys, their eighteenth-century successors are still to be seen today, carefully preserved by the Calder Civic Trust and other bodies.

One important aspect of the woollen cloth industry, which thanks to a change of fashion developed from a long-established craft in peasant communities into a national industry during the mid-sixteenth century, was stocking knitting.[6] For various reasons, separate woollen stockings became fashionable in place of cloth hose at this time and soon a wide range of qualities, textures and patterns developed, to such an extent that the industry remained widespread and important throughout the period. Both men and women were engaged in the craft and they combined it with their normal agricultural pursuits, especially where pastoral farming was dominant. In various parts of the country, men and women knitted as they led their beasts into the fields or walked to market and their products went off to the local market centre. In North Yorkshire, knitters from the Dales sent their pairs of stockings to Richmond. In Northamptonshire they went to Northampton, from Sherwood Forest to Nottingham, and from the fishermen and their wives on the Norfolk coast to Norwich. During the latter part of the period, from about 1650 onwards when labour costs were beginning to rise, the adoption of the knitting frame became more widespread and led to greater productivity. As a result, the use of the stocking frame spread particularly through the East Midlands and was to be found in many farmers' homes. In the three counties of Nottinghamshire, Leicestershire and Derbyshire, for example, the number of frames rose from 140 in 1667 to 3500 by 1727 and, indeed, the first two counties remain important centres of hosiery knitting to this very day.

Other textile industries

During the period under review, four other textile industries flourished at various times and to various extents, namely the weaving of linen, hemp, lace, and silk. As, however, silk manufacture was almost entirely located in the cities, especially in London where it developed from the 1620s onwards, we shall restrict ourselves to considering only the first three. The linen and hemp weaving industries were almost entirely domestic industries, producing linen and hempen cloth for a large number of everyday purposes, including household linen, clothes and for sacks of all kinds. Until the middle of the sixteenth century, most linen used in England was imported from the Continent, especially from Holland, France and Germany. However, from about 1550 onwards, the manufacture of linen cloth became established in Lancashire and Yorkshire, on both sides of the Pennines, where large numbers of poor farmers were employed. Being largely unskilled, they concentrated on cheap, coarse goods for the home market and the finer linens continued to be imported from the Continent. An associated industry was the manufacture of fustians, which was a form of cloth which was both cheap and hard wearing, in which linen was mixed with cotton. Long established on the Continent, it seems to have been first introduced into East Anglia in the mid-sixteenth century by Protestant refugees from the Low Countries. Eventually, however, the industry found a more permanent home in East Lancashire and it flourished around Blackburn, Bolton and Oldham during the seventeenth century. Flax and hemp weaving were also not unimportant domestic industries in those areas where the raw materials were grown: for example, in the fens around the Wash; in the Isle of Axholme, in Lincolnshire, where hemp cloth was made for sacks; in the pastoral areas of Northamptonshire; and in Somerset and Dorset. In other places, flax and hemp weaving was based on imported supplies of the raw materials, as in Nidderdale in Yorkshire where, in the seventeenth century, imported flax was brought along the river from Hull.

Lace-making was another industry which resulted from the introduction of a new fashion. In the mid-sixteenth century, the use of lace to decorate cuffs, collars, and ruffs and as aprons and handkerchieves became very fashionable and by the end of the century lace manufacture had been introduced into rural areas in the south-west and in the south Midlands, apparently as a means of giving employment to pauper labour. By the 1630s, lace-making was firmly established in south Devon, especially at Honiton where Celia Fiennes commented on the making of 'the fine bone lace in imitation of the Antwerp and Flanders lace'; on the Somerset-Dorset border around Yeovil and Sherborne; and in the south Midlands in Bedfordshire and Buckinghamshire, especially around Stony Stratford, Olney, Newport Pagnell and Bedford. It was an industry that very largely employed female labour and, by 1700, lace dealers were asserting that over 100,000 women and children were employed in it. Mention should also be made of the nearby straw-plaiting industry which was centred around Luton and Dunstable in Bedfordshire and in neighbouring Hertfordshire. A craze for wearing straw hats and bonnets developed in the late seventeenth century and the industry sprang up to meet the demand, though it did not achieve a national significance until the nineteenth century.

Mining and metal industries

Mineral production, restricted by geology very largely to the north and west of the country, was already of considerable importance by 1400. The principal minerals that were extracted were coal, iron, lead and silver, tin, copper, salt, and stone and, indeed, the areas being exploited at this time largely coincided with those being worked today (Figure 7).

Coal-mining was active in the fifteenth century, albeit on a small scale, in virtually all the major coalfields of today. Although charcoal was preferred for smelting iron, coal was used by blacksmiths, for lime-burning, salt-making, in baking and brewing, and increasingly as a household fuel. It was commonly known as 'sea-coal', to distinguish it from charcoal, probably because it outcropped near the mouth of the River Tyne, from which it was exported to other parts of the country and especially to London. For the next hundred years or so there was little change in the extent and character of coal-mining; in every coalfield where coal occurred close to the surface it was worked and used locally and only from Newcastle was there as yet any substantial movement of coal. However, towards the last third of the sixteenth century, coal came increasingly to replace wood and charcoal as a source of domestic fuel, largely because of the steadily increasing rise in the cost of wood. For the same reason, coal was also adopted as fuel for an increasingly wide range of industries, especially from about 1600 onwards. As a result, well before the end of the century, its use was largely complete in the production of lime, bricks, glass,

Figure 7 The major extractive industries in seventeenth-century England

soap, salt, starch, alum and copperas, in malting and brewing, in the dyeing of cloth and in the refining of sugar, though it had yet to be employed successfully in the smelting of iron. These developments brought about considerable increases in coal production which, between approximately 1550 and 1700, increased at least several-fold, standing perhaps at 2½ million tons at the end of the period, of which perhaps one third was used for industrial purposes. In the earlier part of the period, the expansion in production derived partly from an increase in the number of small workings, many of which were operated by groups of farmers who combined agriculture with mining. These were especially

127

common in coalfields away from sea transport in areas like the Midlands, south Lancashire and Somerset where the prohibitive cost of transport restricted the sale of coal to a local market and created conditions in which small-scale enterprises could thrive.

This early coal-mining took two main forms: drift mining and by bell pits. Drift mines were dug horizontally or at an angle into the hillside and the coal was dug out by hand by miners using hand picks and by driving wedges into cracks and seams. Necessarily, such operations were restricted to seams at or very close to the surface. The same was true of bell-pits which were shafts sunk down to the level of the coal seam, from which point the miners worked outwards from the foot of the shaft, forming a bell-shaped cave from which this type of mining derives its name. Eventually, as the miners pushed outwards, the whole cave would begin to collapse inwards when it would be abandoned and a new pit sunk (similar pits were used in iron-mining, (Plate 32). Evidence of bell-pits for the extraction of coal is still to be found in places, as in the hummocky mounds in the Forest of Dean, at Coleford in Gloucestershire, and on Catherton Common in Shropshire.

From about 1550 onwards, however, the biggest increases in production took place in the few coalfields that were well placed to export coal to other parts of the country, especially in north-east England, along the lower reaches of the Rivers Tyne and Wear in Northumberland and Durham. Expansion also occurred in the Nottinghamshire coalfield adjacent to the Trent, in Shropshire near to the Severn, in South Wales, and along the Cumberland coast (Figure 7). In these areas, as the seventeenth century wore

Plate 32 The remarkable landscape created by medieval iron-mining: the remains of bell-pits at Bentley Grange, Yorkshire

on, the most accessible coal seams, those close to the surface, were exhausted and deeper shafts had to be sunk, a process which inevitably required much greater capital investment. By the end of the seventeenth century, pits of 120 feet in depth were common and, in parts of north-east England, they occasionally reached a depth of 300 or 400 feet. These deeper mines required the digging and lining of air tunnels, improved ventilation and better haulage and winding gear. However, the problem of drainage remained largely unresolved and a solution was not found until the early eighteenth century when Thomas Newcomen and Thomas Savery devised an effective 'engine for raising water by fire'. Meanwhile, the output of the late seventeenth-century mines had greatly increased and a coal mine which might have been producing a few hundred tons of coal a year before the middle of the sixteenth century could well be producing 25,000 tons a century later. The effect on the landscape was correspondingly greater and Celia Fiennes describes the area around Newcastle-upon-Tyne in 1698 in these terms:

> As I drew nearer to Newcastle I met with and saw abundance of little carriages with a yoke of oxen and a pair of horses together, which is to convey the Coales from the pitts to the barges on the river . . . this country all about is full of this Côale the sulpher of it taints the aire and it smells strongly to strangers; upon a high hill 2 mile from Newcastle I could see all about the country which was full of coale pitts.[7]

The river Tyne was full of colliers waiting to be loaded with coal (Plate 33) which was brought to them by keels from the staithes which were located further up the river and interesting survivals of this busy trade are the famous 'ballast hills' made up of ballast deposited on the river banks by returning empty colliers.

Of the metal industries that flourished in England between 1400 and 1700, iron-making was probably the most important and as society increased its use of iron over the period so the quantity grew and the quality improved. During the fifteenth century, the Forest of Dean was probably the most important iron-smelting area in the country, with the Wealden industry beginning to grow, particularly to meet the needs of the London market. Both areas had abundant iron ore and plentiful supplies of wood for charcoal. In the earlier part of the period, the iron ore was commonly quarried by means of shallow pits or trenches, by groups of about 15 or 20 men, until eventually the pits became flooded or were in danger of collapse, when they moved on elsewhere and started again. This type of quarrying, whose cost was fairly small and could therefore be undertaken by small groups of men, often resulted in the creation of bell-pit ironstone mines, similar to those for coal. The waste material was disposed around the opening of shallow shafts leading to the bed of ore and when the shafts eventually collapsed they left hollows in the centre of the

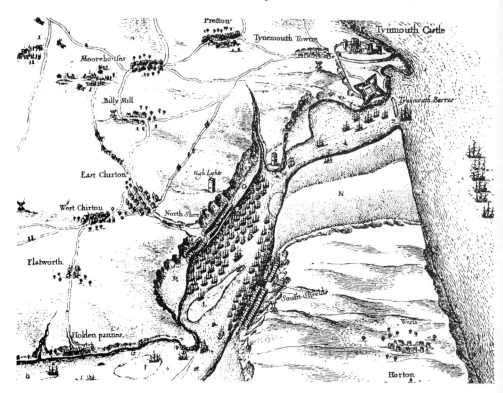

Plate 33 A 1664 map showing colliers waiting in the River Tyne between North and South Shields, to be loaded with coal brought by keels from staithes farther up river

spoil heaps. In some places, iron-making produced an underground complex of caverns, as in the Clearwell Caves in the Forest of Dean, which were heavily worked in the Middle Ages and where the workings are now open to the public.

The ore, some of which was imported from Spain or Sweden, was smelted in a crude furnace known as a bloomery, which was fired by charcoal. The making of charcoal or 'coaling' as it was called is described by John Evelyn in his *Sylva*, of 1664 (Plate 34). Itinerant charcoal burners, or 'colliers', would level a piece of ground in the forest or wood some 20 to 30 feet across. A heap of wood was then constructed with a central chimney and the heap was covered with layers of small brushwood and turf. The wood was set alight and, by various means, the burning was controlled, as the slower the coaling proceeded the better the quality of charcoal it produced. This process had remained basically the same for many centuries both in England and abroad. The charcoal was then delivered to the bloomery where it was used to fire the iron ore. The itinerant 'colliers' who produced the charcoal were extremely skilful and much in demand by the iron founders. They often lived in temporary camps in the forests and a typical camp, with its simple huts and charcoal heaps has been

130

Plate 34
Charcoal-making in the
seventeenth century: an
illustration from John
Evelyn's *Sylva* of 1664,
p. 103

reconstructed at the Weald and Downland Open Air Museum at Singleton in West Sussex. The bloomery produced a soft mass of metal which was consolidated into a bar of wrought iron by repeated hammering, a labour-intensive, and therefore expensive, process. The primitive technology involved has left some inconspicuous remains in the form of heaps of cinder, slag, burnt clay and roasted ironstone and, in the Weald for example, these remains have been meticulously charted by the Wealden Iron Research Group and others. The bloomery produced very limited amounts of wrought iron and required considerable quantities of timber, hence its common location in the forest areas (Plate 35).

From the late fifteenth century onwards, however, two important technological developments transformed the iron industry. The first was the harnessing of water power to drive the forge hammer. Earth dams were thrown up across narrow valleys to create hammer ponds which supplied water with a sufficient head to work the mechanical bellows and hammers of a furnace and forge. These artificial ponds have left their mark in the form of small lakes which in the Sussex Weald, for example, carry such names as 'Hammer Pond', 'Furnace Pond', and 'New Pond'. The second development was the introduction from the Continent of the blast furnace in which the draught was provided by bellows driven by a powerful water wheel. This greatly increased the efficiency and scale of iron-smelting. The first blast furnaces were introduced at the very end of the fifteenth century when at least three were in use in the Sussex Weald, at Newbridge, Hartfield and Buxted on the edge of the Ashdown Forest. These blast furnaces were conspicuous features in the countryside, being by the end of the seventeenth century about 30 feet high, 20 feet square at the bottom, with walls between 5 and 6 feet thick to preserve the heat and with a giant bellows about 20 feet long

Plate 35 A bloomery at
work about 1550, from
the great source book of
medieval mining
practice, Agricola's *De Re
Metallica*, published in
Germany in 1556

driven by a water wheel which stood nearly as high as the furnace
itself. The huge water wheels were partly sunk in pits, the remains
of which can still be seen in places: in East Sussex, for example,
the Ashburnham furnace near Ninfield, north-west of Bexhill,

132

possesses an almost complete wheel pit and at Wych Cross, south of East Grinstead, the Pippingford furnace has a wheel pit where cannon were cast.

Such furnaces could produce between 100 and 500 tons of iron annually. As with the developments in coal mining, so these improvements in iron production added very greatly to the capital costs while at the same time substantially increasing both the scale of the output and the quality of the product. In the fifteenth century, for example, a primitive bloomery produced little more than 30 tons of wrought iron a year; by the mid-seventeenth century, however, large furnaces were capable of producing as much as 750 tons a year and the total English production of bar iron grew from about 10,000 tons in 1600 to 30,000 tons in 1760. Moreover, in addition to wrought iron, it was possible by this time to produce cast iron, that is iron cast into moulds, which although not as strong as wrought iron, was much cheaper to produce so that its use became more widespread. Thus, agricultural and industrial equipment began to be made of iron, household goods such as cast iron kettles and cooking pots became available and a flourishing industry developed in the manufacture of cast iron fire-backs and fire dogs.

The English iron industry expanded rapidly from about 1550 onwards and by the middle of the seventeenth century there were three main areas of production. In the Weald of south-east England, the iron industry supplied the London market and possessed a monopoly of cast-iron guns. In 1607, Norden had noted no fewer than 140 'hammers and furnaces' in Sussex alone, and in 1611 it was estimated that of the 800 'iron-mills' in the country approximately half were in the Weald. During the second half of the seventeenth century, however, the Wealden iron industry virtually collapsed, partly because fuel was becoming increasingly expensive, partly because of a succession of droughts which meant that water power was not always available and furnaces had to be blown out, and partly because of competition from the Continent. Whatever the reasons, the Wealden industry by 1700 accounted for only a quarter of the ironworks in the country.

The second major area of production was the long-established industry of the Forest of Dean. With its advantages of cheap coal, abundant timber and facilities for water transport, especially along the River Severn, the area flourished in the seventeenth century and according to Yarranton, writing in 1677, was producing 'infinite quantities of raw iron' and giving employment to 'no less than sixty-thousand persons'. The third major iron-producing area was the West Midlands, which expanded considerably during the later part of the seventeenth century, though more particularly in the eighteenth century. Iron was produced in Staffordshire, Warwickshire, Worcestershire and Shropshire and according to Yarranton in all these counties

is an infinite quantity of Pit coals, and the Pit coals being near the iron
and the iron-stone growing with the coals, there it is manufactured very
cheap and sent all England over and to most part of the world.

Moreover, much iron was increasingly being used locally in the
highly labour-intensive and fast-growing metal working industry of
the Birmingham and Black Country areas. These included the
manufacture of nails, bolts, locks, keys, wires and scythes.[8] Typical
of these industries was needle-making, which dates from the late
1550s, being introduced into England, like many other new
industries of this time, by Flemish refugees. The scale of
production was small, with a typical unit consisting of a master
employing a handful of journeymen and apprentices, a pattern
which continued throughout the period. The industry originated
in London and Colchester but in the course of the seventeenth
century spread into rural areas, especially in and around Studley
in Warwickshire, about 15 miles south of Birmingham, and in the
surrounding parishes on the Worcestershire border. One reason
for its development here was its favourable location close to the
metal trades of Birmingham and the Black Country.

Another ancillary branch of the iron industry which began to
develop, albeit on a small scale, during the late sixteenth and
seventeenth century, was that of steel-making. Although it was
known as a refined and hardened iron, it was little used in the
Middle Ages and did not assume any importance until the reign of
Elizabeth when Dutch steel workers introduced improved methods
of production into the country. Its production remained very
expensive throughout the period and it was not sufficiently hard
for many specialist purposes. However, by the seventeenth century
a considerable number of small steel works was in operation, using
high quality imported Swedish iron ore as native ones were less
suitable for steel-making. These were located mainly in the west
Midlands around Stourbridge and Birmingham, in the Sheffield
area, and around Newcastle-upon-Tyne where they supplied
innumerable small enterprises manufacturing cutlery, clocks,
watches, pens and other small objects.

Lead, which was usually mined with silver, and tin were two
other important minerals in England throughout the period under
review. In 1400, the extraction of lead ore occurred mainly in the
Mendips, but as we shall see it was later outstripped by production
in the Peak District of Derbyshire, and other areas which
developed later were the Yorkshire dales and further north in the
Pennines, at Alston in Cumbria (Figure 7). Lead was first used for
making cheap, low-grade pewter and for shot and ball. However,
as building increased and became more sophisticated, it was
chiefly used as roofing material, for guttering and water pipes and
for leaded windows. As in the coal and iron industries,
technological improvements in the production of lead ore, such as
water-powered stamping mills and furnaces with water-powered

bellows, which were introduced by enterprising landlords and other mine-owners, resulted both in increased production and lowered costs. As a result, the lead industry spread from the Mendips, especially to the Derbyshire Peak District where it had been mined for centuries on a part-time basis by farmer-miners but which now became the most important centre. Here, the lead had long been mined by means of rakes, deep gullies created by the miners as they followed almost vertical sheets of lead ore. An impressive rake which can be seen today is the Dirtlow Rake to the south of Castleton. By the seventeenth century, however, these more accessible sources of lead had been virtually worked out and the entrepreneurs sought ways of excavating the deeper ores which lay in hitherto unworkable waterlogged veins in the limestone. By means of long adits, or 'soughs', driven into the base of the limestone at considerable cost, the water was released and the lead could be worked. Further north, in the Nidderdale area of North Yorkshire at Greenhow Hill, deep incised valleys made the lead accessible by means of adits, dug horizontally into the valley sides. Here, cottages were built early in the seventeenth century for the lead-miners and their ruins are still to be seen today.

The increased demand for lead for building, especially after the Great Fire of London, resulted in the exhaustion of easily accessible seams. As with coal mining, primitive forms of drainage pumps had been in use in lead mines since the Middle Ages (Plate 36), but in the latter part of the seventeenth century the introduction of more efficient pumping and winding gear enabled deeper mines to be dug in the lead fields. As a result, the mining and processing of lead increased more rapidly than any other form of extractive industry, though its value per ton was relatively low compared to iron. The scale of the increase was such that whereas national output was of the order of 625 tons a year in 1500, it had risen to about 28,000 tons a year by 1700.

Tin-mining was restricted to the south-west peninsula and especially to Cornwall. In the early Middle Ages it was also worked in the western part of Devon, in the streams flowing down from Dartmoor, but by 1400 this source of tin had become largely exhausted and the centre of the industry moved westward to Cornwall. As tin occurred in alluvial deposits, the ore was easily worked by 'streaming', that is extracting the metal-bearing ore from deposits washed down by the rivers, and no elaborate equipment was required. As a result, for the earlier part of the period most tin workings were quite small, and were operated by a small number of tinners, though individual merchants might own a large number of separate mines. However, although some streaming for tin continued throughout the period, the more accessible ores in Cornwall were being worked out by the end of the sixteenth century and underground mining, involving the intervention of the entrepreneur and his capital, had become general. During the fifteenth century the production of tin ran at

Plate 36 A simple
drainage pump, worked
by means of a treadmill
operated by the men on
the left. This illustration
is also taken from *De Re
Metallica*

about 600 tons a year and, unlike lead, production increased only
slowly throughout the period, reaching perhaps 1,500 tons by
1700. This was largely because English tin went mainly for export
and met with fierce competition from Continental producers.

136

However, a proportion of the tin was used at home, mainly for the manufacture of pewter but also for making bells and bronze and brass. Pewter ware was a fairly expensive semi-luxury at first but its use was disseminated more widely by the end of the period. By about 1650, when the demand for tin had begun to increase, most of the alluvial deposits and the shallower veins of ore in Cornwall had been worked out. Deep hard-rock mining became necessary which, as in the other extractive industries, required large investments of capital. Consequently, during the last part of the seventeenth century, tin extraction became increasingly centred on a small number of large tin-mines employing substantial numbers of tin-miners and the small-scale workings declined in number and importance.

A third non-ferrous metal whose mining was virtually unknown until the reign of Elizabeth I was copper. It was closely associated with brass manufacture, brass being an alloy of copper and zinc eminently suited to the making of guns and ordnance of all kinds. The development of copper mining for this purpose was stimulted in the late 1560s with the importation of skilled German technicians. However, its production was very limited and rarely exceeded 100 tons a year. For one thing, the areas of production were Cornwall, the Keswick areas of Cumberland and, to a lesser extent, the Derbyshire Pennines while the chief market was a long way away in London. For another, copper deposits were difficult to work and the refining and manufacturing processes were technically difficult and expensive. Nor was the demand for copper and brass ever very high, their use being largely restricted to artillery and high quality pots and pans. English copper producers found it increasingly difficult to compete with those on the Continent, so that the Cornish mines closed down by the early seventeenth century, and those of Cumberland by the time of the Civil War.

Salt was a vital commodity throughout the period under review, as it had been for centuries previously, as a preservative and seasoner of food, and for use in various industrial processes, such as the curing of leather. At a time when the want of winter feed meant that many farm animals had to be killed off in winter, the only way to preserve their meat was to salt it down. Salt was also widely used in a similar fashion to preserve fish. Appreciable quantities of salt had been obtained since Roman times from the brine springs of Cheshire and Worcestershire and, throughout the fifteenth and sixteenth centuries they were the principal suppliers of fine quality salt which was used for culinary and dairy purposes. This salt, from the celebrated salt workings at Nantwich, Middlewich and Northwich in Cheshire, and Droitwich in Worcestershire, found its way throughout the country. In addition, some salt was made by the evaporation of salt water at certain places around the coast. However, in the fifteenth and sixteenth centuries, these sources produced only a small proportion of the salt consumed in England, and the greater part, especially the coarser salt used as a preservative, had to be imported from abroad, especially from France.

In the salt-working areas of Cheshire and Worcestershire, the brine which was obtained from the underground salt springs was boiled in lead or iron pans for approximately three hours, after which the salt was scraped out of the bottom of the pans with wooden rakes and put into baskets. The production of Cheshire and Worcestershire salt increased steadily throughout the period, though in both areas the industry was relatively small, consisting of little manufacturing pockets in the middle of agricultural districts. However, salt-making on a large scale was not practicable until large salt-evaporating furnaces were devised which burned coal, instead of wood, as fuel. This type of industry developed from the end of the sixteenth century in north-east England, in and around North and South Shields and Sunderland, where some limited salt-making had taken place in the earlier part of the period. Run on capitalist lines, the salt industry of the north-east was employing hundreds of men in the early seventeenth century and, in about 1640, output around the mouth of the Tyne alone was estimated at 15,000 tons a year and that of the whole country at least 50,000 tons. However, the north-east area suffered severely during the Civil War and the Commonwealth and output did not recover until the end of the century. By this time, the rock salt deposits of Cheshire had been discovered and were being exploited on an increasingly large scale. By 1700, English consumption of salt had increased at least three-fold in the preceding 150 years and the country was almost self-sufficient in the commodity.

Other rural industries using local extractive products were the making of glass and pottery, and the smelting of lime, all of which used commonly occurring raw materials but which required very large amounts of fuel. Other less important industrial activities which could be regarded as branches of the chemical industries were the making of alum, copperas and saltpetre.

Although it is generally assumed that the medieval tradition of glass-making in England had largely died out during the fourteenth century, there is some evidence to suggest that a few English glass-makers remained active in the fifteenth century.[9] Glass was made by fusing together silica, which was obtained from coarse local sand, and a vegetable alkali, or potash, which was principally obtained from the ashes of wood or 'fern', that is bracken. Consequently, glass-making at this time was mainly carried out on the edge of those forest areas where the raw materials were readily available. The principal areas of glass-making were in the western Weald, around Chiddingfold on the borders of Surrey and Sussex, and on the fringe of Needwood Forest and Cannock Chase in Staffordshire. The Chiddingfold district had a small industry in the early sixteenth century producing green glass both for windows and vessels while, at the same time, furnaces in Bagot's Park, near Abbots Bromley in Staffordshire, were producing brown window glass. However, these were only very limited in scale, the glass they produced was generally rough and coarse, and the great majority of glass was still imported from the Continent. Moreover, by the middle of the sixteenth century, the small-scale English glass industry was on the point of collapse, partly because of increasing difficulty in obtaining wood for fuel, and partly because there was an increasing demand for the finer kinds of glass which were imported from abroad.

With the great increase in house building in the second half of the sixteenth century there was also a growing demand for window glass and, from the 1540s onwards, various attempts were made to establish a domestic industry in the manufacture of fine glass, French, Flemish and Italian craftsmen, mostly Protestant refugees, being imported for this purpose. Eventually, the industry succeeded in establishing itself and numerous glassworks were set up, mainly in the Sussex and Kentish Weald, but also in Staffordshire and elsewhere in the Midlands. The output of glass increased in the seventeenth century, especially after 1615 when the problem of using coal instead of wood for glassmaking was solved by melting the potash and sand in a container that did not come into contact with the coal. By the middle of the seventeenth century, the country was largely self-sufficient in both window glass and glass for bottles and drinking glasses.

Two other industries which were very largely rural in character during this period were lime-burning and pottery-making. Lime was used for various purposes, including the preparation of leather, for making plaster and for other building purposes and, latterly, as an agricultural fertiliser. It was obtained by burning chalk or limestone in kilns which required large quantities of fuel, originally charcoal from wood but later replaced by coal. As lime was relatively easy to produce, the industry was small-scale and was dominated, at first at least, by individual lime-burners. Production expanded very greatly during the seventeenth century, partly because of the increase in the number of houses being built at this time, but more particularly because of the widespread adoption of the application of lime as an agricultural fertiliser to counteract soil acidity. As wood for fuel became more expensive and difficult to obtain, so lime-burning was one of the first industries to adapt to coal. To facilitate the movement of the raw material, kilns were often sited along rivers or near the coast, especially where there were local supplies of chalk or limestone. For these reasons, kilns became concentrated in areas like Northfleet and Gravesend in the Thames estuary, a location which also granted easy access to the London market. The increasing use of coal as fuel also necessitated larger kilns and towards the end of the seventeenth century some of them became very large and required large investments of capital. However, even at the end of the period, of the thousands of lime-kilns in existence, dotted all over the country, the great majority were relatively small.

The pottery industry, like lime-burning, was scattered all over the country, drawing upon local raw materials such as clay and wood to fire the kilns. The traditional English pottery was unsophisticated, consisting of coarse, heavy and crudely decorated ware such as butter pots, designed to keep cool in summer. Most potters were engaged part-time in the industry and, as in the village of Burslem in north Staffordshire, later to become 'the mother of the Potteries', they combined farming with making pottery. One such farmer-potter here in the late seventeenth century was the grandfather of Josiah Wedgwood (Plate 37). By the end of the seventeenth century, some degree of specialisation was developing in this area and Staffordshire potters were beginning to produce improved forms of red stoneware to meet the increased demand for high-quality goods, providing a foundation on which the eighteenth-century entrepreneurs were able to build a major industry.

Plate 37 The house and pottery of Josiah Wedgwood's grandfather at Burslem, North Staffordshire, in the time of Charles II

Other less widespread extractive industries included those which were based on the manufacture of alum, and saltpetre. Alum was used chiefly as a mordant in the cloth industry, that is a substance to fix the dye to the cloth, and also as a dressing for tanned leather. It was extracted by quarrying from English alum-

140

bearing shales and produced by a process involving the use of considerable quantities of fuel and, as with lime-burning, coal came almost completely to replace wood for this purpose. Typically, the alum house consisted of a large building made of wood, in which the alumstone was smelted over brick furnaces fired by coal. The process was a complex one involving large sums of money and by the seventeenth century, the industry consisted of a small number of large works each employing large numbers of workers. During the latter half of the sixteenth century, attempts had been made to establish an alum industry along the Dorset coast, but with little success, and the main area of production, from the early seventeenth century onwards, was the North Yorkshire coastal area between Whitby and Guisborough, where it was found in large quantities in shales outcropping in the cliffs. A large number of alum quarries still remain in this area at places like Bowlby, Kettleness, Sandsend and Peak and at Ravenscar, near Robin Hood's Bay, a typical alum mine can be seen. Belonging to the National Trust and dating from the early seventeenth century, it shows signs of extensive quarrying and contains the remains of surface buildings, including stone-flagged leaching tanks.

During the seventeenth century, demand for alum grew as the proportion of cloth that was dyed increased, so that by the 1620s production reached about 1,200 tons a year and increased somewhat later in the century. However, it was never substantial enough to meet home demand and much alum, usually of higher quality than the native product, had to be imported from the Continent.

Saltpetre, a form of potassium nitrate, was very important as the principal ingredient in the manufacture of gunpowder. Like other industrial processes, its manufacture was unknown in England until the 1560s, when German immigrants, for a consideration, revealed the hitherto well-guarded secret to English gunpowder-makers. It was made, in a number of scattered small-scale enterprises, from earth impregnated with animal excrement, mixed with lime and ashes. Pigeon-houses, described at one time as 'the chiefest nurses of saltpetre of the kingdom', barns and stables were all useful as sources of animal excrement and by the late sixteenth century, saltpetremen were licensed by the Crown, anxious to ensure a regular supply of gunpowder, to enter and dig in such places. However, the enterprises were almost always on a small-scale and scattered, and never succeeded in meeting the growing national demand. Eventually, from the 1620s onwards, saltpetre was imported in large quantities from India, where it was found in a natural state, and used to make gunpowder at the Chilworth mills near Guildford in Surrey, from 1635 onwards the only authorised gunpowder mills in the country.

Finally, the most widespread of all the extractive industries was probably the quarrying of stone, perhaps the most useful and certainly the most varied of all the minerals extracted from the countryside. Stone is our most beautiful and enduring material for building and we are particularly fortunate in having abundant supplies of it. Extracted from quarries all over the country, by quarrymen who were principally farmers and worked on a part-time basis, most stone was used in close proximity to where it was obtained. Consequently, the use of local stone was reflected in the local buildings, from the lovely honey-coloured Ham Hill stone used over a wide area of south Somerset and north-west Dorset, through the pale golden stone used by the wealthy wool merchants of the Cotswolds, through the grey Barnack stone of Northamptonshire used in homes and churches in the east Midlands (Plate 38), to the famous red Hollington sandstone of Staffordshire, used extensively in that county and also for Hereford Cathedral and for the post-war rebuilding of Coventry Cathedral.[10] Because stone extraction required considerable labour and because it was very

Plate 38 The medieval stone quarries at Barnack, Northamptonshire

142

expensive to transport, only exceptionally fine stones were taken any distance from the quarries, and then to be used only for important buildings. Such quarries included those of Purbeck and Portland in Dorset, and the famous Weldon quarries near Corby in Northamptonshire whose stone was used for King's College Chapel in Cambridge. Typical of these were the quarries on the island of Portland. Portland stone was relatively little used in the Middle Ages and extensive quarrying did not begin until the seventeenth century, when it was popularised by Inigo Jones who used it for the portico of the Banqueting Hall at Whitehall and for the reconstruction of old St Paul's. Really large-scale quarrying occurred here after 1666, when the stone was chosen by Wren for St Paul's and the new city churches after the Fire of London. Because of the scale of the operation, considerable sums of money were involved in the industry and large numbers of men were employed, increasingly on a full-time basis.

Two other very important and widespread industries to be found in the countryside were the milling of corn and the tanning and making of leather. Corn-milling was crucial to the economic life of England throughout the period, as bread remained the staple diet of the majority of its people, and consequently the miller was an important figure in rural society. Corn-mills were a very common feature of the countryside and were to be found in almost every manor and parish. The Domesday Book, for example, lists over 5,000 of them, all water-powered. Since the windmill did not appear in this country until the middle years of the twelfth century, watermills always greatly outnumbered windmills.

Watermills were situated on streams or rivers, often at the lowest point in the manor in order to obtain the maximum flow of water. The stream was usually tapped into a dam or millpond to ensure a more even flow of water and also to increase the head of water in case of a dry spell. Leading into and out of the dam were watercourses, or leats, to fill the dam and operate the mill-wheel. One of the oldest water-powered grain mills to be seen today is the Old Mill at Nether Alderley in Cheshire, belonging to the National Trust and dating from the fifteenth century. Another celebrated watermill, dating from the fifteenth century, and also in the possession of the National Trust, is that of Flatford Mill, on the north bank of the Stour, one mile south of East Bergholt in Suffolk. It came into the possession of John Constable's father and the greater painter worked there for a year. A further splendid and picturesque example is Bourne Mill, near Colchester in Essex, which was built in 1591 as a fishing lodge; also in the possession of the National Trust, its stepped and curved gables are testimony to the Dutch architectural influence which was strong at that time in this part of the country.

Windmills were of two main types: post-mills and tower-mills. Post-mills were the earlier type of windmill and changed little in appearance throughout the period. They were box-like structures containing grinding machinery and the working part of the mill rotated round a central post so that the sails faced into the wind. However, as rotating the whole mill was a cumbersome business, a new mill was invented in the sixteenth century, the tower-mill. In this type of mill the body was a fixed structure and only the cap, with the sails and their gearing, rotated. These mills were usually built of brick, or stone or occasionally of wood, in which case they were also known as smock mills. In addition to grinding corn, windmills were also used, in areas like the Fens, for raising water from one level to another (Plate 39). The windmill turned a scoop

Plate 39 A windmill like those used in the Fens in the middle of the seventeenth century, from Walter Blith's, *The English Improver Improved*, published in 1652

Both
The Millsmade open that the whole Engins may appeare ———

wheel, up to 25 feet in diameter, which could raise water as much as 5 feet.

There are a number of windmills dating from the period still to be seen in the English countryside today. The oldest is at Pitstone, in Buckinghamshire, 3 miles north-east of Tring, and bears the date '1627'. It is of the earlier post-mill type, was working until 1902, and is now in the possession of the National Trust. Other excellent specimens include the restored seventeenth-century post-mill at Brill in Buckinghamshire; a smock-mill dating from about 1650, at Loosley Row, also in Buckinghamshire; and a restored seventeenth century post-mill, still regularly used, at Nutley in East Sussex. Finally, the stumps of many abandoned tower-mills, without their caps, are still to be found scattered about the countryside and, where the windmills have disappeared completely, their sites can sometimes be found from the mounds which formerly held post-mills and from field names like 'Mill Field' and 'Windmill Furlong'.

The manufacture of leather was particularly important as, together with wood and wool, it was one of the three natural resources which was virtually indispensable to medieval society. Indeed, it was second only to wool cloth as our most important manufacturing industry. Leather was used for clothes, especially boots and shoes, for boxes and chests, bags and purses, for book covers, for saddles and harness, for buckets, and for many other purposes. By 1400, the curing and tanning of animal hides into leather and the making of leather articles of various kinds was widespread throughout England, both in urban and in rural areas. Although the leather industry was mainly concentrated in the towns, especially London, most villages, for example, would contain a leather worker who operated on a small scale, obtained his own skins and worked them up into finished articles used in the agricultural community. Tanning was a complex, lengthy process, requiring much water and large quantities of oak bark. For these reasons older tanneries were situated near streams, rivers, or wells and tanners were frequently found working alongside the charcoal burners in the forest areas. Hides were tanned by suspending them for months in pits containing tanning liquor, a mixture of water and ground oak bark, and by the seventeenth century the process had become more commercialised, with large 'tan yards' being constructed, containing stone-lined pits some of which remain today. Over the period, the demand for leather products greatly increased, as did that for virtually all consumer goods, and with it the processing and working of leather. As in the fifteenth century, the great majority of the industry was centred in the towns, especially London, but the countryside, too, benefited from the expansion. Moreover, unlike some of the other industries described above, the period witnessed little technological development in the making of leather goods. This was partly because the process was an intricate one involving

145

much manual skill to which mechanisation was less applicable and partly because labour, which was the most important factor in its production, remained cheap and abundant throughout the period. Thus, leather-making in the countryside remained a domestic activity, carried on largely by the individual craftsman. Moreover, there is reason to believe that the proportion of leather goods deriving from the countryside rose considerably during the seventeenth century.

Finally, the manufacture of paper was another industry partly based in the countryside. Until the invention of printing in the late fifteenth century, the market for paper in England was relatively small, though it had begun to displace vellum and parchment as writing materials. Gradually, through the sixteenth century the demand for writing paper increased, though it was an expensive commodity, and also for brown paper as wrapping paper. Neither, however, was manufactured in England and both had to be imported from abroad. Sporadic attempts were made to start paper manufacture in England, from the end of the fifteenth century onwards, but with very limited success. Indeed, it was not until a century later than a German immigrant obtained the lease of two existing paper mills on the River Darenth, near Dartford in Kent, and manufactured and sold various types of paper over an appreciable period of time. By the 1630s, other paper mills were in operation such as those in Cannock Chase in Staffordshire, near High Wycombe in Buckinghamshire, and at Yatton Keynell in Wiltshire. However, they produced mainly the coarse brown paper used for packing, so that almost all the paper for writing and printing had still to be imported. Gradually, during the last part of the century, the number of paper mills increased, to reach 50 or so by 1670, and over 150 by the early eighteenth century. By this time, they were also producing the poorer qualities of white paper. A seventeenth-century paper mill can be seen today at Wookey Hole, near Wells in Somerset; powered by water, it was largely rebuilt in the nineteenth century.

Thus, the years from 1400 to 1700 witnessed considerable changes and developments in industries located in the English countryside. England began the period with an economy dominated by agriculture and with only a small proportion of its population engaged in industrial pursuits, mostly on a part-time basis, combining mining or pottery-making, for instance, with farming. As the population grew, especially in the second half of the period, so economic and industrial activity diversified in response to the greater demand for consumer products at home and for woollen cloth abroad. At home, by the seventeenth century a market for non-essential consumer goods had emerged which was larger than any which had previously existed and which stimulated the development of native manufacturing, which though relatively small compared to that which was to occur in the Industrial Revolution was nevertheless very significant. These developments took three principal forms.

Firstly, the scale of basic industrial activities such as coal-mining and iron-making expanded considerably, partly as a result of technological innovations. The effect of this expansion was to require larger and more elaborate plant and equipment which became increasingly expensive so that these industries could less and less be carried on by small-scale workers and became more entrepreneurial and capitalised. The extractive industries, such as coal, iron, tin and lead mining, all became characterised by deeper and larger mines which required more capital for drainage, ventilation and other purposes associated with larger-scale production. Secondly, there was a growth in industries producing new consumer goods which often successfully captured markets previously supplied by imports. This development became marked after the middle of the sixteenth century and applied, for example, to industries such as the manufacture of woollen stockings and lace products, the production of metal goods, the manufacture of glass, and the manufacture of linen cloth. All these industries were to be found operating in the countryside, on a domestic basis.

Thirdly, during the late sixteenth and early seventeenth centuries, water power increasingly became the basis of industrial development and entrepreneurs placed very high reliance on water resources generally. In the Tillingbourne valley of Surrey, for example, where the River Tillingbourne ran westwards for about ten miles before joining the River Wey just above Guildford, river water provided a source of energy driving grain and textile mills, trip-hammers for iron, brass and wire manufacture and also wheels for the making of gunpowder, saw-milling, paper-making and knife-grinding.[11] In addition the water was used for leather tanning, for the floating of meadows, and for such popular features of seventeenth-century gardens as canals, cascades and waterfalls.

Lastly, some parts of the country began to lose something of their agricultural character and to become increasingly indus-trialised. Typical of these was south Staffordshire which in the fifteenth and sixteenth centuries had been essentially a pastoral region, concentrating mainly on stock-rearing. As this activity consumed only part of the farmer's time, it permitted the development of a dual economy whereby the peasant both kept livestock on a few acres of land and also ran a small forge in which he made metal goods. As the seventeenth-century progressed, however, so the agricultural and industrial activities within the region became increasingly divorced and the latter became large-scale entrepreneurial activities employing increasing numbers of workers on a full-time basis. More and more men became wholly dependent on work in industry and those maintaining a stake in the land could no longer compete on equal terms and were having to give up their agricultural activities. Although industry remained

147

essentially domestic in character, as competition became more and more intense, men were increasingly required to work excessively long hours in their cottages, often for very little reward. By the seventeenth century, this had already become characteristic of the woollen industry of large parts of Wiltshire, Somerset and East Anglia. Thus, developments foreshadowing the factory system of the Industrial Revolution could by 1700 be clearly discerned both here and in other parts of the country such as the north-east coalfield and the North Staffordshire Potteries.

CHAPTER 7

Roads and rivers:
movement in the landscape

Throughout the period considered in this book, England was an underdeveloped country. Perhaps the greatest bar to economic expansion was the limited transport system which the country possessed. Inland transport, which alone concerns us here, was determined very largely by topography and other natural limitations, as the techniques for overcoming them, by laying down tarmacadam roads or by cutting canals, for example, were still undeveloped. The two major forms of transport were by road and by river, and each will be considered separately. In addition, there was a small number of tramways, or wagonways, which were primitive railways serving coal mines, consisting of wagons running on wooden rails, and these, too, will be described at the end of the chapter.

Roads and tracks

In 1400, as throughout the Middle Ages, roads must have formed the backbone of the transport system and were therefore fundamental to the country's economic well-being. Relatively little has been written about their location, writers on the topic confining themselves largely to describing travellers, the state of the roads and the means and safety of travel.[1] Little attempt has been made to describe the road network and to see where the roads were, partly perhaps because of the lack of documentation and partly because the medieval road system has left very little by way of archaeological evidence.

The chief source of information on the geography of the late medieval road system is the Gough map of about 1360 (Plate 40) which depicts some 2,940 miles (4,730 km) of roads covering most of England (Figure 8), and there is no reason to suppose that any substantial changes had occurred by the fifteenth century. However, the Gough map, while probably reasonably accurate, is an incomplete copy of an earlier map and does not include at least a few roads which were certainly in existence at the time, including the London to Dover section of Watling Street, the road from York to Newcastle, and that linking Southampton with

Winchester. What it does show, however, is that London was then, as now, the principal focus of routes. Moreover, almost 40 per cent of the routes shown are along the lines of Roman roads, although in many cases travellers avoided the hard surface of Roman roads where they survived, and instead developed later roads on the softer ground alongside them. Those routes which did not follow Roman roads developed as the result of the continual passage of traffic and, in effect, 'made and maintained themselves'. They were legal rights of way more than physical tracks and, if they became impassable, the traveller had the right to diverge from them even if it meant trampling through crops.

Figure 8 The routes of the Gough map of about 1360

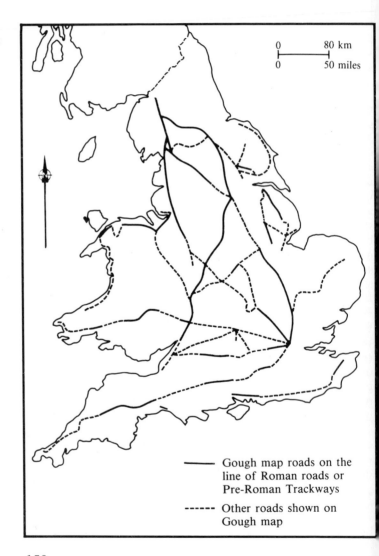

0   80 km
0   50 miles

—— Gough map roads on the line of Roman roads or Pre-Roman Trackways

----- Other roads shown on Gough map

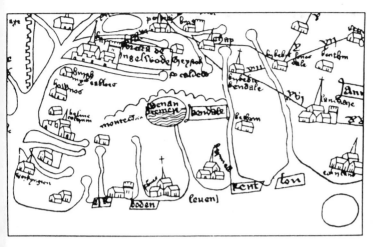

Plate 40 An extract from the Gough map of about 1360 showing part of Cumbria and the roads leading south from Carlisle

However, it seems likely that the lines marked on the Gough map represented actual roads on the ground. In any case, it is clear that the economic development of England during the Middle Ages had led to numerous roads and tracks coming into existence, so that virtually every part of the country was reasonably accessible to a major routeway. However, the art of making roads remained rudimentary throughout the period, the principles upon which the Roman roads were constructed having been forgotten, and it was not until the later eighteenth century that solid, weatherproof roads were once more constructed. On the other hand, solid road bridges were built in the fifteenth century and others rebuilt, with their timber structures being replaced with stone ones. Good examples include the three-arched bridge across the River Derwent at Cromford in Derbyshire (Plate 41), the Barnard Castle Bridge which crosses the River Tees between Barnard Castle and Bowes in County Durham, and the St Ives Bridge across the River Ouse in Cambridgeshire, reconstructed of Barnack stone about 1414. Although this system of major routeways was probably inadequate, even in winter, for the amount of traffic that wanted to use it, it is also true that it did bring every part of the country within a fortnight's ride of London and it did make possible a centralisation of national government without parallel in Western Europe.

However, there seems little reason to doubt that the general condition of roads in the fifteenth century left much to be desired, even though to judge from the silence of most contemporary documents on the topic, the majority of travellers regarded the poor state of the roads as inevitable and unworthy of comment. Certainly, the roads managed to accommodate a considerable variety of traffic, mostly consisting of teams of pack-horses and of horse-drawn carts. England's biggest exports, wool and woollen

151

Plate 41 The fifteenth-century bridge across the River Derwent at Cromford, in Derbyshire

cloth, were taken by road to the ports; raw materials for building, like wood and stone, would be transported in carts; many travellers, both on horseback and on foot, used the road system; and large numbers of animals, probably outnumbering men and women, were driven along them. The responsibility for maintaining the road system generally devolved upon the various landowners, or the towns, through whose property the roads ran and the actual keeping of the highways in repair was the traditional responsibility of the local inhabitants. It is unlikely that this responsibility was assiduously attended to and it probably amounted to little more than clearing verges and filling up holes. It is hardly surprising, therefore, that especially in winter many roads fell out of repair, became covered with water and were virtually impassable. Moreover, the gradual decline of the manorial system in the course of the fifteenth century led to a corresponding decline in the care devoted to roads and bridges due to the shortage of labour at this time and the changes in landholding. Both in the fifteenth century and, indeed, in different places and at different times throughout the period, roads and highways were rendered hazardous by robbers and highwaymen. As early as 1401, for example, conditions in the West Midlands were so bad that the Crown sent a special commission to enquire into reports that

certain evildoers, scheming to hinder the king's lieges, merchants and

152

others going by roads and highways . . . to the markets of Colleshull, Birmyngham, Walshale, and Duddeley in the counties of Worcester and Warwick, from buying and selling corn, victuals and other necessaries, there assembled in divers conventicles, and veiling their faces with masks, with garments turned in the manner of torturers, and carrying machines called 'glandmeres' and other instruments, lay in ambush and assaulted the king's lieges going to and from the markets and put them and their horses to flight so that the women and children riding on the horses, with sacks filled with corn fell off, and some died, and some were injured, and cut the sacks and scattered the corn along the roads.[2]

Throughout the period covered by this book, the packhorse and packmule were among the principal means of transporting merchandise. Indeed, in some of the hillier parts of the country, such as the Peak District,[3] they were often the only means of carrying goods. A much favoured breed of packhorse was the Galloway, which though small was strong and accustomed to rough country. Packhorses normally carried their loads in two panniers or baskets, one on either side of a special type of saddle, called a 'crook'. In a typical pair of these baskets a packhorse could, for example, carry 2½ hundredweights of coal. The routes which the packhorses followed were known as packhorse ways, or packways, and frequently as saltways, from the most commonly transported commodity. The packhorse travelled in single file, in 'trains' commonly consisting of forty to fifty horses, headed by a packman or sumpter astride the first which was belled. As a result, the packhorse train could follow the tracks which were too narrow for wheeled traffic and the sure-footed horses could pick their way over upland country, and for this reason were very widely used in these areas. The 'ways' used by the packhorse trains were frequently paved, over the softer ground at least, and these sections were often known as 'causeways'; over the Pennine moorlands, for example, big flagstones were laid down to create a single-width paved path. In order to carry the trails across rivers, packhorse bridges were built and maintained: as they carried a single file of horses, they could be quite narrow and steeply humped to leave room for the river in times of flood (Plate 42). The packhorse trails and saltways formed a network criss-crossing the length and breadth of the country and enabled the packhorse trains to cover long distances. For example, Daniel Defoe, writing in 1700, describes the 'fish-trains' which carried fresh salmon from Workington and Carlisle in Cumberland down to London and, as the fish arrived as 'fresh as they take them', the whole journey could not have taken more than 3 days.

The packhorse trails have left their mark on the contemporary landscape in a number of ways. In the upland areas, the tracks were often characterised by 'crosses' or 'stoops', consisting of rough stone pillars which helped the trains to find their way in bad weather. These have given their names to places such as 'Badger

Plate 42 The medieval packhorse bridge at Danby, North Yorkshire

Stoop', 'Hollow Mill Cross' and 'Mid Causey Stone' which mark the routes of former packhorse trails.[4]

The saltways were particularly important and well-used, as salt was a vital commodity in the preservation of food and as such essential to daily life. The salt was purchased by salters from the areas of production, such as Cheshire and Worcestershire. They followed regular routes with their packhorses to the places where they sold the salt. These routes, or saltways, are still quite often commemorated in placenames embodying the word 'salt' such as Saltersford, Saltersbridge and Salters Well. In Cheshire, for example, the saltways linked the three 'wiches' – Northwich, Middlewich and Nantwich – through various 'salt' placenames to towns beyond (Figure 9).

The other important long-distance trackways that existed throughout this period were the drove roads, or drovers' roads, which were distinguished from packhorse ways by their much greater width, extending from 40 feet to as much as 90 feet wide.[5] Although they reached their peak in the eighteenth century, they had been in existence long before then, albeit on a smaller scale. Droving first became of national importance when cities began to outgrow the food supply available in the neighbouring countryside and there is evidence of cattle being driven from Wales to London during the fourteenth century. However, it was not until the latter part of the sixteenth century that drovers became so numerous that it was felt necessary to control them by a Statute which

154

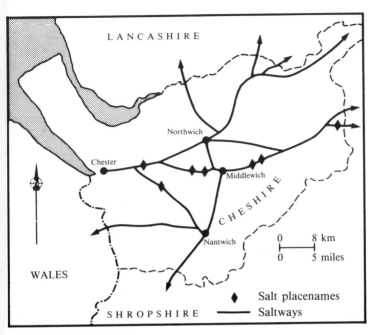

Figure 9 The saltways of Cheshire (based on W.B. Crump, 'Saltways from the Cheshire Wiches', *Lancashire and Cheshire Antiquarian Society*, vol. 54, 1939, pp. 84–142)

required them to have a licence which was renewable annually. The main animals that followed the drove roads were cattle and sheep, though oxen were also moved in this way – hence the drove road was occasionally termed 'ox road' or 'ox way' – as were geese and pigs, though these usually covered shorter distances. Cattle were driven in herds of not more than 200 animals with a drover to every 50 beasts, herded along, then as now, by dogs. Sheep, on the other hand, were driven in much larger flocks, sometimes consisting of as many as 2000. The major, long-distance drove roads seem to have converged on London, especially from Wales in the west, and from Yorkshire and Scotland in the north. However, they were common all over the country though, like all the roads which existed at this time, they are usually impossible to date. The majority were probably relatively short, carrying largely local traffic.

In addition to the roads there were complex networks of tracks and trackways which surrounded virtually every village and hamlet in the English countryside, leading from one village to the next, from village to town, and from the village to its fields, pastures, wastes, meadows and woodlands (Figure 10). These networks of medieval tracks can be categorised into three main types. The first consisted of unfenced tracks in the open field manors which led from the villages to the strips and which usually ran along the headlands between the strips. Secondly, in the wood-pasture areas and on the moorland edges of the Pennines and the south-western

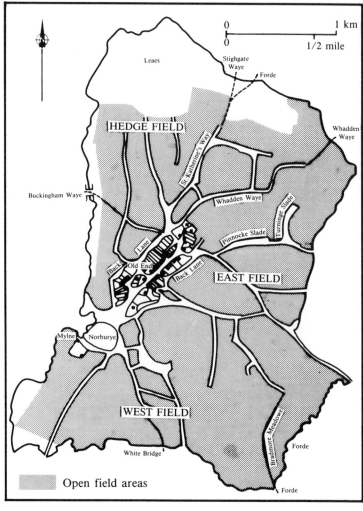

Figure 10 The roads and tracks of Padbury in Buckinghamshire from a map of 1591 (based on M. Beresford and J.K. St Joseph, *Medieval England – An Aerial Survey*, Cambridge University Press, 2nd edn, 1979)

uplands where there were enclosed fields bounded by hedges or stone walls, countless lanes wandered amongst them, enabling farmers to reach their fields or pass through them to the upland pastures. Thirdly, in the mountains and moorlands and in the unreclaimed fenlands and marshes, there were unfenced tracks or short drove roads along which farmers took their animals out to summer pasture and back in autumn and which were used by the villagers exploiting the marshes for bracken, peat, or fish. All three types of tracks have left some evidence of their existence in places on the contemporary landscape.

As the economy improved during the sixteenth century, so the amount of traffic along the roads must have increased correspondingly. Although many of the bulkier commodities – such as wood, coal, building stone, hay, bricks and lime – were moved where possible along the rivers and by sea around the coast, the volume of packhorse and cart and wagon traffic had increased substantially by the late 1530s when John Leland was travelling round the country, as can be inferred from the minute attention he pays to bridges and causeways.[6] Where possible, the roads followed the outcrops of well-drained limestones and sandstones, but in some parts of the country it was impossible to avoid outcrops of clay and alluvium entirely and, here, raised causeways were often built. Leland, who traversed many of them, describes the section of the important road between London and Banbury in Oxfordshire where it leaves the dry chalk for the impermeable Gault Clay at Wendover in Buckinghamshire in the following terms, 'There is a Causey made almost to pass between Alesbury at it, els the way in wett time as in a lowe stiffe Claye were tedious and ill to passe.'[7] Other notable causeways included those across the Trent valley at Swarkeston, south of Derby (Plate 43), across the Thames between Oxford and Hinksey, and across the Nene near Oundle in Northamptonshire. The overall network of major roads at this time was probably much as it had been in 1400. It seems to be accepted, however, that there was a rapid decline in the condition

Plate 43 The medieval bridge and causeway, about three quarters of a mile long, across the River Trent at Swarkeston in Derbyshire

157

of the road network between the late 1530s when John Leland was writing and some forty years later when William Harrison was complaining that some highways, 'within these five and twenty years have beene in most places fiftie feet broad according to the law . . . now they are brought into twelve, or twentie, or six and twentie at the most.'[8] Certainly Leland made little complaint about the roads in his day, but this may have been a matter of temperament as much as anything else. Nor is it certain that Harrison's animadversions applied to the road network generally. However, some decline seems likely by the 1580s, partly because of the rapid increase in traffic during the previous 40 years, and partly because of the effects of the dissolution of the monasteries. The monks travelled widely between their scattered estates and, perhaps for this reason, monastic landowners seem to have been reasonably conscientious in maintaining the major roads that ran through their manors; however, the lay successors to their estates were much less inclined to maintain the roads in good condition.

The Tudor administration, on the other hand, was concerned to ensure that the roads, on which so much of the economy depended, were kept in a reasonable state and in 1530 Henry VIII enacted a Statute empowering Justices of the Peace to enquire into 'all manor of annoyances of bridges broken in the highways, and to make such process . . . for the reparation of the same against such as owen to be charged.'[9] Like so much other Tudor legislation, the Statute was largely ineffective and in 1555 the first general Highways Act was passed, 'for amending highways, now both very noisome and tedious to travel in, and dangerous to all passengers and carriages.'[10] This first significant move towards state control placed the obligation for maintaining the roads in good condition where it had long rested, namely upon the parishes through which they ran. The Act created a system of road maintenance whereby each parish was required to appoint two surveyors of highways, unpaid and holding office for a year. Under their direction, householders could be compelled to work on the repair of the roads for four days a year, though others could commute their labour for a money payment or by sending others in their place. If the parishes failed to keep their roads in good condition, they could be fined at quarter sessions. Another similar Act in 1563 raised the period of labour to six days a year.

It is very difficult to determine how effective the Act was, but it seems likely that many parishes refused to carry out the work required of them, on the not unreasonable grounds that it was unfair to expect them to labour on roads for the benefit of people passing through, and others were unable to cope with the increased amount of repairs engendered by the greater volume of traffic using the roads. All in all, it seems unlikely that the state of the roads nationally was greatly improved by the effects of the legislation.

However, the growing interest in roads in the latter half of the sixteenth century is reflected in the publication of road tables, which first appeared in 1541, as appendices to 'chronicles'. These tables also give some indication of the network of major routes in existence at the time. The first tables describe nine roads, with their stages and distances, radiating from London: variously, to Walsingham in Norfolk; Berwick, Caernarvon; Cockermouth in Cumbria; Great Yarmouth; Dover; Saint Buryan (Plate 44); Penzance in Cornwall; Bristol and St Davids in Dyfed. By 1570, roads to Southampton, Nottingham, Lincoln, Boston, Carmarthen, Cambridge, Oxford and Rye had been added to the tables and a number of cross-country routes had also appeared. These early tables may have been compiled as a guide to post routes and stages, rather than as a general guide for travellers or carriers, but in either case they give us no information about the condition of the roads or the goods that they carried. Moreover, it was 1593 before the English Mile was defined by statute. Increased travel also resulted in the production of more detailed maps, although

Here foloweth the wape from Douer to London.

From Douer to Caunterbury.	xii.myle.
From Caunterbyry to Sittyngboyne	iii.myle.
From Sittyngboyne to Rochester.	viii.myle.
From Rochester to Grauisende.	v.myle.
From Grauisende to Dertfoyde.	v.myle.
From Dertfoyde to London.	xii.myle.

Here foloweth the wape frõ Saint Buryen in Cornewell to London.

From S. Buryen to the Mount.	xii.myle.
From the Mount to C. Trury.	xx.myle.
From C. Trury to Bodman.	xx. myle.
From Bodman ta Launston.	xx.myle.
From Launston to Ocamton.	xv.myle.
From Ocamton to Crokhoynwell	x.myle.
From Crokhoynwell to Excetre.	x. myle.
From Excetre to Honpton.	xii myle.
From Honpton to Charde.	x . myle.
From Charde to Crokhoyne.	vi.myle
From Crokhoyne to Shyrboyn.	x.myle.
From Shyrboyn to Shaftisbury.	xii.myle.
From Shaftisburye to Salisbury	xviii.myle.
From Salisbury to Andeuoy.	xv. myle.
From Andeuoy to Basingstoke.	xvi.myle
From Basingstoke to Hertfoydbyyge.	viii.myle.
From Hertfoydbyyge to Bagshot.	viii. myle.
From Bagshot to Stanes.	viii.myle.
From Stane to London.	xv.myle.

Here foloweth the wape from Byystowe to London.

Plate 44 A page from a road table published by William Middleton in 1544. It describes the roads from Dover and St Buryan in Cornwall, to London

159

the first county maps, produced by Christopher Saxton in his atlas of 1579, contained no highways. The first cartographer to produce maps for the specific use of travellers was John Norden who marked roads on many of his maps, though they are not to be trusted in detail. In any case, these maps were not road maps as such and did not contain sufficient detail to guide the traveller along the road system. One of the first guides or roadbooks was John Norden's *An Intended Guide for English Travellers*, which appeared in 1625 and was subsequently re-issued several times.

The increased traffic along the roads in the second half of the sixteenth century included both regular carrier services between the main towns and also substantially greater numbers of passengers. Carrier services had been in existence as early as the late fourteenth century and had achieved a degree of regularity; for example, cloths were carried regularly from Kendal to Southampton each year from 1492 to 1546. More widespread services developed from the mid-sixteenth century onwards and by 1600, for example, a thrice-weekly carrier was operating between Ipswich and London. Carriers took goods of all kinds, as well as passengers, letters, money, and bills of exchange. In this way, considerable loads were being moved across the country. In addition, letters had been carried by a system of post-horses since Henry VIII's time and, in 1548, the postage rate was fixed by law at one penny a mile, extremely expensive by the standards of the time. New postal routes were gradually introduced over the remainder of the period.

Early in the reign of Elizabeth, new four-wheeled long-wheel base wagons drawn by some 8 horses and carrying between 60 and 70 hundredweights were introduced from Holland. Unfortunately, the effect of these heavy wagons on the road surface was so deleterious that few parishes could afford the constant repairs. As a result, in 1618 a limit of 5 horses was imposed on four-wheeled wagons. This does not seem to have been very effective and in 1630, Charles I tried, with no more success, to prohibit altogether the use of four-wheeled wagons. By this time, the first coaches or carriages had appeared, also from Holland, which were able to give travellers with money a degree of comfort. Previously, travellers rode on horseback or in appallingly uncomfortable carts whose bodies rested directly on their axles. Now, carriages were in use with the body slung in straps above the axle, thereby giving a much greater degree of comfort.

The growth of road traffic throughout England continued during the seventeenth century. Carrier services increased both in number and in geographical spread and it is estimated that the capacity of the carrying industry, as measured by the output of regular, scheduled services, more than doubled in the period from 1637 to 1715.[11] For example, England north of Lancashire and Yorkshire was without a carrier service to London in 1637, whereas by 1715 it had six services a week. The enormous growth of London during the seventeenth century undoubtedly led to a substantial increase in carrier services from the metropolis along the major routeways to towns all over the country. Goods were transported by packhorses and by wagons, with the former probably carrying the majority of the merchandise. The wagon was a more efficient method of road transport, if measured in terms of horsepower, and a new larger stage wagon, with a swivelling front axle, was introduced on to English roads at some time before 1650. In addition to goods, wagons were also increasingly used to carry passengers and by the first third of the seventeenth century, the stage coach had begun to supersede the long wagon or wain which had served to convey passengers since about 1550. The stage coach was a wagon drawn by six or more horses which could carry some twenty passengers, together with miscellaneous goods, at a speed of two or three miles an hour. John Taylor's somewhat primitive directory of carriers, his *Carriers Cosmography*, published in 1637, lists over 200 carriers who were regularly transporting passengers, letters and goods, from London inns to all parts of the country. By the last quarter of the seventeenth century, their numbers had increased by at least 50 per cent. Gradually, the share of carrying capacity transported in wagons rose during this period, especially in the last two decades of the seventeenth century. This increase in wagon traffic has recently led some economic historians to conclude that the state of seventeenth-century roads was not as parlous as has hitherto been made out and that, at worst, to allow a complex network of scheduled public carrying services to operate successfully, they must have served the country's needs reasonably well.

But it was not only the carrier services which increased in number and volume during the seventeenth century. Mail services gradually developed and, in 1635, four regular services were established between London and Oxford, Bristol, Colchester, and Norwich respectively. In addition, a number of postal services were available along some cross-country routes. By this time, the cost of letter-carrying was much reduced, with the rates varying from 2 pence for distances up to a mile to 8 pence for the five-day journey from London to Edinburgh.

Ever since the end of the Middle Ages, the country's roads had been traversed by itinerant dealers and a great variety of manufactures, especially cloth, food, craft products and, particularly after 1550, imported goods was moved around the country by pedlars, hawkers, tinkers or 'Manchester Men', as they were called. The hawker with his wool, yarns and cloth had especially carved out for himself a recognised niche in the rural economy.[12] The numbers of such dealers increased considerably in the seventeenth century and, by this time, they had come both to provide important retail outlets for a wide range of goods and also to represent a significant part of the traffic on the roads.

The harmful effect of all this increased traffic on the state of the

161

roads must have been considerable and conditions were worsened by the derelictions of the Civil War. It is hardly surprising, therefore, that particularly after 1650, repeated attempts were made to improve the highways. In 1654, for example, Cromwell introduced an Ordinance which began by stating the obvious, namely that, 'the several statutes now in force for mending highways are found by experience not to have produced such good reformation as was thereby intended.'[13] It, therefore, decreed that in the case of important roads the Justices of the Peace could levy a rate upon neighbouring parishes with which to hire labourers and carts to repair the roads. They could also impose fines upon those who damaged the roads by using too heavy wagons on them. Then, in 1663, a major development occurred in the history of English roads when the first Act of Parliament was passed permitting the levy of tolls for the repair of a highway on travellers who passed along, thus ushering in the turnpike era. In this first instance it enabled the Justices of the Peace for Hertfordshire, Huntingdonshire and Cambridgeshire to levy tolls for the repair of that part of the Great North Road which passed through their counties. In this fashion, the first turnpike road appeared when the first tollgate, or turnpike, was erected at Wadesmill in Hertfordshire, and others followed along the same stretch of road. A second Act, dealing with Hertfordshire only, followed in 1665, and soon other roads were similarly dealt with on the turnpike principle, including that from London to Harwich in 1695-6 and two smaller stretches of road in Sussex and Gloucester a year or two later. In all, seven Acts of Parliament authorising Turnpike Trusts were passed between 1663 and 1700. However, it was the eighteenth century that was to witness the great expansion in the establishment of turnpike roads. Moreover, the setting-up of local Trusts in the early eighteenth century did not necessarily result in any considerable improvement in the state of the roads, as there were as yet no marked improvements in the methods of road construction and most repair work still consisted of filling in potholes, levelling ruts and digging and recutting drainage ditches. In these early days of the turnpike system, there were no road engineers and the Trustees and their surveyors largely proceeded by trial and error.

Nevertheless, the passing of these first Turnpike Acts was of great significance in that it ushered in a system which became well established in the next century and which brought about many improvements. Perhaps the most significant of these was the way in which the turnpikes frequently reduced the former multiplicity of tracks to a single line. Previously, main routes in many instances consisted of two or three alternative ways across a specific part of the country. As only one route was turnpiked, which was then used by the majority of traffic, so the lines of many of our present trunk roads were finally delineated. A clear picture of the network of major roads in existence towards the end of the seventeenth century is given by the excellent roadbook, or road atlas, the *Britannia* of John Ogilby, prepared at the request of Charles II and published in 1675. Ogilby surveyed a hundred main roads in England and Wales and in his road atlas presented them as strip maps with each mile numbered and furlongs represented by dots and marking topographical features and villages along the routes (Plate 45). His meticulous work showed a spider's web of eleven

Plate 45 An extract from John Ogilby's road atlas of 1675, *Britannia*, showing the route from Bristol to Weymouth

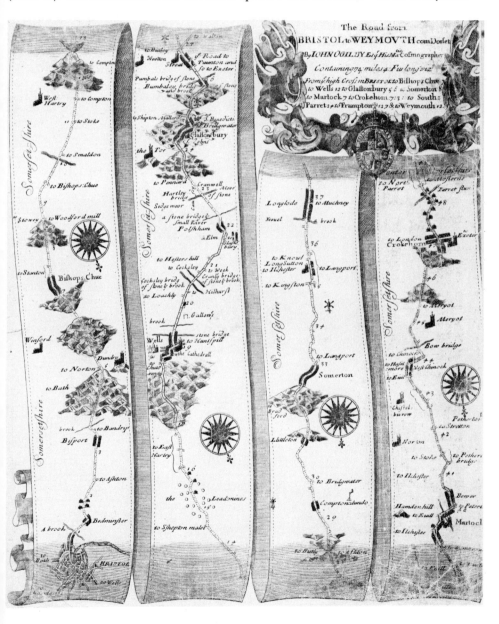

main roads leading out of London to virtually every part of the country with an extensive system of cross-country roads linking them together at many points. In broad terms, however, the system and its layout were essentially the same as that portrayed in the Gough map three centuries before (Figure 11).

Rivers

Throughout the three hundred years from 1400 to 1700, rivers carried much of England's internal trade, though exactly how

Figure 11 The road system of seventeenth-century England (based on H.J. Dyos and D.H. Aldcroft, *British Transport*, Leicester University Press, 1969, p. 32)

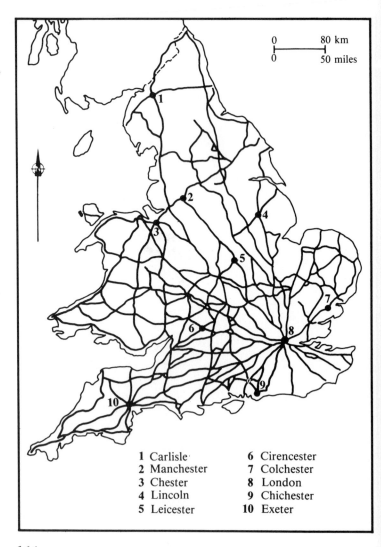

| 0 | 80 km |
| 0 | 50 miles |

1 Carlisle	6 Cirencester
2 Manchester	7 Colchester
3 Chester	8 London
4 Lincoln	9 Chichester
5 Leicester	10 Exeter

much it is very difficult to determine. For the earlier part of the period, there is very little information on the state of the rivers, their navigability and the nature of the cargoes which were carried on them. However, the five major rivers of England – the Severn in the west, the Thames, the Trent, the Great Ouse and its tributaries, and the Yorkshire Ouse in the east (Figure 12) – were all major transport arteries. Moreover, they were all tidal rivers, so that passage along them, within the tidal limits, was free and common to all.

As it was cheaper, as measured by mile per ton, if slower, to carry goods on rivers, it is very likely that bulk cargoes were sent

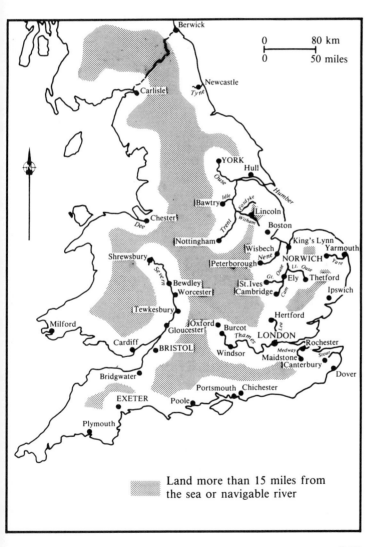

Figure 12 The navigable rivers of England about 1600 (based on L.T.C. Rolt, *Navigable Waterways*, Longmans, 1969, facing p. 1)

by river wherever possible. For example, along the Yorkshire Ouse, large quantities of corn were carried downriver to be transhipped at Hull: this cargo emanated not only from York, which was the tidal limit, but from other shipping points along the river such as Selby, Cawood, and Bishopthorpe. In the opposite direction, a common cargo was Tyneside coal, which was brought from Newcastle to Hull by coastal colliers and transhipped into countless smaller vessels such as keels and sloops and taken up-river to Selby and York. Other important bulk cargoes carried on all the major rivers included building materials, such as wood, stone, and lime. The precise extent of the navigable river system of England in the first half of the period, from 1400 to about 1550, is very difficult to determine. Even the five major rivers were obstructed by mills, fish-garths, that is enclosures for taking and preserving fish, and weirs which impeded the passage of barges and boats. Moreover, the openness of some rivers, like the Severn, to adverse weather conditions, 'where by sundrie perils oft overtake such as fish or saile in small vessels on the same',[14] was another hazard, as were river-pirates with whom the Severn, in particular, was infested. In the fifteenth century, for example, they were particularly active in and around Bewdley in Worcestershire, whose watermen tried to reinforce their hold on the trade of the upper part of the river by virtual acts of piracy. Despite its defects, however, the Severn was a very important traffic artery. By the second half of the sixteenth century, it was navigable as far upriver as Shrewsbury, which was served by shallow-draft Severn 'trows', and below the town was a string of river ports as far as Bristol, upon which the Severn trade was centred. In the 1570s, for example, Bristol was sending up the river large quantities of imported French wine, probably the single most important item, together with iron, oil, tin, and items of food and clothing. Downstream, the major commodities were barley malt and grain and, in addition, wool, leather and cloth were also shipped in considerable quantities.

The Thames was navigable by sizeable barges as far up river as Reading in Berkshire, and by smaller boats and barges to Burcot just south of Oxford. From the latter, goods were carried overland to Oxford, though there seems to have been some local river traffic still further upstream, possibly as far as Lechlade, just over the county boundary in Gloucestershire. According to Harrison, writing in the 1570s, the Thames was much superior to the Severn, 'in length of course, bountie of water, and depth of channel'. Trade on the river was dominated by corn and coal, and by vast quantities of foodstuffs for the London market. In addition, the Medway below Yalding in Kent carried into the Thames Wealden iron and timber.

The Trent was navigable as a major waterway and, apart from the important crossing at Newark, unobstructed by bridges as far upriver as Nottingham, though there were ferries crossing the river at various places between there and the sea. The only one of its tributaries that was navigable was the Idle, as far upriver as Bawtry, near Doncaster. The Trent had possessed another 'tributary', the Fosse Ditch which ran from Torksey to the Witham at Lincoln and enabled timber to be carried to the city from Nottinghamshire. However, it appears to have fallen into disuse by the early sixteenth century and later attempts to make it navigable came to nothing. Like most of the English rivers, the Trent was much obstructed by weirs, mills and kiddles (stake-fences set in the river to catch fish). Nevertheless, considerable trade was carried on along the river and the more important cargoes included coal, shipped down river from Nottingham,; timber; Derbyshire lead, from Bawtry down the Idle and the river Trent; cutlery and metal goods from Sheffield, by the same route; large quantities of grain; and imports of wine, food, and dyestuffs, up to Hull and then up the Trent to Nottingham.

Further south, the Great Ouse and its tributaries provided another very important commercial river system. The Ouse itself was navigable at least as far upriver as St Ives and, of its tributaries, the Cam was navigable as far as Cambridge, and there was also some traffic on the Little Ouse and the Lark. In addition, the river was linked to the Nene at Wisbech, and the Nene itself was navigable as far as Peterborough. Among the more important commodities carried upriver on the Great Ouse network were coal, wine, fish, salt, iron and foodstuffs, mostly brought into King's Lynn by sea. Downriver, the chief cargoes appear to have been corn, butter and cheese.

The Yorkshire Ouse was navigable by larger vessels at least as far as York, which was its tidal limit, and beyond that as far upriver as Boroughbridge. Among its tributaries, it is possible that the Don was navigable to Doncaster and the Wharfe to Tadcaster. According to one authority, at least, grain was being carried in the fourteenth century by boat from Tadcaster to Doncaster to Hull, for transshipment.[15] On the other hand, another writer on the subject states categorically that in Elizabethan times, the Wharfe did not appear to have been navigable and that the Don had no direct access to the Ouse. In either case, traffic on the Ouse depended in large part on the port of Hull: goods going downriver were transhipped there for export or for carrying by coastal vessels to other parts of the country; and sea-borne goods entering Hull were transferred into boats and barges for passage up the Ouse. Among the chief commodities that moved down-river were lead, grain, cloth and possibly butter. Upriver, a greater variety of cargo was moved including coal from Newcastle; the raw materials for the cloth industry including oil, madder, woad and alum; foodstuffs and furniture from London; corn; and salt.

In addition to these five major river systems, other smaller rivers also carried traffic. Perhaps the most important of these were the three East Anglian rivers centred on Great Yarmouth, the Yare, Waveney and Bure. The busiest of these was the River Yare which was navigable as far upriver as Norwich. It carried coal upriver from Great Yarmouth to Norwich, as well as wine, the raw materials needed for making cloth, foodstuffs, corn and tin, and bricks and tiles. On the return journey, the most important cargo by far was cloth. As we have seen, the Medway was navigable as far as Yalding and bore Wealden iron and timber. Iron was also carried on the Sussex Rother above Rye and on the Arun above Arundel. The Itchen had been made navigable from Southampton as far upstream as Alresford in Hampshire by the Bishop of Winchester very early in the thirteenth century, and the Hull River was navigable from Hull upriver to Wansford. In addition, many other smaller rivers around the country must have been utilised for local traffic, including the Exe serving Exeter and the Parrett serving Bridgwater in Somerset.

Although river transport was slower and, due to the circuitous nature of so many English rivers, substantially further than road transport, it was also considerably cheaper, at least for bulk cargoes. For this reason, as the economy grew in the sixteenth century so attempts were made to extend and improve river carriage. These essentially took two forms: the improvement of those parts of the rivers which were already navigable; and the making navigable of unnavigable rivers or parts of rivers. However, these early attempts were largely abortive and it was not until the second half of the sixteenth century that successful endeavours were made to increase and improve the extent of navigable rivers. A half-hearted attempt was made very early in the sixteenth century to render the Kentish Stour navigable from the sea to Canterbury but to little avail. Acts of Parliament were passed during the reign of Henry VIII to stimulate the dredging and clearing of obstacles from rivers, but these measures were largely ineffective as locks and weirs were needed to render rivers navigable and in the field of river engineering, as in many other technical spheres, England was well behind its neighbours on the Continent. Moreover, entrepreneurs wishing to develop rivers for navigation often faced the opposition of landowners who owned the river banks, and of mill-owners and fishermen, and also experienced difficulty in raising money to finance river improvements. However, in the 1560s, a major technical advance in river engineering occurred with the building of the first new locks in England, on the Exeter Canal. These locks, called mitre-gated pound locks, had been known in Italy since the end of the fifteenth century but the knowledge took a long time to reach England. The short canal at Exeter, which started just below the town and ran for about three miles before rejoining the River Exe, could only carry small boats, so that goods had to be loaded into or out of sea-going ships at Topsham. Despite its difficulties and its relatively limited scale, the Exeter Canal with its three pound-locks represented a marked advance in conception which foreshadowed the many artificial cuts by which river navigations were later improved, especially in the eighteenth century. The original locks at Exeter have long since been replaced, but the canal basin is still to be seen with its handsome Customs House built in 1681 and the Exeter Maritime Museum, with an excellent collection of vessels from all over the world.

Meanwhile, during the earlier years of the reign of Elizabeth, two further Acts of Parliament granted powers for improving rivers. The first, in 1571, entitled the town of Stamford in Lincolnshire to make the River Welland navigable as far as the sea, an entitlement which for various reasons was never taken up. The second Act, also passed in 1571, was more successful. It empowered the lord mayor, commonalty and citizens of London to bring the River Lea to London by a cut made at their own expense. Between 1571 and 1581, the 'New Cut' was duly dug, at a cost of possibly £80,000, and consisted of a straight canal from Hoddesdon in Hertfordshire to Bow, parallel with the meandering main river channel. It included at least one pound-lock, at Waltham Abbey, and, in addition, an embankment was built near the mouth of the river to exclude sea water from the valley and direct it into the new cut. The effects of these engineering works were to raise the River Lea to the position of a leading commercial waterway and to cleanse the upper part of the river from Ware to Hoddesdon.

Early in the seventeenth century, moves were made to improve navigation on the Thames and in 1605 an Act of Parliament was passed to clear the Thames of weirs and obstructions as far up river as Oxford. However, the Act was apparently unsuccessful and a further Act was passed in 1624 to extend navigation for barges on the Thames beyond Burcot through Abingdon to Oxford. This time, the measure eventually succeeded and the improvements had certainly been effected a decade later. Another of the great rivers of England on which improvement works were carried out at about this time expressly for the purpose of navigation was the Great Ouse. Arnold Spencer of Cople in Bedfordshire was the entrepreneur behind the scheme and he set out in 1628 to improve a stretch of 16 miles of the Great Ouse between St Ives and St Neots. He appears to have completed his work, which included the construction of six 'sluices', in the next 3 or 4 years, though he never personally achieved his further ambition to make the river navigable for another 7 miles as far as Bedford. This later development had to wait until 1689 for its fulfilment. Between 1634 and 1638, other private individuals were able to carry out improvements to rivers including the Lark in Suffolk, the Tone in Somerset, the Warwickshire Avon, and the Soar in Leicestershire. Typical of these individuals was William 'Water-Work' Sandys of Fladbury in Worcestershire who undertook to make the Warwickshire Avon navigable from its junction with the Severn at Tewkesbury to a point near Coventry. Despite considerable opposition and various setbacks, by 1640 Sandys had opened the Avon for navigation for a stretch of some 20 miles from Tewkesbury to Stratford-on-Avon, with the aid of 12 sluices and a number of locks. A year later the river was navigable to within 4 miles of Warwick and, although the stretch to Coventry was never completed, the Avon was soon carrying much traffic, especially large quantities of coal.

Perhaps the finest work of river improvement during the seventeenth century, from an engineering point of view, was the Wey Navigation in Surrey, extending from the Thames at Weybridge to Guildford. Engineered by Sir Richard Weston of Sutton in Surrey between 1651 and 1653, it covered a total stretch of 15 miles. Because the river fell no less than 86 feet from Guildford to Weybridge, Weston had to build 10 pound-locks, 4 weirs, and construct an artificial cut 7 miles long. He also built 12 new bridges in the course of the work and altogether set an example for the more ambitious works of river improvement which were to follow in the next century. Some remnants of this seventeenth-century work are still to be seen, including a flash, or flood, lock at Weybridge, now in the possession of the National Trust. This was a primitive form of lock, predating the pound-lock, consisting of movable timbers fixed horizontally in a gap in a weir.

Following the restoration to the throne of Charles II, many Acts relating to river improvements were passed, including a dozen in the four years between 1662 and 1665. This spate of legislation was due partly to the growing demand for agricultural products, especially grain, and partly to the example provided by Continental engineers. Among the rivers which were improved during the 1660s were those which drain into the Severn Basin, including the Wiltshire Avon, the Stour, the Salwarpe, the Wye and the Lugg; the Welland and Great Ouse which drain into the Wash; the Hampshire Itchen; and the Mole in Surrey. One of the leading engineers involved in this work was Andrew Yarranton who, in addition to making the Worcestershire Stour navigable from Stourbridge to Kidderminster in 1662 and helping to extend William Sandys' Avon Navigation from Bidford to Stratford, was a staunch advocate of river improvement in such works as his book *England's Improvement by Sea and Land*, published in 1677.

More parliamentary legislation followed in the 1670s, dealing with the Cornish Fal, the Wey, the Witham, the Waveney and the Bedfordshire Ouse and, in the last three or four years of the century, Acts were passed, almost for the first time, for rivers further north including the Aire, the Calder, the Trent and the Dee. The main reason for the promotion of these schemes by entrepreneurs was to facilitate the carriage of bulk commodities such as coal, wood, iron, lead, timber, cloth, and agricultural products. As we have seen, on many rivers there was a two-way traffic consisting of agricultural products travelling downstream and the raw materials for industry moving upstream. Perhaps the single most important commodity in the traffic of many rivers, such as the Aire and the Calder, was coal, which was becoming increasingly in demand both as an industrial and domestic fuel. However, it was during the eighteenth rather than the seventeenth century that river and canal navigations were developed primarily to make the movement of coal easier.

In the meantime, the late-seventeenth-century developments greatly increased both the extent of navigable river waterway and the amount of traffic carried on them. For example, Yarranton stated in 1677 that the Severn was navigable as far as Welshpool, and in about 1694 that percipient observer Celia Fiennes commented that from Oxford to Abingdon she 'rode along by the Thames side a good way which was full of Barges and Lighters.' By this time, barges on the lower reaches of the Thames, and on the Severn, had become larger and more elaborately rigged and were capable of carrying up to about 80 tons. In addition, the Thames grain barges, the largest in use in the country, could carry up to a hundred tons. On smaller rivers, small squared-rigged open sailing barges were common, their sails augmented by teams of 'halers', men who dragged them along the towpath, or by horses. As has been observed, the advantage of river transport was its relative cheapness compared to road transport and some idea of the comparative costs can be gained from the assertion made at the end of the seventeenth century that it was possible to send goods for 300 miles on the Thames for only 10 pence, whereas to send the same goods 30 miles overland from Hitchin in Hertfordshire to London would have cost 3 shillings. While there may have been a substantial element of exaggeration in this assertion, there are nevertheless good grounds for believing that at this time freight rates on rivers were considerably lower than those on land.

Just how far this reduction in cost helped to foster economic growth it is impossible to say, but it was probably only to a limited extent. However, the various improvement schemes for extending water transport, implemented between about 1550 and 1700, did provide transport in land-locked regions and probably more than doubled the effective capacity of England's inland waterways. The actual extent of navigable rivers also grew considerably, from 685 miles in the period 1600 to 1660, to 960 miles at the end of the century. These developments paved the way for the much greater improvements, especially the coming of the canal network, that were to follow in the eighteenth century.

Tramways

Tramways, wagon-ways, or trackways, as they were variously known, were primitive forms of railways, consisting of parallel

171

wooden rails laid on open wooden sleepers, along which wagons of coal were pulled by horses. The first recorded reference to a tramway is to 'railes and bridges' in a coal mine near Nottingham in 1597. Early in the seventeenth century, a similar system operated at Broseley in Shropshire, to take coal down to the river Severn, and also about this time tramways are first mentioned in the Tyne Valley, the area where they were to reach their maximum development. The reason for the introduction of tramways was to overcome the difficulty of transporting coal by the normal means, for as Lord Middleton, a mine-owner of Wollaton Hall in Nottingham, put it in 1610 when speaking of transporting his coals 'we will bring them down by raile ourselves, for the Strelley cartway is so fowle as few carriages can passe'.[16]

The major development of tramways began to take place in the north-east coalfield in the period after 1660. Here the topography was particularly suitable. The wagons were sent along the rails down the gentle gradients to the staithes, or coal wharves, on the banks of the Tyne where the coal was loaded on to ships. On the way down, the rate of descent of the full wagons was controlled by hand brakes, and on the way back the empty wagons were pulled up the slope by horses. This method of transporting coal became very common in Durham and Northumberland, especially along the banks of the rivers Wear and Tyne, though it was not until the eighteenth century that an extensive network developed.

CHAPTER 8

The English countryside in 1700

In some respects the English countryside had changed little in appearance over the long period of three hundred years that had elapsed since 1400, while in others it looked very different indeed. The cultivated landscape of Middle England, for example, still largely consisted of the open fields divided into the innumerable corrugations and wrinkles of ridge and furrow, farmed in the communal manner which had persisted for many centuries (Plate 46). But, even here, changes had occurred and, alongside the great open fields were to be seen the separate, hedged fields similar to those with which we are familiar today. In 1700, they were largely the product of the relatively recent conversion of woodland, waste and heath, made possible by new methods of clearance, drainage and fertilisation and the introduction of relatively new crops, such as turnips and clover, suited to their lighter soils. Over the country as a whole the preceding three hundred years had seen a considerable expansion of the area being farmed.

Precisely how much of England was cultivated in 1700 it is impossible to say for, in this respect as in so many others, there was a complete absence of accurate statistics. Gregory King, writing in 1698, estimated that England and Wales together consisted of almost 40 million acres, which is 1,600,000 in excess of the mark, a relatively small proportion given the circumstances in which he was writing. Probably his other more detailed estimates show a similar relatively small margin of error. Thus, he estimated that 9 million acres were given over to arable, with a further 2 million acres of fallow, 12 million were pasture and meadow, 6 million were forests, parks and commons, 10 million heaths, moors, mountains and barren land, 1 million acres were devoted to what he termed 'homes and homesteads, orchards, churches and churchyards', half-a-million were rivers, lakes and ponds, and another half-million were devoted to 'roads, ways, and waste land'.

If we assume that his estimate of 9 million arable acres for England and Wales was not too far out, that represents more than three-quarters of the present-day cultivated area which was

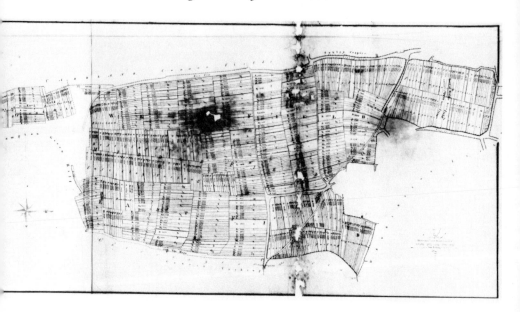

Plate 46 A section of the
open fields at
Wedhampton, near
Devizes in Wiltshire.
Although this map was
made in 1784, it shows
the pattern of tenants'
holdings much as they
must have appeared a
century earlier. The
Wedhampton fields were
not enclosed until the
nineteenth century, by
Act of Parliament

required to feed a population of about one-eighth of its present
size. However, crop yields still remained relatively low even if they
had risen, probably by more than a third, since 1400. The major
field crops were as they had been for centuries, primarily cereals
consisting of a large variety of wheats and a rather smaller variety
of barley, together with either black or white oats, peas and beans.
According to Gregory King, the cereal crops of England and
Wales annually yielded a harvest of not more than 70 million
bushels, a mere fraction of what is obtained by farmers today. By
1700, as we have seen, other crops had been introduced,
especially root crops, including turnips which were used mainly for
animal feed, and potatoes. Three types of turnips – round, long, or
yellow – were being grown by the farmer in 1700 and their great
significance lay in the fact that he could feed them to his stock so
that instead of being unable to keep them all alive in winter, as was
previously the case, they could be kept in good condition
throughout the year. The previous fifty years or so had also
witnessed the introduction from the Low Countries of the new
artificial grasses such as clover, sanfoin, lucerne, trefoil and rye-
grass, but these were grown only by a small minority of the more
adventurous farmers, principally in the areas of enclosed fields.

As we have seen, the slow but steady enclosure of the open
fields went on throughout the seventeenth century, so that by 1700
a greater proportion of lowland England was devoted to 'severall'
fields than had ever been the case before. In the place of the great
open fields were relatively small irregular fields – the straight lines
of parliamentary enclosure had yet to appear on a substantial

174

scale – bordered by quickset hedge of whitethorn, blackthorn, crab, holly and elder. Within their enclosures, fields were devoted separately to arable and pastoral farming. Manure from the stock in fields, as well as those who were yarded up during the winter, was increasingly spread on the arable fields to increase their fertility. A wide variety of other products was also being increasingly used as fertilisers, including chalk, burnt lime, marl, sea sand and seaweed, soap, ashes, soot, rags and salt.

The animal population of the country had also changed considerably since 1400. Gregory King meticulously records 4½ million cattle in England and Wales, 11 million sheep and 2 million pigs, approximately half to a third of present-day figures. Though very inferior animals by today's standards, they were nevertheless, at their best, a marked improvement on previous breeds of animals. Another common feature of the countryside was the warren and King assumes that no fewer than 1 million rabbits and conies inhabited England and Wales, together with 24,000 hares and leverets.

It is important, however, not to over-estimate the extent and significance of the newer and more productive methods of farming, for the sad truth was that the great majority of farmers were, in Charles Wilson's words, 'conservative, illiterate and suspicious of newfangledness'. Even by 1700, only a small proportion of the more enlightened farmers were growing turnips, for example, and clover was even more narrowly used: at this time the principal source of clover seed was still the Low Countries and one estimate is that only sufficient seed was imported to sow a mere 4,000 acres, or 1 in every 2,250 acres of land under crop cultivation. In some of the principal farming regions of the country such as the Midlands, communal open-field farming practices were naturally resistant to the introduction of new methods and the progress of enclosure, with its legal encumbrances, was a slow, costly and cumbersome business, frequently accompanied by social unrest.

However, in other parts of the country, major changes were taking place and by 1700 a marked degree of regional specialisation had established itself. In the home counties, such as Hertfordshire, Middlesex, Buckinghamshire and Bedfordshire; in the West Country, especially in the areas adjacent to Exeter and Bristol; in East Anglia; and in Kent, farming had developed which in terms of technique and productivity was in advance of most of the rest of the country. These were primarily areas where either no open fields had existed or which were enclosed at a relatively early date. As a consequence, they had been almost completely enclosed and their owners were among the first to adopt the new flexible methods of husbandry, alternating arable and pasture. In parts of East Anglia, with their lighter soils, the fields, some of them quite newly enclosed from heath or waste, were particularly suited to the newer root crops. Here, too, the recently reclaimed Fenlands were highly productive. In East Anglia, the latter part of the seventeenth century witnessed a broad change in the English countryside: due to the entrepreneurial endeavours of such landlords as the Walpoles at Houghton, the Cokes at Holkham and the Townshends at Raynham, grassland was being put down to arable and sheep were giving way to corn. Elsewhere, change was also taking place, if by modern standards at a very slow pace. In Wiltshire, on the southern edge of the chalk lands, wheat was replacing barley and on the heavy clay of the Midlands, especially in Leicestershire and Northamptonshire, grass was being grown for cattle and horse-rearing. In the western parts of the country, dairy produce was dominant, as it had long been, and dairy farms in Wiltshire, Somerset and Gloucester produced large quantities of milk and butter, while in Cheshire and Somerset a thriving cheese industry had established itself.

Another form of agricultural specialisation which was well developed by 1700 was that of market gardening. On small intensively cultivated plots, especially in the vicinity of the large towns of southern England which were the principal markets for their produce, horticulturalists grew an increasingly wide range of fruit, vegetables and herbs. Fruit-farming had also become profitable in some parts of the country in the seventeenth century and, by 1700 was well established in Kent, Hertfordshire, Worcestershire, Gloucestershire, Herefordshire, Somerset and Devon. Orchards were commonplace in these counties and apples, pears and cherries were grown in large quantities. In addition, a wider range of cash crops had developed by this time and the English farmer was growing increasing supplies of industrial crops such as cole-seed, flax, hemp, woad, and teasels. Cole-seed was particularly valuable in that its oil could be used for lamps and for preparing wool, its straw made into cakes which were used as fuel, and the seed itself could be fed to sheep. Hops was another commercial crop that had become increasingly popular and, by 1700, extensive hop fields were to be found in Kent and Sussex, Suffolk, Essex and Hereford.

The increase in the area of land under farming by 1700 had been accomplished in two main ways: by the reclamation of marsh and swamp; and by 'assarting', or clearing of woodland, heath and waste. The former was the most spectacular example of the extension of farming land, adding in all several million acres. The largest reclaimed area was in the Fenland of East Anglia, which had been transformed from a watery land devoted largely to fishing and fowling to one of the richest arable farming areas in the country, made up in William Hamson's words of 'roughly three-quarters of a million acres of land unsurpassed in productivity anywhere in these isles'. Elsewhere, up and down the coast of England, especially around the Wash and the Thames estuary, other smaller areas of land were reclaimed from the sea and converted to farming.

Woodland, heath and moor areas had similarly been brought under the plough or put down to grass as new farming land was won from old forest, park and waste. Instead of being converted into open fields, much of this newly obtained land was sub-divided into separate, hedged fields, drained and manured and, where suitable, sown with root crops. Many of the royal forests had been largely denuded of their trees, so much so that towards the end of the seventeenth century, an observer remarked of the work of the royal foresters in the New Forest, 'so much destruction the forest is more like a woodyard than a wood . . . scarce any tree left in the forest without a badge of their cruelty.'[1] Fortunately, the wastefulness of these depredations had sunk home by the end of the century so that replanting had become the order of the day both here and in the other principal royal forest, the Forest of Dean.

This reclamation of swamp and woodland was undertaken by all kinds and conditions of men, from the great aristocratic landlords, through the squires who held large or small areas of land, to the yeomen and tenant farmers. Just how much a part the greater landowners played in the shaping of the English landscape it is difficult to say, except that it was a considerable one and, by 1700, the numbers of substantial estates had both increased and were also growing larger in size. Standards of upper-class living had risen considerably, especially in the latter part of the seventeenth century, and great mansions like Chatsworth in Derbyshire and Dyrham Park in Gloucestershire had recently been erected, surrounded by their extensive gardens and parks and adding their own architectural character to the Tudor and Jacobean palaces which had preceded them. More typical of the end of the seventeenth century, however, were the smaller pleasant, more comfortable houses that were springing up all over England. Bearing the architectural stamp of Christopher Wren, they testified to a new wealth and a new elegance. In Charles Wilson's words,

> Much of the social history of England in these years is the history of the life that went on within such houses – the purchase of tapestries, of Dutch and French furniture and marquetry work, of marbles and mirrors, of paintings, clocks and vases, of sumptuous meals of unbelievable length served by a growing army of servants, black as well as local, of topiary gardens, ponds, statues, grottoes and parks.[2]

Some of the wealth of these great landowners flowed from the industrial development that was increasingly occurring within their lands. By 1700, the extractive industries had expanded greatly and landowners like Lord Dudley on his Black Country estates and the Leveson Gowers on their property at Whitehaven in Cumbria derived increasingly large sums of money from the exploitation of the coal reserves beneath the ground. By the beginning of the eighteenth century, some industries had waned while others had waxed. Among those that had collapsed entirely or had seriously declined were the cloth industries of Hertfordshire and Suffolk and iron and glass production in the Weald. On the other hand, the relative importance of industry in the north and west of England had increased substantially, especially in the seventeenth century, enhanced by the mining of coal and metal ores. In these regions, industries had grown up which were dependent on large quantities of fuel, especially coal, such as salt extraction in the north-east and glassmaking, both here and in Staffordshire. Upland England, north and west of the Exe-Tees line, also possessed abundant water-power, more and more being utilised in industrial processes, and contained some of the remaining forests which still possessed substantial reserves of wood for use as fuel. These raw materials helped to increase the production of iron-making in such areas as the Forest of Dean, the west Midlands and south Yorkshire.

In industry, as in agriculture, the beginnings of regional specialisation of production were clearly to be seen, and although most industrial workers were still also part-time agriculturalists, in a few places industry was demanding their services full-time. This was true, for example, of some of the cloth-manufacturing districts in the West Country and East Anglia, and metal-working enclaves in the west Midlands. Nevertheless, not too much importance should be attached to this, nor to the growth of industry in the north and west as opposed to the south and east. In 1700, as three hundred years previously, the basis of the English economy was still agriculture and not industry, though the relative importance of the latter had undoubtedly grown considerably. The majority of workers in industry still retained their roots in the countryside and were still part-time farmers. It was to be another 75 years or so before the English landscape witnessed the coming of industrial-isation in the modern sense. However, the basis of that development had already been laid by 1700.

Finally, England in 1700 had a much larger and more effective network of communications than had been the case three hundred years earlier. While road surfaces may have improved relatively little since then and were not to do so substantially until the coming of surfaces like tarmacadam in the latter part of the eighteenth century, nevertheless the number of roads in use and the volume of traffic along them had both greatly increased. A significant pointer to the subsequent development of the road system was the setting up of the first Turnpike Trusts in the latter part of the seventeenth century. One major stimulus to the growth in road traffic was the enormous expansion of London, from which the main roads radiated, as they had since Roman times, and whose population sucked in and issued forth a substantial proportion of the industrial and agricultural products that moved along the roads. One important and growing part of this traffic was provided by the carrier services which had multiplied considerably, notably in the second half of the seventeenth century. In 1700, as in 1400, the horse remained the main 'engine' of road communication. However, improvements had been effected both in the size and also the comfort of the wagons which it pulled.

Throughout the period under review, the major rivers of England carried much of the country's internal trade, especially the five principal ones – the Severn, the Thames, the Trent, the Great Ouse, and the Yorkshire Ouse – and their tributaries. By 1700, successful attempts had been made to extend and improve river carriage, both along these major rivers and other smaller ones. New forms of sluices and locks were introduced and stretches of rivers were canalised. The effect of these improvements was greatly to increase the extent of navigable rivers and consequently the traffic, most of it bulky in nature, that moved along them.

England in 1700 was, thus, a very different country from that which existed in 1400. It was both more populous and more prosperous, though the improvements in living standards did not extend to a growing class of paupers, including many landless poor dispossessed by the growing capitalisation of agriculture. The greater prosperity was attributable partly to an increase in agricultural and industrial productivity which created a surplus for export well beyond England. In addition, rising standards of living led to a growing demand for 'colonial imports' such as sugar, tobacco, pepper and saltpetre. The nature of this export and import trade, protected both by legislation and a growing naval power, is not the subject of this book, but nevertheless the growth of overseas trade brought in wealth and new ideas which inevitably left a strong imprint on the landscape. New crops and new agricultural techniques, derived especially from the Low Countries, were slowly but surely improving the quality of English farming, just as new technologies, stimulated by the growing scientific curiosity which was such a feature of the second half of the seventeenth century, stimulated manufacturing production. Although in 1700, as in 1400, agriculture remained the source of income for the great majority of the people, the stage was set for the industrial and commercial explosion that was to occur before the eighteenth century had run its course.

Further reading and references

FURTHER READING

During the past twenty years, the numbers of books and articles on the English rural landscape, in its many aspects, have multiplied considerably and it is neither possible nor desirable to list them all.

However, I have drawn extensively both on books which deal generally with the economic and social history of the period and also on those which can be categorised as treating the agrarian history and historical geography of England between 1400 and 1700. These are as follows:

General books on economic and social history

Clay, C.G.A., *Economic Expansion and Social Change: England 1500-1700*, 2 vols, Cambridge, 1984.
Coleman, D.C., *The Economy of England, 1450-1750*, Oxford, 1977.
Gregg, Pauline, *Black Death to Industrial Revolution: A Social and Economic History of England*, Harrap, 1976.
Thomson, J.A.F., *The Transformation of Modern Britain, 1370-1529*, Longman, 1983.
Wilson, C., *England's Apprenticeship, 1603-1763*, 2nd Edition, Longman, 1983.

General books on agrarian history and historical geography

Baker, A.H. and Harley, J., *Man Made the Land*, Rowan & Littlefield, 1973.
Beresford, M.W., *History on the Ground*, Alan Sutton, 1984.
Cantor, L.M. (ed.), *The English Medieval Landscape*, Croom Helm, 1982.

Darby, H.C. (ed.), *An Historical Geography of England Before 1800*, Cambridge, 1969.
Dodgshon, R.A. and Butlin, R.A., *An Historical Geography of England and Wales*, Academic Press, 1978.
Finberg, H.P.R. (ed.), *The Agrarian History of England: IV, 1500-1640*, Cambridge, 1967.
Kerridge, E., *The Agricultural Revolution*, George Allen & Unwin, 1967.
Thirsk, Joan, *The Rural Economy of England*, Hambledon, 1984.
Yelling, J.A., *Common Field and Enclosure in England, 1400-1850*, Macmillan, 1977.

In addition, I have made considerable use of a number of standard works on specific aspects of the English landscape during the period under review. These are as follows:

On **Villages**, Maurice Beresford and John G. Hurst, *Deserted Medieval Villages*, Lutterworth, 1971; on **Country Houses**, Olive Cook, *The English Country House*, Thames & Hudson, 1974; on **Woodland and Forest**, Oliver Rackham, *Ancient Woodland*, Edward Arnold, 1980; on **Parks**, Leonard Cantor, *The Medieval Parks of England: A Gazetteer*, Loughborough University, 1983; on **Gardens**, L. Fleming and A. Gore, *The English Garden*, Michael Joseph, 1979 and John Harris (ed.), *The Garden: A Celebration of One Thousand Years of British Gardening*, 1979; on **Industry**, A. Burton, *The National Trust Guide to Our Industrial Past*, George Philip, 1983, D.C. Coleman, *Industry in Tudor and Stuart England*, Macmillan, 1975, J.W. Gough, *The Rise of the Entrepreneur*, Batsford, 1967, and A. Raistrick, *Industrial Archaeology, an Historical Survey*, Eyre Methuen, 1972; and on **Roads and Rivers**, H.J. Dyos and Aldcroft, *British Transport*, Leicester UP, 1972, B.P. Hindle, *Medieval Roads*, Shire Archaeology, 1982, and L.T.C. Rolt, *Navigable Waterways*, Longman, 1979.

Where these books are cited in the references, only the authors' names and the pages are given. For all other books and articles, full details are included.

Finally, the volumes of the *Victoria County History of England* contain much invaluable information and the various county volumes in *The Making of the English Landscape* series, published by Hodder & Stoughton, are also very useful.

REFERENCES

1 The English countryside in 1400

1 M.M. Postan (ed.), *The Cambridge Economic History of Europe: I, The Agrarian Life of the Middle Ages*, 2nd Edition, Cambridge, 1966, p.571.
2 R.A. Butlin, *The Transformation of Rural England, c 1580-1800*, Oxford, 1982, p.43.

3 Barrie Turner, *A History of Shropshire*, Phillimore, 1983, pp.27-8.
4 Gregg, p.45.
5 Oliver Rackham, *Trees and Woodland in the British Landscape*, Dent, 1976, p.71.
6 H.S. Bennet, *The Pastons and their England*, Cambridge, 1970, p.258.
7 R. and M. Beckinsale, *The English Heartland*, Duckworth, 1980, p.73.
8 Christopher Dyer, *Lords and Peasants in a Changing Society: The Estates of the Bishopric of Worcester, 680-1540*, Cambridge, 1980, p.172.
9 J. Hatcher and T.C. Baker, *A History of British Pewter*, Longman, 1974, p.210.
10 F.M. Stenton, 'The Road System of Medieval England', *Economic History Review*, vol. 7, 1936, p.6.

2 Sheep or men? The cultivated landscape in the fifteenth and sixteenth centuries

1 Clay, II, p.2.
2 Dyer, *op.cit.*, p.5.
3 Thomson, p.15.
4 John Fitzherbert, *The Book of Husbandry*, 1523.
5 Dodgshon and Butlin, pp.128-30.
6 P.D.A. Harvey (ed.), *The Peasant Land Market in Medieval England*, Clarendon Press, 1984, p.261.
7 Yelling, p.51.
8 J.R. Wordie, 'The Chronology of English Enclosure', *Economic History Review*, Second Series vol. 36, 1983, pp.483-505.
9 Butlin, *op.cit.*, p.43.
10 Michael Reed, 'Enclosure in North Buckinghamshire, 1500-1750', *Agricultural History RReview*, vol. 32, 1984, p.135.
11 L. Fox and P. Russell, *Leicester Forest*, Edgar Backus, 1948, p.96.
12 Lord Francis Hervey (ed.), *Suffolk in the XVIIth Century, the Breviary of Robert Reyce, 1618*, 1902, p.35.
13 G.E. Fussell, *The Old English Farming Books from Fitzherbert to Tull, 1523 to 1730*, Crosby Lockwood, 1947, pp.15-16.
14 L.T. Smith (ed.), *The Itinerary of John Leland in or about the years 1535-1543*, 5 vols, Centaur, 1964.

3 Agricultural improvement: the cultivated landscape in the seventeenth century

1 John Broad, 'Alternate Husbandry and Permanent Pasture in the Midlands, 1650-1800', *Agricultural History Review*, vol. 28, 1980, p.78.

2 Carolina Lane, 'The Development of Pastures and Meadows during the Sixteenth and Seventeenth Centuries', *Agricultural History Review*, vol. 27, 1979, p.25.
3 A. Yarranton, *England's Improvement by Sea and Land*, 1677.
4 C. Morris (ed.), *The Journeys of Celia Fiennes*, Cresset Press, 1947, p.31.
5 Finberg, p.176.
6 Walter Blith, *The English Improver Improved*, 1652.
7 Broad, *op.cit.*, p.93.
8 G.B.G. Bull, 'The Changing Landscape of Rural Middlesex', Unpublished PhD, University of London, 1958, pp.170-1.
9 Morris, *op.cit.*, p.43.
10 H.C. Darby, *The Changing Fenland*, Cambridge, 1983, p.93.
11 V.H.T. Skipp, 'Economic and Social Change in the Forest of Arden, 1530-1649', in Joan Thirsk (ed.), *Land, Church and People*, British Agricultural History Society, 1970, p.110.
12 Skipp, citing Camden.
13 R. Trow Smith, *English Husbandry*, 1951, p.148.
14 Wilson, p.145 citing John Houghton, *Collection, 1681-3*, 1727, p.83.

4 Settlements and buildings in the countryside

1 Douglas Moss, 'The Economic Development of a Middlesex Village', *Agricultural History Review*, vol. 28, 1980, pp.104-14.
2 R.K. Field, 'Migration in the Late Middle Ages: The Case of the Hampton Lovett Villeins', *Midland History*, vol. 8, 1983, p.42.
3 Lawrence and Jeanne Stone, *An Open Elite? England 1540-1880*, Clarendon Press, 1984, p.329.
4 Alec Clifton Taylor, *English Parish Churches as Works of Art*, Batsford, 1974, p.95.
5 R.W. Brunskill, *Traditional Farm Buildings of Britain*, Victor Gollancz, 1982, pp.80-2.
6 M. W. Barley, *The English Farmhouse and Cottage*, Routledge & Kegan Paul, 1961, p.46.
7 Turner, *op.cit.*, p.50.
8 J.H. Bettey, *Rural Life in Wessex, 1500-1900*, Moonraker Press, 1977, p.98.
9 C.J. Harrison, 'Elizabethan Village Surveys: A Comment', *Agricultural History Review*, vol. 27, 1979, p.82.
10 J. Kennedy (ed.), *Madeley, A History of a Staffordshire Parish*, University of Keele, 1970, p.39.
11 J.C. Cox and C.B. Ford, *Parish Churches*, Batsford, 1961, p.99.
12 Kenneth Lindley, *Chapels and Meeting Houses*, John Baker, 1969.
13 Ralph Dutton, *The English Country House*, Batsford, 1962, pp.49-50.

14 H.M. Colvin (ed.), *The History of the King's Works, IV: 1485-1600*, HMSO, 1982.
15 Ian Nairn and Nikolaus Pevsner, *Sussex: The Buildings of England*, Penguin, 1965, p.195.
16 Philip A. Crowl, *The Intelligent Traveller's Guide to Historic Britain*, Sidgwick & Jackson, 1983, p.310.
17 Sacheverell Sitwell, *British Architects and Craftsmen*, Pan, 1960, p.136.
18 L. Butler and C. Given-Wilson, *Medieval Monasteries of Great Britain*, Michael Joseph, 1979, p.26.
19 Martin S. Briggs, *Goths and Vandals*, Constable, 1952, p.20.
20 Beckinsale and Beckinsale, *op.cit.*, pp.88-97.
21 Geoffrey Wright, 'Northumberland, The Middle March', *Out of Town*, July 1985, p.32.

5   Woodland: forests, chases, parks and gardens

1   Gareth Lovett James, 'In the Country of the Bodgers', *Out of Town*, July 1985, p.4.
2   C. Rawcliffe, *The Staffords, Earls of Stafford and Dukes of Buckingham, 1349-1521*, Cambridge, 1978, p.61.
3   Finberg, pp.xxix-xxx.
4   H.R. Schubert, *History of the British Iron and Steel Industry*, Routledge & Kegan Paul, 1957, p.222n.
5   C.E. Hart, *Royal Forest: A History of Dean's Woods as Producers of Timber*, Clarendon Press, 1966, p.71 and p.73.
6   Ernest Straker, 'Ashdown Forest and its Enclosures', *Sussex Archaeological Collections*, vol. 81, 1940, p.123.
7   Charles Chenevix Trench, *The Poacher and the Squire*, Longman, 1967, p.90.
8   Rackham, p.155b.
9   Darby, pp.398-9.
10 Desmond Hawkins, *Cranborne Chase*, Victor Gollancz, 1980.
11 Victoria County History, *Staffordshire*, vol. V, 1959, p.59.
12 John Manwood, *A Treatise of the Laws of the Forest*, 1615, p.18.
13 Leonard Cantor, *The Medieval Parks of England: A Gazetteer*, Loughborough University, 1982.
14 Bryan E. Coates, 'Parklands in Transactions: Medieval Deer Park to Modern Landscape Park', *Transactions of the Hunter Archaeological Society*, vol. 9, 1969, p.137.
15 Roy Strong, 'The Renaissance Garden 1500 to 1640', in Harris, pp.13-14.
16 F.E. Halliday (ed.), *Richard Carew of Antony*, Andrew Melrose, 1953, p.106.
17 Hawkins, *op.cit.*, p.46.
18 Hugh Prince, *Parks in England*, Pinhorns, 1967, p.2.
19 Harris, *op.cit.*, p.17.
20 D.M. Palliser, *The Staffordshire Landscape*, Hodder & Stoughton, 1976, p.101.

6 Industries in the countryside

1 Finberg, p.426.
2 C.M.L. Bouch and G.P. Jones, *The Lake Counties, 1500-1830*, Manchester UP, 1961, p.132.
3 Richard Muir, *Shell Guide to Reading the Landscape*, Michael Joseph, 1981, p.314.
4 C. Morris, *op.cit.*, pp.245-6.
5 Raistrick, p.97.
6 Joan Thirsk, *The Rural Economy of England*, Hambledon, 1984, p.237.
7 C. Morris, *op.cit.*, p.209.
8 S.R.H. Jones, 'The Development of Needle Manufacturing in the West Midlands before 1750', *Economic History Review*, Second Series, vol. 31, 1978, p.359.
9 D.W. Crossley, 'The Performance of the Glass Industry in Sixteenth Century England', *Economic History Review*, Second Series, vol. 37, 1984, p.426.
10 Norman Davey, *Building Stones of England and Wales*, Bedford Square Press, 1976, p.7.
11 P.F. Brandon, 'Land, Technology and Water Management in the Tillingbourne Valley, Surrey, 1560-1760', *Southern History*, 1985, p.76.

7 Roads and rivers: movement in the landscape

1 Hindle, p.5.
2 J.T. Gould, *Men of Aldridge*, G.J. Clark, 1957, p.35.
3 A.E. and E.M. Dodd, *Peakland Roads and Trackways*, Moorland, 1974, p.66.
4 Raistrick, pp.128-9.
5 W. Addison, *The Old Roads of England*, Batsford, 1980, p.70.
6 Christopher Taylor, *Roads and Tracks of Britain*, Dent, 1979, p.139.
7 Darby, p.341.
8 William Harrison, 'Description of Britain', *Holinshed's Chronicles*, 1586, i, p.192.
9 H.S. Bennet, *op.cit.*, p.136.
10 *Ibid.*
11 J.A. Chartres, 'Road Carrying in England in the Seventeenth Century: Myth and Reality', *Economic History Review*, Second Series vol. 30, 1977, pp.73-88.
12 Carl Bridenbaugh, *Vexed and Troubled Englishmen, 1590-1642*, Clarendon, 1968, p.221.
13 Darby, p.427.
14 T.S. Willan, *River Navigation in England, 1600-1750*, Oxford, 1936, citing Harrison, *op.cit.*, i, p.117.

15 Darby, p.264.
16 Raistrick, p.137.

8 The English countryside in 1700

1 British Library, Egerton MSS 3351, 1671.
2 Wilson, p.155.

Index